SERVICE CREW

The Inside Story of Leeds United's Hooligan Gangs

CAROLINE GALL

MILO BOOKS

First published in hardback in 2007 by Milo Books
This paperback edition published in March 2009

13-digit ISBN 978 1 903854 84 6

Printed in Great Britain
by Cox & Wyman, Reading

MILO BOOKS LTD
The Old Weighbridge
Station Road
Wrea Green
Lancs PR4 2PH
United Kingdom
www.milobooks.com

To all the boys no longer with us. We don't have to mention names, you know you've never left us.

— Eddie Kelly

CONTENTS

FOREWORD

IT WAS ONLY a few months after my book about Birmingham City's football crew, the Zulus, had gone on sale when word reached me that the Leeds firm was interested in telling their own, long-awaited story. I was actually driving along the M621 into Leeds on other business when I got a phone call from one of the Zulus to say Leeds had been in touch with him. David George, from the Junior Business Boys, the younger Zulu mob, had been speaking to some of them while researching for his own book. I told him I was driving and he said he would call back and that it was good news.

A few weeks later, I found myself standing in a cold Leeds city centre on a wintry February morning, waiting for my first glimpse of Leeds' main man, Eddie Kelly. As I struggled to keep warm, I saw a solitary figure coming down the street towards me and guessed straight away that it was him. No taller than me – 5ft 5in – I was initially surprised at his diminutive stature. He cut a benign figure but I soon came to realise that it hid a steely character as game as anybody, verbally as well as physically. Eddie, in his late thirties, headed the Very Young Team, who emerged in the mid-Eighties as its infamous forerunner, the Service Crew, was beginning to fade away. A respected figure who led from the front, Eddie told me that a four-year banning order stopping him from watching matches had persuaded him to help write a book instead. He also accepted that football hooligans were fast becoming an endangered species and 'decent' battles now happened just once or twice a season.

Eddie's fiery and quick-witted character shone out through our meetings and I got the impression that he was a man who did and said what he wanted, a man destined to be a leader. It was Eddie who would lead me deeper into the world of the Leeds hooligans. We soon met up with an older lad, Benny, in a nearby coffee shop. Benny represented those that first started going to football matches in the raucous and rampaging Seventies. The two of them set about telling me how they had come to the decision to finally let the exploits of the Leeds United massive be immortalised in print.

The Leeds firm occupies almost legendary status in the annals of hooligan history and I felt flattered to be asked to write their story. Dressed in a sharp suit, Benny was friendly and easy-going and said he felt that if a book was to be written, then honesty was the key. That meant giving other notable firms their fair dues. They didn't want a lopsided account which did nothing but glorify Leeds even when the facts told a different story. Equally, they felt they had been overlooked in other books, with their exploits often played down. Having written about the Zulus, I was particularly keen to hear what the lads had to say about the infamous battle at St Andrews in 1985, at which a teenage Leeds fan tragically lost his life.

I listened intently as they outlined the chain of events on and off the terraces of Leeds United FC over the past four decades. They told me how the Leeds mob was essentially made up of lads from many different areas who would all come together on a Saturday at 3pm. Such unity, however, was sometimes short-lived and other firms have commented on how Leeds would have been indestructible had they only been able to keep together. It wasn't until the late Seventies that all the firms merged into one and the Leeds legend was truly born. There have been the inevitable rows and fall-outs between various areas over the years and this fractured nature even meant the firm overlooked some potentially lucrative side work running the doors at some of Leeds' most popular venues.

Leeds are one of the last of the major firms to have a book written about them and inevitably it has been a lengthy and detailed process. I have interviewed nearly forty lads over the past eighteen months, to-ing and fro-ing up the M1 from my home near Birmingham. I found the Leeds lads to be a hardy bunch, true Northerners with a dry sarcasm underpinning their constant banter. I found their honesty refreshing and they were keen to tell it as it is, warts and all. I spent hundreds of hours in their company, travelling to matches home and away and to several social gatherings. I found myself driving to Brighton, Salisbury and Leicester to meet people who had valid stories to tell about their time with one of the biggest names in football hooligan history.

Foreword

Thanks must go to the lads I have interviewed, in no particular order: Eddie, Benny, Sean, Alan from Cow Close, Jack, Dave and Pete from Shipley, Neil, Paul and Brian from Leicester, Johnna, Diddie, Zoz, Shoot, Steve W, Moose, Dean from Oldham, R, DS, Pat, Derek, Gouldy, Flare Gun Foxy, Gilly, Scottie, Stevie Li, Crombie Boy, Musky, Wayne, Little Terry, Skiz, China, Tobin, Griff, Sheeba, Ronnie, Paul M, John from south Leeds and Dave M from Bradford, and to Raffs, Wuggy and Simon Hulme for their photographs.

CLUB BACKGROUND

LEEDS UNITED JOINED the Football League in 1920 and yo-yo'd between Division One and Two for several decades until former England centre forward Don Revie was appointed player-manager in 1961, heralding a golden era for the club. After four seasons in charge, Revie took the West Yorkshire club out of Division Two and into an unprecedented period of success. With greats such as Billy Bremner, Norman Hunter, Peter Lorimer and Jack Charlton – who first played in 1953 with 'Gentle Giant' John Charles – Leeds United were the top English side in the late 1960s and early 1970s. Between 1961 and relegation to Division Two in 1982, Leeds won the FA Cup and League Cup once, the Inter-Cities Fairs Cup twice and reached the finals of the European Cup and European Cup Winners Cup. They won the League twice, in 1969 and 1974, were FA Cup finalists four times and Inter Cities Cup runners-up once.

In 1965, three seasons after staving off relegation to the Third Division, the club reached the FA Cup final and a crowd of 100,000 saw Bill Shankly's Liverpool beat Revie's Whites 2-1 during extra time at Wembley. However, in 1968, Leeds became the first English Club to win the Inter-Cities Fairs Cup, now UEFA, with victory over Ferencvaros. The 1967/68 season was particularly memorable as they beat Arsenal 1-0 to win the League Cup and were semi-finalists in the FA Cup. The following season they were League champions and then won the Charity Shield in 1969 after beating Manchester City 2-1. They also reached the semi-final of the European Cup and the final of the FA Cup, which was won by Chelsea after a replay.

The Revie team was known for physical toughness as well as great skill and some could argue that the trouble caused by supporters off the pitch resembled the aggressive nature shown by Leeds players on the pitch. Most of the team in the Revie era went on to become internationals – by the early Seventies the squad contained seventeen full internationals – but also developed a reputation for too often falling at the last hurdle. The team recorded the song 'Marching On Together', which became the club's anthem, for the 1972 FA Cup final, in which they beat Arsenal 1-0. But after reaching the Cup final again in 1973, fans were stunned to see their team lose 1-0 to Division Two side Sunderland.

The 1973/74 season saw the team go a record twenty-nine games undefeated and win the League, finishing five points clear of Liverpool. But Revie was lured away by the offer of becoming England manager in 1974, which would have resounding impact on the club and its fans. Revie's successor was Brian Clough, who infamously lasted a few weeks before being replaced by former England captain Jimmy Armfield, who guided the squad to the European Cup final in 1975. That memorable, for all the wrong reasons, night in Paris saw the club banned from Europe for the next three seasons.

Within a few years, the best players had moved on and finding replacements to match the prowess of the great Revie team proved impossible. While support for the club was still huge, Leeds slipped to Division Two in 1982 after a riotous match against West Brom. The Eighties brought a succession of managers, including former players Eddie Gray and Billy Bremner. Bremner took Leeds to the 1987 play-off final, only to see them lose after extra-time. He was later sacked with Leeds struggling once again near the bottom of the Second Division.

Howard Wilkinson was appointed in October 1988. Leeds finished tenth in the 1988/89 season and finally managed to climb back into the top flight a year later, with Gordon Strachan the top goalscorer. Attendances began to increase and in 1992, under Wilkinson, Leeds captured their first League title since 1974 by pipping their detested rivals Manchester United. The club also got a taste of European Cup football in the first year of the Premiership but exited in the early rounds. They did go on to win the Charity Shield by beating Liverpool 4-3 thanks to a hat-trick from Eric Cantona and a fourth from Tony Dorigo. But Wilkinson was on his way after inconsistent performances and losing in the League Cup final to Aston Villa in 1995/96.

He was replaced by ex-Arsenal boss George Graham, not long after a controversial episode over him receiving illegal payments from a football agent. Graham left to join Spurs after just two years and David O'Leary was appointed as the nineteenth manager for Leeds, which would mark another extraordinary few years for the club. He was followed in succession by Terry Venables, Peter Reid, Kevin Blackwell, interspersed with three caretaker managers before Dennis Wise arrived in 2006. By 2007, the club was in League One.

1

SHIPLEY SKINS

IF IT BEGAN ANYWHERE, it began in Shipley. For the thousands of 'lads' who have been involved in football hooliganism while following Leeds United, the mill town of Shipley in West Yorkshire is where its origins lie. In the Sixties and Seventies, it was home to the Shipley Skins, a group of mates who grew up together watching Leeds. From about 1965, a hardcore of about fifty teenagers started going to matches together. They soon built up a robust reputation, and not just within Yorkshire. Stories about their exploits were whispered on the terraces, like the time at Manchester United when they went dressed in sheepskin jackets with hammers stashed inside, or about the lad who was deported after a European match, which was unheard of in the late Sixties.

The Shipley lads would eventually be followed by a new generation, with the infamous European Cup final in Paris in 1975 marking the occasion when the original lads, by now in their twenties, saw that a younger group had arrived. And so the cycle went on through the years, leading to the emergence of the Leeds Service Crew later in the Seventies, the Very Young Team in the Eighties and, more recently, the Infant Hit Squad. But back in the Sixties, that unknown future lay a long way ahead. Jack, Dave and Pete, three original Shipley Skins, are now aged in their fifties, and the story below is drawn from their recollections of those original 'bovver' days.

Shipley is about three miles northwest of Bradford and was part of the county of West Riding before it was abolished in the mid-Seventies. Coming under Bradford's administrative jurisdiction wasn't welcomed by locals but made no difference to the lads, who classed themselves as Shipley before anything else. Those that had jobs either worked in the mills or had apprenticeships and the sole purpose of their earnings was to pay for them to watch Leeds United.

They started hanging about at the Seven Seas cafe before drinking in the Bull public house, which soon became known for miles around as their headquarters, mainly because it was the only pub they were allowed in. They would fight with other lads who came to drink in and around Shipley or go to neighbouring towns to find them. They grew up alongside Mods, bikers, rockers and the odd Teddy Boy, as well as a gang of boot girls who were every inch as rough and tough as they looked. The bikers in particular had a big following in Shipley in the form of Satan's Slaves. Some bikers actually turned to them for help in dealing with another local group of skinheads causing them grief. They came into the Bull asking for protection and the trouble stopped once the Shipley lads put out the word that the bikers were all right.

The first skinhead they ever saw was actually a Londoner, a Chelsea lad called Tommy H. They were amazed by the way he dressed, with his shaven head and Ben Sherman shirt with braces. They got to know Tommy from their football trips to London and met his mates Mick Greenaway and Eccles, both big names at Chelsea. They would stay on drinking with them in London after matches and would take them out around Bradford when they came north, and they remain good mates with Tommy today. He later moved up north and would travel to Chelsea matches with the lads when they were going south. When Greenaway worked in the ticket office at British Rail, he sorted tickets out for the lads through Tommy.

The skinhead fashion was a revelation to the Shipley lads. Previously most had sported long hair and wore tie-dye T-shirts or grandad shirts – mainly so people couldn't grab hold of their collars – braces and combat jackets. They would shop at Millets and all invested in £1 pairs of black Army-issue boots, which meant everyone could hear them marching down the road. They also favoured US Army gear worn by soldiers in Vietnam, complete with blood stains. But once they had met Tommy H, they were soon off to Whitakers hairdressers in Bradford to get their locks shorn. Jack and Dave were actually suspended from work without pay until it grew back while mothers apologised to neighbours for the state of their sons' hair. Men in pub tap rooms, dressed in their three-piece suits after a hard day's graft in the mills, literally dropped their pints when the lads entered. When Dave told his mum that he wanted Doc Martens and Levi Sta-press for Christmas, she had no idea what they were. They soon discovered Levis were impossible to buy in the north of England at the time. They would pester the staff in Henry Smiths, the local clothes shop, asking if they had any Ben Shermans and, if not, when would they.

Their new appearance was instantly intimidating. When Man City came to Leeds, the lads got off the bus by the Peacock pub near the ground and watched City scatter when they saw them. The new movement was heralded in one national newspaper around 1967/68 with the headline: 'The Skinheads Are Coming.' *The Shipley Times and Express*, whose motto, according to the lads, seemed to be 'if you farted you were in it', wrote several articles about them, portraying them as loud and brash young men who went to places they shouldn't. Despite the racist reputation skinheads acquired, black lads went around with the Shipley lads and on Sunday nights they would all be at a soul night in Keighley as well as similar events in Bradford. They listened to reggae and ska and didn't consider themselves racist. They felt that in the end their West Indian mates drifted away from them by the early Eighties, but it was not down to any racial tension.

Dave B was one who never converted to the skinhead style of dress and kept his long hair and 'amusing' dress sense. In the Bull one Friday night, the lads met to discuss ambush tactics ahead of a visit by Manchester United. The next day, Dave decided he was going to wear only a pair of ripped jeans – no socks, no shoes, no shirt. In the end they raided his mum's wardrobe and he tore the sleeves off a fur coat and walked to the ground 'looking like Cher'. When the Red Army came pouring out of the Scratching Shed over to the Kop, most of the Leeds fans parted but the Shipley lads stood. The Mancunians completely bypassed Dave, obviously unsure what to make of him, while his mates laid into their hated northern rivals.

Another well-liked character was General Jows. He was one of three lads who were arrested and sent home after a match in Anderlecht in the late Sixties. He became entangled in barbed wire by the pitch as Leeds fans tried to get to Anderlecht and the police discovered he had no passport, money or ticket on him, as he had blagged it all the way. His antics eventually led to him having to spend a couple of hours at an attendance centre every Saturday so the authorities could keep an eye on him during games. He would still go through to Leeds on a Saturday morning to welcome any visiting fans, returning before the match began.

Generals Jows organised a battle with Man United by the train station in Leeds one year. The station was at that time surrounded by goods yards rather than the car parks and buildings that stand there now, and he got a couple of hundred lads to hide in the alleyways while he and several others went to meet United. They found two police officers at the station dealing with over 1,000 United fans. The Shipley lads, numbering about thirty, were cunningly wearing red and white scarves and told United to follow them, as they 'had Leeds on the run' nearby. The Red hordes followed, only to be led over a bridge into the yards where the rest of the Leeds mob appeared with pieces of wood. Hatred towards Man United stemmed partly from an apparent bias in the northern media, which was predominantly based in Manchester at that time. Despite Leeds' achievements it seemed Man United could do no wrong in the papers and this exacerbated the loathing that other clubs felt as well.

Mick C was another Shipley legend, thoroughly rated by others. A couple of weeks after Sheffield Wednesday knocked Leeds out of the FA Cup, in 1969, about 100 lads went down to Queens Park Rangers. Mick was living in London at the time and went to meet them. When they returned to their coaches after the game, a mob of 'London United' were waiting for them. They had met this strange cartel before, a mix of Spurs, Arsenal, West Ham and QPR hooligans who came together to attack northern fans. The one notable absence was Millwall, who actually joined up with Leeds at a West Ham game once.

In the ensuing free-for-all, Mick slashed a lad across the face. He got away and the police arrested someone else for it. When they got back to their coaches, numerous windows had been put through. The driver told them they had about ten minutes while he cleaned up, so they got off and went running after the London mob again. They didn't have a clue where they were going and were chasing lads all over the place, through some flats occupied mainly by West Indians, who didn't like seeing white skinheads on the rampage.

They stopped in the early hours at Leicester Forest East, the only service station that allowed football coaches to pull in at the time and which soon became known as the place to catch fans travelling north or south. They got there so late after the problems in London that they met coaches of West Ham going up to Huddersfield early for an FA Cup match. They were the last people West Ham expected to see at 4am and the lads gave the Cockneys a kicking, chasing some along the hard shoulder and others through some turnip fields. The Leeds crew then decided to go straight to Huddersfield and hang about there for the match. They went in the Cowshed end, fought with West Ham again and didn't get home until Sunday dinner time, having set off on Friday.

For London trips, the lads found a pub near Scotland Yard called the Clarence and used it as their meeting place once they were more organised. They would typically take the midnight train from Bradford, then go to Covent Garden at 5am, as the pubs were open there for market porters and the like. Despite most being only sixteen years old, they could get served, and would later wander around the streets before ending up in the Clarence, which was run by a Yorkshireman who employed Yorkshire lasses behind the bar. It eventually became known as a Leeds pub and the London United mob turned up there a couple of times looking for trouble. The Leeds lads once heard tapping on the windows and looked out to see West Ham drumming cut-throat razors on the glass. It was shit or bust, so they smashed up some bar stools, and hurled them out the windows and did what they could to fend them off.

They were in there on another night after a match when a smartly dressed bloke came in and asked if they would like to go for a drink with him. He said he was a lieutenant colonel and invited them to his soldiers' mess nearby. Curious but wary they went with him, thinking he could be someone who took a shine to young boys. He led them out of the pub, into a building and up some stairs, and soldiers saluted him as he passed. They discovered that a Yorkshire regiment was having a presentation evening there and they were told they had two hours to eat and drink whatever they wanted from a huge buffet before the guests arrived. Other soldiers were milling about in kilts and dinner jackets, while they were there with their scarves tied around their wrists. They had never seen anything like it but wasted no time in tucking in.

From the age of about fifteen, most of the Shipley Skins were pretty independent and their parents never batted an eyelid when they said they were going to London. They faced QPR, Spurs, Arsenal and West Ham most years and they were always good days out, with a couple of hundred travelling down. 'It was like the summer holidays, when you go out in July and play until September, then you come in to get warm and then go to school. That's what it was like for us,' said Jack. 'Things are so different now, in every sense.' West Ham was always a bit hairy and so there was a sense of relief that they had got away trouble-free after a match in 1967 – until their Tube train pulled in at a stop and it was wall-to-wall with Hammers. They got done but two older lads, Shep and Wilkie, put up a good fight and saved a few from a bigger battering. Shep and Wilkie were in their twenties when the rest of the lads were just teenagers and they didn't look like stereotypical hooligans at the time. Shep had rotten teeth, long, straggly hair and always wore a scruffy combat jacket, while Wilkie's signature look was a leather jacket with tassels on the back and sleeves. They were fearless rogues.

Chelsea was always another lively fixture and a Shipley lad was stabbed by West Ham after a game at Stamford Bridge. When Chelsea came to Elland Road, the lads decided to wait at the station for their special to arrive. The first lot of Chelsea skinheads they encountered moved out of their way, which gave them a bit of confidence, so they went to find more on the platform. They were doing well until a guy in a long coat pulled out an axe, causing them to split up and leave before he did some serious damage.

Jack and Dave B decided to hitch to Chelsea for another match. Afghan coats were all the rage and Jack wore his while Dave had his mum's fur coat. They struggled to get lifts at first and ended up dossing down in a sheep pen – minus the sheep – by the M62 for a few hours before trying again. They went in the Shed among the Chelsea fans, who were dressed in Sta-press and leather coats and couldn't believe how these two northerners looked. Undaunted, they announced, 'We're Shipley' – and, in their own words, 'got kicked to shit'.

Leeds soon learned to play on their caveman image when playing down south, a response to the 'soap and water' chant that was aimed at them by the supposedly flash Cockneys. In 1970, they played Sutton United in the fourth round of the FA Cup at their ground in leafy Surrey. The locals looked astonished at the hordes of Yorkshire fans descending on their tiny ground. The Yorkshiremen joked that they lived in caves and huts, and when the locals shared some oranges with them, one visitor told them that in Yorkshire they ate the peel, not the fruit, and gave them a demonstration. 'You can take the lad out of Shipley but you can't take Shipley out of the lad, never ever,' says Dave.

Arriving at grounds well before kick-off was the done thing, to let the opposition know they were on their territory. They would be in the Clock End at Arsenal or Newcastle's Gallowgate by midday. It wasn't one way either – other mobs did it to them. Local rivalries also built up, although the nearest clubs were much smaller than the mighty Leeds, who were dominant on the pitch at that time. On a train to Nottingham once, they were treated to a rousing chorus of 'We hate Shipley' when they stopped at Sheffield. Their reputation was such that the two rival Sheffield groups – United and Wednesday – made a point of waiting together for the special to come through because they hated Shipley that much.

Ahead of a match at Nottingham Forest in the late Sixties, the magazine *Charlie Buchan's Football Monthly* proclaimed, 'Leeds ready to set fire to Forest.' When part of the ground did indeed catch fire, Leeds fans got the blame. A big song at the time was 'I Am the God of Hellfire' by The Crazy World of Arthur Brown, and lads were singing it as they ran across the pitch away from the fire. Such misbehaviour was par for the course. Returning from away matches on the train usually meant someone pulling the emergency cord and several hundred disembarking down an embankment near their home, as it was easier for the Shipley lads to do that than go all the way into Leeds on the train and then come back out again. It got to be such a regular occurrence that train drivers would slow down approaching Shipley.

By 1975, a new set of young lads had emerged. The Shipley lads were in their mid-twenties and some had already had enough. Dave B announced in the pub one day that he was pissed off with it all, finished his pint and left, choosing to go travelling across the US, Alaska and India instead. General Jows suddenly stopped going in the early Eighties and hasn't been since. The debacle that surrounded the infamous 1975 game in Paris – ticket problems with the club, rioting, a ferry strike that trapped many at Calais – also saw many 'not bothered' about going any more. The younger group that they had been mixing with from Seacroft and Harehills – Vallo, Eddie C, Collar, Wagga and Big John – were coming into their own and Shipley were happy to take a back seat.

'We don't say we took the world on, we got a kicking over the years, but you've got to be there to run,' said Jack. 'We did things that nobody had done before and from 1968 we organised things and it all picked up after that. We'd get thrown out of grounds and climb back in again. It was about having a fight and going back to the pub afterwards and knowing when enough was enough. None of us were bullies, just jack-the-lads. We were a group of kids that grew up together and I don't know if it was the time we were brought up in or what, but Shipley was a crazy little town.'

* * *

Of course, Shipley was not the only hotbed of football violence at Leeds. Other youths from other areas had also succumbed to what would later be termed the 'English Disease'. One of those now goes by the nickname Crombie Boy:

The first time I threw a punch in anger at a football match was against Man United, season 1968/69, when I was just thirteen. No surprise that it was Man United, given the bitter rivalry between the clubs, on and off the pitch. Think about this though. Man United were European Champions at the time, the first English club to lift the trophy. I had watched the final on TV the previous season and I genuinely wanted Man United to win it and so did all my mates. We just didn't have that hatred for them then that so many Leeds fans have nowadays – and the feeling is mutual. They were English, so of course we wanted them to win. But that season, I found out what is now common knowledge. They have far more than their fair share of arrogant shithead supporters.

Man United may have come to Elland Road as European champions but they were having a mediocre season, while Leeds were going great guns at the top of the league. A team at the top of the league deserves respect; they gave us none. I was walking along Elland Road wearing my colours when these two gobby Mancs started taking the piss out of me. I guess they were fifteen or sixteen years old. When one of them started to insult our top player, Billy Bremner, it was more than I could take and I lamped him between the eyes, a beauty. You should have seen the look of shock on both their faces. I scarpered pretty damn quickly before they could compose themselves and come after me. This was a new feeling, and it felt good.

Man United always turned up in large numbers, the Red Army. They were a real handful for us, because of sheer numbers, but eventually our young lads grew old enough to take them on, and we started to turn them over at Elland Road. I always loved to hate the bastards after that season.

Clockwork Corner was at the corner of the Lowfields and the South Stand – the Shed in those days. Away fans usually went in the Shed. One of the lads that stood on Clockwork Corner was a dwarf. He was also a skinhead. His typical matchday wear would be eighteen-hole, cherry red Doc Martens that finished just below his knee, Levi's Staprest, also finishing just below his knee, a Jaytex checked shirt and braces. All this was topped off with a white, blood-and-graffiti smeared butcher's coat.

We played Man City at home in the 1971/72 season and beat them 3-0, a very good City team, with the likes of Summerbee, Lee, Young, Donachie and Corrigan. In fact we did a double double over the Mancs, beating City away 1-0 and beating the Rags 1-0 away and 5-1 at home. At the home game with City, a group of us were on Clockwork Corner giving their lads some stick. The dwarf-skinhead was stood on one of the crush barriers really giving the big ' un, or in his case the littl'un. City were going mental. Luckily for us this was before it became fashionable to lob darts and kung-fu fighting stars at each other.

Fast forward to next season and Man City away. A group of us met up at Leeds Station for an early start. There was Terry B from Woodhouse, who believe it or not used to split his time between watching Leeds and the love of his life, Man Utd! There was Dave T, who always got stuck in and who became a Muslim a good few years ago. Shep and Matches might have been in the mix, two Ebor Gardens lads. I don't remember Vallo, another Ebor lad being there, and Eddie C definitely wasn't there or we wouldn't have run later! Other were Phil W, who later went to live on a kibbutz, Stewart R, who became a National Front candidate, Tim H, Kelly the hammer-carrying Liverpool fan on the run from the law, and Pete S. Pete had a few months earlier appeared in the News of The World. The headline was 'The Toff is a Tough'. It was one of those exposés on football hooligans and was along the lines of, 'Don't be fooled by these dandies with their long black coats, silk handkerchiefs, razor-creased trousers, shiny black shoes and rolled umbrellas, they're causing mayhem on the terraces.' Pete got some real stick from us for that, on account of him being soft as shite.

We got to Manchester and merged with another group that included our friend the skinhead dwarf. He was wearing a green Harrington this time, so he didn't stand out as much in a crowd....yeah, right...We got on a bus, made our way up to Moss Side well early and eventually ended up *in a pub. I was seventeen and skint, so I usually had to cadge drinks off the others if it wasn't near payday. I don't know what made us go to Moss Side, a stupid idea, we were clocked straight away. We sat in the tap room of a pub and the lounge, which was empty when we came in, started to fill up with some nasty looking locals.*

The dwarf had gone to the bogs when three City lads walked into the tap room, with another fifty clocking us from the lounge. This City boy looks at Terry B.

'I know you, don't I?'

Terry gives it, 'Don't think so pal,' in his best Denton and Gorton accent. Just in the moment when it's about to go off, in walks the dwarf. Of course the City lad at the front recognises the little twat from the previous season – well you would, wouldn't you?

'And I fucking DEFINITELY know you, you cunt!'

Cue a hail of glasses and chairs from City in the lounge. We got out of there sharpish, but the thing is, dangerous as it was, we were in stitches laughing as we were running, and I don't remember City following us. I never did see that dwarf lad again, I bet City caught him though. He's probably in one of the concrete columns in the Manchester Ring Road.

Other notorious gangs were as keen as the Shipley Skins to make their mark. Cow Close, to the east, and Seacroft and Harehills, to the west, also rose to prominence among the Elland Road hooligan army. By the early Seventies, Cow Close had about forty lads while Harehills could amass 150, although not all would be from that area. Lads like Vallo, Eddie C, Trevor and Cockney Steve soon became well known and a regular forty from Harehills would drink in the notorious Precinct pub in the city centre.

The Seacroft Skins numbered up to seventy, along with the Striped Jacket Boys, twenty mostly long-haired lads who favoured striped boating jackets for a time. The Gipton lads, the East End Park Boys, the Postie Boys from the York Road, the main route into Leeds from the east, and the Oakwood and Roundhay areas could also pull sizeable firms by the mid-Seventies. Some of the Harehills lot were part of a scooter gang called Lulus, which emerged in the late 1960s and took its name from a café in the city where they congregated. It was an exclusive and awesome gang, with members seemingly handpicked. Lulus were Mods from all over the city as well as so-called townies as members, and drank in the Three Legs and a couple of other city centre pubs. Their numbers reached about 200 and while some did go to football, many were seen virtually as gangsters.

The café shut midway through the decade. It was a formidable haunt and younger lads, like Alan from Cow Close, would dare each other to walk up to it or go in. He went in once but was glared at so much he gulped down the piping hot tea he had ordered and left. 'They were very, very hard bastards,' he recalled. 'When Lulus were in town I was about fifteen and they were a few years older. Once, about forty of us, all aged fifteen to seventeen, decided to go and give it to them in this park one day. We'd got a few lasses with us and we got off a bus and walked up to the park. There was a kid with us from Lawnswood called Sean who was a bit older and he'd had trouble with some Lulus in the past. When we got there, a gang of about thirty came running up to us from the bottom corner of the park. One lad with Lulus, Chip, pulled out a knife, then Sean went into his girlfriend's bag and got out a bread knife, but they chased us off and we got on the same bus back, it was over that quick.'

Further to the west of Leeds, another scooter gang formed in the mid-Seventies, made up of teenagers from Calverley, Farsley and Stanningley. The LS28 Squadron, its name taken from the local postcode, was about sixty-strong and thrived on music, football and scooters. There was yet another scooter gang, older than them, whom they held in high regard: the Gemini was originally made up of forty or fifty lads from different areas and had a fierce reputation. They were seen as elite scooter boys and are still going strong today.

Most of the LS28 Squadron had known each other since school and grew out of smaller groups like the Cross Kids Gang in Calverley, between fifteen and twenty youths who got together to take on the neighbouring Calverley Axe Men, who were Bradford City fans. These little entrepreneurs would also wrap 10p pieces in Sellotape, have them weighed in a local bakery and use them as 50p pieces in cigarette machines. They would sell on the cigarettes and also charged people to park their cars on match days. They became expert in the practice of using wires in slot machines, which funded days out for many lads around the country. They watched their team with silk scarves around their necks, wearing Levi jeans, Church's brogues and Harrington jackets. Other opponents for them were lads from the Ravenscliffe Estate in Bradford, which was behind Calverley. Sometimes full-scale fights were organised and they found themselves taking on up to forty lads. They would fight on a hill nicknamed the Bunny Run and if you were slow you could take a kicking, although the rows were generally 'respectful'.

The LS28 went to matches all over the country on their scooters and got to know a lot of York lads who were called the York Saxon Scooters. Their soundtrack of the time was deep, black soul and their dress code morphed into three-star jumpers, luminous socks, flares and Doc Martens. The ultimate look on a Saturday night was a long leather trench coat. Some embraced the Northern Soul scene at all-nighters and at a venue called the Canine Club. It opened all night and the lads could play their own music.

Gradually the LS28 got to know a wide circle of people, including the Seacroft and Cow Close lads, with similar views, likes and dislikes. They eventually made the city centre their home and became 'townies'. Leeds was a tough city in the Seventies – 'rough and not many pubs' was a common complaint. Watering holes like the Peel would be frequented by gangster types, as would the Hostelers, which had an upstairs where the Harehills lot would drink and, later, most Service Crew lads. The older men from Cow Close, like Manny, Mick Steel, Jed, Jeff Keeton and Wally Newton, would also drink in the rougher establishments in the city centre at weekends. Saturday nights meant the Mecca nightclub in the Merrion Centre, where the infamous Eddie C from Harehills jumped off the balcony into a crowd of black guys once, unhappy at them having too much of the dance floor.

'The town lads originally numbered about fifty: Seacroft with

Zoz, Crabby, Battler, then Wortley with the likes of Watty and Popey, they had a big firm,' said Stevie Li, a respected lad from the Chapeltown area. 'East End Park were the scallies, you could always tell them, and then there was the Harehills lot and my lot. There were a few areas that didn't have much input into the town thing: Middleton didn't and the Ollerton Moore lads never joined up with us. Seacroft had so many lads because it was such a big estate and Harehills had the biggest mob in the late Sixties and early Seventies because it was the most densely populated area per square mile in Yorkshire, terraced streets and all that. They are in the north and in the south there was Beeston, Bramley and Wortley. The biggest input into our firm was from those five areas. Before we all went together in the mid-Seventies, after a game or even during there would be a kick-off with people from others areas, lads running over and having a go. I couldn't put my finger on one thing that brought us all together. One year people wouldn't go with other firms then the next we were all together.'

2

MARCHING ON TOGETHER

'NO FUCKER MOVE. They're not getting past us.'

Forty lads obeyed and spread out across Wembley Way, waiting for their opponents. Not many believed Manny when he said, 'They're not getting past us', but they prepared themselves for the ordeal ahead. It was going to be one hell of a battle. It was the 1972 FA Cup final, they were playing Arsenal, and they were about to confront overwhelming odds.

The coachload of Leeds hooligans from the Cow Close area had already received warning of what was coming when between 100 and 150 breathless lads sprinted past them. At first they thought the running lads were Arsenal, and braced themselves for a ruck – until the leader gasped, 'We're Leeds. There's about two thousand Arsenal up there and they've knocked hell out of us. We're off.'

The Cow Close lads had arrived in the capital in the early hours and kipped in Hyde Park. They had already had an eventful day, rousing some tramps in the park to play a game of football and then mixing it in Trafalgar Square with a smaller group of Chelsea, who had given a good account of themselves. The only one among them with a ticket for the final had been nicked and looked pretty glum as he was driven away in a Black Maria.

On Wembley Way, they faced a different proposition. Masses of Arsenal came into view, a sea of heads bobbing up and down as they ran towards Leeds. As they closed in, Leeds could make out individuals dressed in the bizarre get-up from *A Clockwork Orange*: white coats and bowler hats, with one side of the face painted red and the other white with a ring of eye-liner around one eye. Some were carrying sticks. Arsenal's hooligans were known to be no mugs either away or at home, and as there were now possibly 2,000 of them heading towards a vastly outnumbered Leeds contingent, the situation looked dire.

The Leeds lads silently stood their ground, prompting a few anxious looks among the Arsenal front line. The Londoners started to slow down and then stop, shouting, 'Arsenal,' and jeering, 'Come on.' One ran up with a stick in his hand and brayed a Leeds lad called Paul over the head, snapping the stick in the process. Paul bent down, picked up half of the stick and stuck it in the lad's face.

Uncertainty filled the air for a few seconds before everyone went for it and piled in. Manny ran into the middle and nutted two Arsenal lads – he was renowned for his head-butting – and they both hit the deck. The Arsenal parted at the front under the Leeds charge and punches and kicks came lashing in from both sides. The fighting was intense as Leeds waded in, forcing the Arsenal firm back by sheer determination. They knew they had to give their all or face being wiped out. The rear of the London group started to retreat, giving Leeds momentum as they attacked anyone in front of them. Their opponents broke and were chased them off to the sides or over a nearby wall, before turning to make a stand at the top of Wembley Way, prompting more scuffles.

The cops appeared and Alan and Dougie C were nicked and put in back of a police van with three Arsenal lads. One of the Arsenal lads asked for a cigarette or a light and that was enough to start another tussle. They started wrestling with each other before a copper got in the back to calm things down. They were kept in the stationary van until about ten minutes before kick off, when the back doors were flung open and they were told, 'Right, I could have you, you, and you for affray, now get out of here and piss off.'

Bereft of tickets, Alan and Dougie scoured the area for a tout to roll. Dougie managed to get a ticket while Alan harangued a Scouse lad in a long Mac who said he had one but it was for his mate. He eventually caved in minutes before kick-off when his mate didn't show. The three of them found their seats but fifteen minutes in the bloke said he was going and Alan thanked him for the ticket. Surprised, the bloke said, 'Give us the money for the ticket then.'

'I ain't got any money, you never mentioned money,' Alan replied.

'You cheeky little bastard. Keep it and have a fucking drink on me,' he said, and left.

They later saw Billy Bremner lift the FA Cup in its centenary year, thanks to a single goal by Allan Clarke. The jubilant lads regrouped and went back to Trafalgar Square, where it kicked off with another large group of Arsenal. Several needed hospital treatment, including one lad, Dennis H, who cut his hand on a bottle after fleeing from an Arsenal fan who pulled a knife on him. Some waited for those being treated but Alan decided to head off to find the others. He was relieved to hear the familiar sound of Leeds chants as he walked down the road but as he turned a corner he encountered several Arsenal skinheads instead. Some had the same black eyes and painted faces as before and they took one look and set off after him. He saw a taxi in the middle of the road at some lights and opened the door and practically fell onto a couple holding hands inside. The surprised driver said, 'What you doing?' He told him to look behind him and after a quick glance he said, 'Fucking hell,' and put his foot down. Alan escaped and looks back on that day with pride, when so few battled with so many.

Leeds United's defence of the FA Cup the following year was the setting for more high jinks, as Crombie Boy recalled:

On Saturday, 13 January 1973, we had been drawn away to Norwich City in the third round of the Cup. I got a call on the Thursday before the game, saying an overnight coach had been organised, leaving from the Corn Exchange, midnight Friday. Meet in The Hyde Park Pub first, on to town for some grub, and off on the coach. Am I in? Too fucking right mate! Friday 12th, payday's three weeks away, and I'm skint again, blew most of it at Christmas, our kid won't lend us anything, so desperate measures need to be taken.

I worked on Blenheim Terrace in those days, and had a key to the office. So on Friday night, about 7.30, I'm in the office. I had just about enough money to cover tonight's meal, and tomorrow's costs, but nowt left for tonight's ale. I knew where the petty cash box was though, and had managed to get a set of keys cut. Being the 'daft lad' – the junior in the office – I had been sent out to buy the fucker in the first place, and now my key cutting exercise was about to pay off. I nicked two quid, and that was me sorted. Beer was only about twenty pence a pint back then.

I strolled on up to the Hyde Park pub to save on the bus fare, got there and it was full of familiar faces, amongst them Terry B, Roger the DJ, a big half-caste lad and a dead ringer for the singer in Mungo Jerry. Roger was a great disc jockey and had competitions at his DJ nights where he'd give away ten singles at a time for answering music questions. Trouble was, he was nicking the records from Music Hire Group, his daytime employers, and he got caught and did time for it. About twenty of us used to meet at the Hyde Park on Friday nights, mainly Woodhouse and Meanwood lads. It was a student pub but they kept themselves to themselves, and so did we.

After a few bevvies, it was down to the Golden Gate for a chinky. We were regulars and they used to treat us well, knowing that if any gobby out-of-towners started trouble while we were there, we would sort it for them. Then we ambled out to the Corn Exchange, piled on the coach, and after the first hour or so, the beer did its job, and most of us were kipping. None of us had ever been to Norwich before, we hadn't played them since the season we got promoted, 1963/64, and we were looking forward to defending the cup we'd won at Wembley the previous May.

About half four in the morning, the driver managed to find somewhere to stop in the middle of nowhere, and with no cooked food on sale, we had to make do with robbing a few choccy bars and having a piss, although at least one of our party had managed to do that in his trousers, in his drunken stupor. We piled back on the coach and were on our way through the Norfolk country lanes when we heard the familiar nerr nerr, nerr nerr of the sirens, and saw the flashing blue light behind us. A patrol car pulls us over. Just as this is happening, some fucker starts offering handfuls of coins out to everyone, 'Pass it round, pass it round.' At the same time, he opens a coach skylight and places an object on the roof. We all see what's happened: one lad has only gone and nicked the collection box for the blind from the piss stop. I know I'd nicked something earlier too, but morally this was different, in my mind anyway.

The coppers got on the coach, two right carrot crunchers. This was probably the biggest event in their careers. They searched the coach but couldn't find the collection box. We're all sat there with change in our pockets, the older, bigger-style coins, twopence pieces like manhole covers, ruining the cut of my Brutus jeans! Plod can't find any proof, but these straw munchers aren't as thick as they look. 'The person who did it will own up, or we'll nick you all, and hold you in the cells till the match is over,' says one. 'Sort it out amongst yourselves, we'll be back on the coach in five minutes.'

Now we all liked the lad who nicked it, another game-as-fuck lad who always led from the front, but no way were we gonna be nicked for that and eventually he caved in and gave himself up and we were on our way. Time for just one more stop though. Some poor milkman, doing his rounds on a quiet, pitch black Norfolk morning, whistling cheerily to himself and looking forward to an early morning shag with his missus after his shift, when we all pull up at the side of his float, all with mouths like a Turkish wrestler's jockstrap. Within minutes, all his milk and orange juice is gone – but paid for in coins – and it's back to the depot for him before he can complete his round.

We finally get to Norwich and are off in search of breakfast. As the day goes on, we end up in the pub near the station. We weren't expecting any opposition from Norwich and we didn't get any. They simply weren't in our league. I do remember some poor Norwich lass trying to take the piss and having her jeans ripped off and lobbed in the river. Bit harsh that, I thought – for about five seconds.

We got to the match late, as usual. The entrance to the ground was like the old Lowfields, up some stairs, and into the back of the stand. Both the away support and Norwich's *main end were in the same stand, we were right next to each other but separated by a high metal fence and a gangway. One of ours went off for a piss and a bit of an exploration, and came back all excited. 'Guess what, if you go back down the steps, and round a wall at the bottom, you can get in to their section.' Now Norwich had been giving it the big 'un from behind the fence, so we thought, fuck it, let's have some fun. About fifteen of us made our way round, no coppers, no stewards, and sidled in behind them.*

Okay, here goes: 'Hello, hello, Gelderd aggro, Gelderd aggro!' A sea of faces turns towards us and we're straight into them. They completely panicked, and only about two stood. The rest surged forward, away from us, like the tide going out, and the two who stood were soon on their toes. The old bill reacted quickly enough, and we saw the line of helmets making their way up towards us, battling against the bodies that were trying to get away from us. The coppers really didn't have a clue in those days, and we were long gone by the time they arrived. They stayed at the back of the Norwich fans in case we came back for more.

Nothing else happened and the game was a draw. On the 17th the replay at ours was a draw, on the 20th we beat them in the league, and on the 29th, the second replay, we beat them 5-0. I think they were sick of the sight of us by then.

Despite the number of faces appearing on the terrace scene from different areas of the city in the early part of the decade, none would say they called the shots. There was no unified mob to organise, as each area went separately to matches in vans or on the special trains and did their own thing. Nevertheless, Leeds were taking massive followings pretty much everywhere in the 1970s, apart from Manchester, Liverpool and London, where it was felt they were not organised enough to go with a big enough firm to take on the locals. It wasn't until a visit to Chelsea in 1975 that Leeds made their first major show of an organised firm in the capital. The Chelsea leader, Babs, was already well known, as was another sizeable lad called Tiny, though Chelsea didn't themselves travel to Leeds firmed up in the early Seventies. Equally when it came to venturing to London, Leeds fans felt exposed and intimidated. Chelsea would always infiltrate their huge away end and bully Leeds – and no doubt other visiting mobs.

But in 1975, about 1,500 went down on specials trains. At half-time, when some Leeds gathered by a hotdog stand, Chelsea were spotted congregating by some steps, prompting thirty or forty lads to pile into them. 'To me that was a result,' said Scottie, one of the respected Harehills lads. 'It was a main mob and word spread.' However, after the match the lads split up, resulting in about sixty walking to Fulham Broadway station, where they encountered 200-300 Chelsea. 'We got smashed,' said Scottie. 'We were running down the escalators and onto the concourse. We ran everywhere. Three of us got on the first Tube out and didn't even bother to see if it was the right train. We finally managed to get to Kings Cross and then back to Leeds. But we were pleased that we had made a show in London for once.'

Each Saturday now guaranteed mayhem home or away, with the police unable to control it, which allowed an air of confidence to exist. There were also minor feuds going on within the Leeds supporters between the different towns, which were invariably settled, with or without a fight. It took the next generation of lads – the Service Crew – later in the decade to properly bring together the numerous towns in West Yorkshire.

One time when Harehills did mingle with another group was at Cardiff in the fifth round of the FA Cup, in February 1972. As at Wembley against Arsenal, it was also one of only a few occasions in the early Seventies when an immensely outnumbered group of Leeds stood against an overwhelming opposition. About forty Cow Close arrived on an old bus at 6am, after a six-hour journey. Harehills arrived at the same time but parked at the other end of the road, near the bus and train station. The two groups briefly walked down the road together before going their separate ways in search of locals.

Cow Close, many dressed in Crombie overcoats, settled in a café near the train station, venturing outside every so often to attack small groups of locals coming in on trains. Kick-off was at noon but the constant pockets of fighting saw three Leeds arrested by 8am. At about 10am they set off for the ground, with scuffles breaking out en route, and then boldly walked round Ninian Park before repeatedly passing by the turnstiles, braying Cardiff as they arrived.

Inside the ground, several Cardiff fans ran onto the pitch before kick-off and laid down a Welsh flag with 'Cardiff' emblazoned in the middle. Two lads, Billy and George, from the Wortley and Farnley areas decided to retaliate and ran on with Billy's Union Jack. George nutted one of the Cardiff lads and started wrapping him up in the noticeably long scarf that he was wearing, while Billy removed their flag and laid the Union Jack down instead.

At half-time, a lad called Franksie announced he was going in their end and another said he'd try it too. The pair slid behind a hotdog van and clambered up by some railings at Cardiff's end. The Cow Close lads could see them about to launch themselves into the rampaging home support, whose attention was on Leeds and who were throwing coins, with a row of police dividing the two firms. Franksie and his mate waited a few more moments before they dived in. They got absolutely battered but were applauded later for their efforts.

Shipley Jack said, 'The Cardiff lads were game and overwhelmed Leeds in the ground with their numbers and booming chants of "We hate the English". The fashion at the time was to wear berets and one of our Shipley lads, Dave T, kept having his nicked by the Cardiff fans and every time he'd run into them to get it back he got a hammering. Leeds were battered back into a corner and each time they fought back they'd get hemmed in again. For many it was the hardest day out they'd ever experienced and remains that way today.'

The Harehills crew decided to head off after the game but two of them, Eddie and Chip, stuck with Cow Close, which was unusual but was accepted on this occasion. Not far from the ground, Cardiff came running down some railway lines to attack Leeds, many armed with ripped-up fencing. Some had also relieved a nearby café of its crockery before getting onto a bridge, from where plates, cups and saucers rained onto an angry Leeds mob who couldn't get at them. The lads reached the station about half an hour after the match and as they approached their coach, hundreds of Cardiff appeared again and surrounded them. Some coppers were between the two groups but struggled to handle Cardiff because of their numbers. Dennis H took charge. 'Right, if we go down, we go down fighting,' he roared. 'Everyone listen. When I point that way that way with my brolly, that's the way we're gonna go and when I point that way, that's the way we're gonna go.'

Most wondered how the hell thirty-five lads could stand a chance against several hundred baying for their blood but they listened intently. Five had already melted away, presumably to get the train with the remaining normal supporters, something that hadn't gone unnoticed. Cardiff were getting at them through the coppers all the time and when a gap appeared between them and the police, Dennis shouted everyone forward. They battered Cardiff back a good twenty yards before Dennis pointed his brolly and shouted, 'This way,' and they charged again in another direction. It was vital Leeds stayed on their feet and stuck together, and as they made repeated charges their Welsh foes began to disperse, eventually running off. 'That's the best I've seen,' said one of the Welsh coppers. 'Now get out of here.'

As Alan recalled, a small number fronting a larger number can put the opposition on the back foot. 'That was adrenaline. If you had gone down at any time or not got stuck into anybody then we would have got it, but because we all said we were going to do it, we went for it. I've always thought if you front somebody there is only a handful of them that will have a go. There might be two hundred but only a few at the front will want to have a go and if you get them down, the rest are on the back foot straight away.'

For most games at Elland Road in the early part of the decade, the lads would go in the Scratching Shed, which later became the South Stand. The Lowfields Corner Boys existed from 1970/71, after the new development of the Kop, which opened around 1969/70 at the north end of the ground and then became the Leeds end. Previously the north end was an open terrace occupied partly by home fans and partly by away fans, while the Shed had been the main Leeds end. The Lowfields corner became popular as it was adjacent to the Shed, which had now become the away section. It offered the opportunity for those who wanted trouble with the away fans to be closer to them, although the main Leeds support was accommodated in the new Kop. The numbers congregating in the Lowfields corner differed depending who Leeds played: more for Man U, Liverpool or Newcastle, for example, who brought bigger followings than other teams.

Local groups would often chant their own songs at matches: 'We are the Harehills Boot Boys' and similar songs from the Seacroft Skins and the Bramley Boys. But by 1973/74 the mob started to coalesce as inter-area rivalries became less important. Manny, Freddie and Jimmy were part of a group who organised the Shed Bus, which contained a select few who were deemed good enough to travel together. When the Shed was used for away fans, some Cow Close and Harehills still went in there, getting turfed out from time to time but managing to kick out the visiting contingent on odd occasions. Two ends Leeds didn't try to take were the Kop at Anfield and the Stretford End at Old Trafford, as both were just too big and daunting.

Fashion-wise Leeds was a bit barren with only a few clothes shops worth visiting. Class was one, just down from the Viaduct pub, which was popular with the Mods, and some went to Spencers, which was out towards Burley. The suedehead look took hold in the early Seventies, with lads growing out their hair and wearing Docs, Harringtons, Sta-press, loafers and Crombies. Others chose 'Rupert the Bear' trousers, tank tops with matching cardigans and, after *A Clockwork Orange*, some sprayed their boots silver and gold. In its turn, the suedehead look eventually disappeared as musical tastes shifted to glam rock, David Bowie and T-Rex.

Clothes mattered. Alan from Cow Close can still remember having a new green and gold V-neck jumper bought from Class ripped by a copper at a match at Huddersfield, when Leeds were banned from playing at Elland Road for four games after violence the previous season. 'Trouble started as soon as we got off the train and into the town centre pubs, much to the annoyance of one lad, the Welsh Warrior, named after a horse he would back, who had just put a bet on in a nearby bookies,' recalled Alan. 'Huddersfield came out of their pub and we piled into them, knocking them all over. The older lads decided to stay in town for a session and about eight younger lads left to start carrying on in their end. Me and a lad called Paul Sykes were the first in and were amazed at being able to walk through the middle of thirty Huddersfield and lean on a barrier. Five more Leeds entered as a lad went up to them, ordering them out of the end. They refused and started punching until two coppers appeared and grabbed me, ripping my jumper. I pushed them away but was dragged out and given a beating behind a corrugated part of the ground before being thrown in with Leeds.'

On a match day, some would buy rail platform tickets and sneak past the police to lie in wait for visitors the moment they arrived. Many teams brought big followings to Leeds. Thousands with their scarves would pour through the station at weekends after getting off the specials. The locals would wait on an iron bridge that spanned several platforms and would launch themselves into the unsuspecting fans from above, sending them tumbling down the stairs and sometimes joining them – as they didn't always get things their own way.

'When Burnley came to Leeds in 1974, they came out of the train station but were attacked under the bridge outside,' recalled one veteran, 'prompting them to all run back inside and get on a train home. That was the plan most of the time at Leeds. Lads would wait for fans to get under the bridge, which spans the main road as you enter the city centre from the motorways, then get a group in front and a group behind. It's really dark underneath and the acoustics are excellent so when lads are attacked from both sides all they can hear is "Leeds, Leeds, Leeds" booming in their ears. Because of the echo it also makes it sound like there are more lads than there actually are.'

When Chelsea arrived one year, revenge was sought on one lad in particular who had done a good job of pointing out Leeds fans at Stamford Bridge earlier in the season. Back then, Leeds fans wouldn't always stand together at grounds and this conspicuous black youth, in white Sta-press with a big afro, used a walking stick to point them out. After one fierce battle that spilled out onto the pitch, Alan from Cow Close and a few others decided, 'That bastard is getting it when they come to Leeds.'

So when the fixture came up, eight or ten lads bought platform tickets and waited on a bench for them to arrive. They saw a group coming over the bridge and Alan recognised the guy straight away. They waited until they were level and then 'banjoed them all over the place'. Alan and a mate ended up chasing their target onto a train but had to jump off before it departed. As it pulled out with the now-relieved Chelsea lad on board, the Leeds boys asked a platform guard where it was going. He said straight to Liverpool, no stopping.

Leeds United's hooligans would develop a reputation for racism, but by no means all of them subscribed to it. Manny and Wally, two Cow Close legends, were members of the Socialist Party in the city, one as president, the other as secretary. Mick, a lad from Armley, stood for election with the National Front one year and needed twelve nominations, so some of the lads put their names down. Somehow Manny and Wally got a photocopy of the nomination form and slapped one up on every corner in Armley with 'These Men are Wanted' underneath the names. Alan had signed it and was extremely relieved his name couldn't clearly be made out. He was later on a bus when he saw Mick, who had two biggish NF lads with him from Bradford. They were at the back of the bus and Alan sat two rows in front, chatting to them, when Manny and Wally got on and joined them. One of the lads must have made some racist comment or joke and they got absolutely annihilated by Manny and Wally. Mick got a few cracks as well just for knowing them. The two Bradford lads were told never to come to Leeds again.

However, lads can remember seeing the far-right *Bulldog* magazine being sold outside Elland Road next to the Socialist Workers Party representative brandishing copies of *Socialist Worker*. Politics was explosive in the Seventies, with issues like immigration at the forefront. People were swayed one way or another and a definite right-wing element existed amongst the Leeds lads.

Age difference is important when you are young, and Manny and Wally were seen by the younger lads as 'proper men who didn't give a fuck'. They were in their twenties in the early Seventies and word spread about their antics. Manny once downed a bottle of vodka before wading into the Spurs end with another lad, eventually being dragged out by a copper who was amazed at their behaviour. A lad called Bivver remembers feeling mightily relieved when Manny and a few others came into a pub full of Blues in Birmingham. Bivver had gone down on a minibus but the landlord in the first pub they went to said he didn't want any Leeds in and told them about somewhere else to drink. They moved on but as they propped up the bar more and more Blues came in. Bivver, a big lad himself, knew what was coming as he saw more locals hanging around outside. When Manny, Wally and another lad called Jed walked in, he had never been so thankful to see anyone come through a door. He immediately felt they could take on anyone. Bivver told Manny he reckoned they were going to get chinned but Manny turned round and said, 'Who wants it then?' complete with his dead-man's stare. No one said anything, no punches were thrown and that was how it stayed.

At Wolves, Leeds went in their end, forcing the police to segregate it half-and-half. At half-time, Wally said he was going to the toilets, which were in the Wolves section. No-one else was keen to battle their way through to them but one lad, Scafey, known as General Scafe because he liked to think he was a bit of a leader and order lads about, followed Wally a few minutes later. As he walked into the bricked, open toilet, he could hear fighting and stuck his head round the door. Wally was dusting himself down and three lads were laid out on the floor. Scafey left him to it and came back and told the others but when Wally returned he never said a word about it – which added to his reputation. 'Manny and Co had an aura about them,' said Alan. 'A photo of them in Paris in 1975 shows their attitude: We do what we want and don't give a fuck.'

Some lads would go to matches in Jed's pop van when he worked for drinks firm Scot's Pop. Anything up to twenty-five lads would pack into the back. They were stopped by the police after going to Nottingham Forest and when the officers opened the back, a gaggle of drunken lads fell out. The cops just shoved them back in and told them to get going.

Wally, Manny and Alan got more than they bargained for when they went to lowly Peterborough, in the fourth round of the FA Cup, in January 1974. They arrived by coach and Alan walked to the train station to meet Woody and Mick, from Armley. Mick got off the train with a piece of three-by-two with a little flag on the end of it. As they walked up the road debating which pub to go in – as two had already been smashed up since Leeds's arrival – twenty black youths came round a corner. Mick stood in the middle of the road, shouted, 'You black bastards,' and started hitting out with his piece of wood. The other two had to get stuck in after that but soon realised these lads were pretty tough. Mick and Woody ran to get reinforcements from one of the pubs while Alan did his best to fend them off. He knew he had to remain standing no matter what. He grabbed one lad who was thumping him, pushed him into the middle of the others and tried to escape. Unfortunately he ran in the wrong direction – straight into the main bunch. He hit two of them and tussled with others but was then hit with a full house brick. He went down and took a few more kicks before staggering up and away.

Still dazed, he went back towards the station where the others appeared with eight or nine helpers, but their attackers had gone. They told Alan he looked like he'd been run over. His nose was splattered across his face and his eye was swollen. During the game he got more and more vexed as the pain kicked in. The fact that Leeds were winning comfortably did nothing to quell his anger and ten minutes before the game ended he said he was going 'to look for one of those bastards'.

He went out and was walking near a bridge when he heard someone shout, 'Alaaaan!' He looked over and saw Billy – who had left the game to rob a shop he'd had his eye on – on a wall on the bridge thirty feet up surrounded by several lads, with two trying to push him off. Alan decided here was his chance for revenge so he darted over and attacked them but once again he found they were no pushovers.

Three more wandering Leeds saw what was happening and joined in but Peterborough did well, getting the better of the lads for a time. The fighting lasted about five minutes before Wally, Manny and another lad turned up and helped flatten five or six of the locals. Yet some of them got up and came running after Leeds as they walked off to get their coach. 'They were game,' said Alan. 'They got it again, but they were game.'

One of the biggest Leeds mobs Alan can remember seeing was against Wolverhampton Wanderers in the semi-final of the FA Cup, at Maine Road in April 1973. Wolves came around the ground and tried to get in the Leeds section, leading to a 'right set-to'. When they got out, eight Leeds followed nine or ten Wolves lads and repeatedly attacked them all the way back to the station, which was a long walk. Each time the Wolves 'got done' they would come back for more. But when they neared the station, Wolves came running back saying, 'There are loads of Man U coming down the road, stay with us.'

They walked up to the end of a big, wide road together and there they saw a huge mob. 'I've never seen one as big as that – there must have been about five thousand of them, it was huge,' says Alan. 'You couldn't see the back of the mob and they were pouring downhill. It was amazing. You could hear the footsteps getting louder. Then I recognised a kid at the front from Farnley who was wearing a sheepskin and I thought, that's Trevor! It's Leeds! Well, the Wolves lads were off after a bit. They looked scared and they went.'

It was a different story when Alan and Tony were at Wolves and got split up from the main group of Leeds. They ended up in the city centre with three other lads when they spotted a large group of black lads coming towards them near a church. One of the three said, 'Right, nobody runs,' to which Alan and Tony said they had no intention of running. The lads got closer and the next thing Alan knew was the wind blowing in his hair as the three 'heroes' ran past them. He and Tony looked at each other in disgust and then took a battering from the locals. Alan managed to get away with eight of them in pursuit. He ran into a car park which was a dead end and feared the worst, as some of his assailants had knives.

He went up some stairs out onto the roof of a building and lay down in the pitch black in a puddle, hoping they would disappear. They couldn't find him but he stayed there for half an hour to make sure, soaked but relieved.

Descending the stairs, he didn't know which way to go and as he set off in one direction, he walked in front of the black gang again. He ran across a road, clambered over a fence and encountered two Alsatian dogs, so he jumped on a fire escape, went across another roof and climbed down a lamppost out into another street. He eventually found the railway lines further on and followed them, catching up with the others who were all wondering what the hell had happened to him.

* * *

Popular drinking establishments in the city in the Seventies were the Tam O' Shanter, later called Hoagies, the Three Legs and the Vine. When Newcastle came to Elland Road on Boxing Day, 1972, rumours spread quickly that their coach was parked up by the Tam O' Shanter and their mob was drinking inside. Scouts were despatched and returned confirming they were there, along with the police. Leeds weren't sure if Newcastle would get back on their coach or walk to Elland Road. In the event, they walked – only to encounter an ambush by 300-400 Leeds on Boar Lane, by Trinity Church. Fights broke out in the middle of the road in front of passing cars and shoppers, much to their dismay. Cockney Steve grabbed one lad up against a car and clocked him straight on the jaw, knocking him out cold on the road. Bystanders were panicking, with some screaming, and the small police presence could not contain the trouble. Newcastle were 'smashed to pieces' before Leeds scattered into the city centre.

Middlesbrough were enjoying life back in the First Division when Leeds took 8,000 to Ayresome Park in February 1975, with around 1,500 on one special train. Things went smoothly en route to the ground, with no locals trying anything, so most took it for granted that it would be the same afterwards. Invigorated by a Leeds victory and not worried by a minimal police presence, up to thirty lads headed in the direction of the train station, with others going in the opposite direction for coaches.

Scottie from Harehills walked down the road with two workmates, Alan and Craig, to get a train. They noticed a bit of trouble in a nearby park and decided to 'see what the crack was'. There were no police around and they soon realised groups of Leeds were getting run all over the place by the locals. They were quickly spotted and on the lam themselves. They were nearly split up but ended up jumping over a wall into a graveyard with a couple of others. They ducked down with a mass brawl taking place just yards away and snuck through the graveyard, wondering how they were going to get away without being seen. Debating what to do, they decided to hide their scarves in their Harrington jackets and risk it.

They managed to avoid trouble until they reached a road leading to the train station, where masses of Boro were gathering. They would have to walk the gauntlet. Scottie managed to reach a shopping precinct a few hundred yards from the station and a massive feeling of relief washed over him, until he heard from behind, 'Get the Leeds bastard!' He'd been sussed. He noticed an optician's shop and tried to run inside but only made it to the doorway before he was hit on the head and kicked by several Boro. He clung onto the door as best he could to shield himself from attack while the women inside the shop did their best to push him out. He took a hefty kicking on the floor until a copper appeared and stopped the beating.

With a broken nose, cuts and bruises, Scottie was escorted to the station, with the copper asking him to point out his assailants on the way. 'That was never going to happen,' said Scottie, but he went along with it, pretending to examine faces in the crowd to no avail. He made it to the platform, boarded the train and made it back home to Leeds with another tale to tell. 'Boro had a good mob that day and over the years we have had some big offs with them,' he recalled. 'On the whole they are a main mob who are always up for it.'

Crombie Boy is another old-school lad who rates Boro:

December 23, 1978 was Middlesbrough at home. I loved the games with Boro because you always knew it would go off. We started the day in the Windsor Castle pub, now the Leeds Riflemans. Back then, we had a lot more casual supporters because you could just turn up and pay on the gate. So before you ordered taxis, you'd do a quick ask round the pub, 'Anyone else fancy coming today?' There would always be three or four 'Yeah, nowt better to do' types who would come along for the laugh. Remember as well that the boozers used to shut between 3pm and 5.30pm.

Taxis ordered and off we went. Among our number was Ally G. He's a quiet lad now and doesn't go anymore, but he was a right battler in his day, big frizzy ginger afro head, you couldn't miss him. Skanny was with us, a Leeds fanatic with a fierce temper and a pride of all things Leeds. One time we were playing Derby away. We hitchhiked and got there about 2.45. The Leeds section was full, gates locked, so we went round to their end and just got in. We decided to make our way quietly to the front and get the coppers to squeeze us in with the Leeds fans. We squeezed our way about halfway down the terraces when Derby's Leeds-born player Kevin Hector fouled one of our players. Skanny went apeshit, it was a personal insult to him that a Leeds lad would play for anyone else and, boy, didn't he let everyone know. 'HECTOR YOU FUCKING TRAITOR, YOU FUCKING SHITHEAD.' A big gap suddenly seemed to open up around us as I grabbed him and made a dash for the front and we got out with all limbs intact.

Anyway, back to the Boro game, 'Big D' Derrick H was with us, and a couple of members of HM Armed Forces, estate lads on leave – funny, half of our estate seemed to be in the Army, Navy or Air Force. These two were in the Paras and game as anything. We got to Elland Road about 2.55 and it went off with Boro straight away, even numbers, about eight a side. We sussed them and steamed in. They didn't run, and we had a right go. I was piling into one lad when his mate, some stocky fucking ship welder or chemical mixer, caught me with a big right hook and I was on my arse. Luckily Alistair whacked him before he could follow up. Eventually everyone got a bit tired and sort of mutually backed off, but a good scrap with bumps and bruises on both sides.

We got in the Kop and pushed and shoved our way up to our usual place in front of stanchion five. After five minutes, I was starting to feel the after effects of the whack I'd taken, so I got into the gap behind the stanchion, which was our usual pissing post at half time, and spewed up. I felt better after that. After the game (we won 3-1) we made our way to the bar in the West Stand. We liked going in there because the windows in there were right above the away players' exit to their coach and we used to have great fun shouting abuse from above and taking the piss. It was because of stuff like this that Elland Road got its rep as a hostile place.

After the crowds had cleared we made our way onto Elland Road. We knew there'd be some Boro about, taking their time, stuffing their faces at United Fisheries, hunting for an off licence. The police didn't have it all wrapped up anything like they do now. We weren't disappointed. There they were, at the bottom of Wesley Street, a whole coachload, about forty lairy-looking cunts, scruffy bunch of inbred smog monsters gathered around the coach. There were about twenty of us now. They clocked us and started to walk, then run towards us and we deliberately backed off up the hill, till the front runners were near to us, pie-eaters behind, and the odds were even. We ran back at them and got the better of them as we were fighting downhill. Then their reinforcements caught up, and we backed off again. This happened two or three times until their numbers eventually backed up right up to the top of the street.

Now there just happened to be a shop right at the top of the street and just inside the door was a pyramid pile of tins of baked beans on special offer. The same thought occurred to all of us, and with a tin in each hand and all pockets full, we charged Boro right back down the hill, with tins of beans *whizzing round their heads, and chased them right back to their coach. At this stage, only about half of them wanted a pop back at us, while the other half were scrambling around trying to retrieve the beans, not to throw back at us but for Saturday night's supper! By the time the poor shopkeeper had called the cops and the sirens were approaching, we made our excuses and left.*

Scottie and his mates hung on the coat-tails of older lads from Harehills like Trevor H, Vallo and Eddie C, after going to matches at an early age and being exposed to their antics. For a League Cup match at home against Liverpool in November 1972 he saw plenty of 'good lads' in action in what turned out to be a huge brawl. The match was called off thirty minutes before kick-off due to bad weather. Many Leeds fans were already at the ground when they heard the news, so they decided to head back into the city centre. They were by the Holbeck Park Stadium end when they saw a huge crew of Liverpool fans at the bottom of Holbeck. It appeared the Scousers and their police escort didn't yet know the match had been cancelled.

The police officers scrambled to get between the two groups, but with about 500 Leeds and about 1,000 Liverpool, they had little chance of stopping what quickly became a riot. Fighting raged up and down the road for almost thirty minutes, according to those who were there, with more Leeds arriving behind the initial mob and joining the fray. Eventually Leeds managed to push back the Scouse hordes until more police quelled the disturbance and marched the visitors back to the train station.

An unruly teenager, Scottie ended up in a detention centre for four months, then a borstal for a further seven in 1973, before finally serving four months in the young offenders' wing of Manchester's Strangeways Prison. He was arrested four times in just a couple of seasons and fined £150 for three incidents and a whopping – for those days – £200 for trouble at Stoke. Finally sentencing him to six months, magistrates told him he was 'a bit of a menace'. He joined several other Leeds lads in Strangeways who had been detained at Her Majesty's pleasure for various offences.

Football rivalries continued inside and while the experience was not pleasant, it did no harm to his reputation when he was released in 1976.

At Chelsea in September 1978, he was stabbed after a 3-0 victory to Leeds. A fight developed in a ramped area when a group of 150 Chelsea tried to steam Leeds but they were having none of it and refused to budge. There some good boys there like Trevor H and Freddie and it was 'proper on-top', with everyone having a go, punching and kicking. It lasted only a short time before the police restored order, and as he walked away Scottie was aware of a warm feeling on his backside. He realised that in the melee he had been jabbed.

While groups from most areas still went to away matches separately, one lad from Bradford was going completely alone. Johnna, a huge Adam and the Ants fan, was heavily into the punk scene and was used to brawling at gigs, where there was rarely a police presence. Although he was starting to get to know others from Bradford, he would usually go to matches on his own with his scarf tied to his wrist. But after witnessing an episode of trouble at Middlesbrough around 1975, he realised he was much better off as part of a group. He was stood by a hotdog van when Boro and Leeds appeared, throwing bricks. He and the hotdog guy had to duck and dodge the missiles and later as he walked past a pub he saw a Leeds fan get ejected via a window.

Johnna started going in a van with the likes of Benny and Silver from Bradford for the occasional away game, and eventually for pretty much every away game. After trouble at Everton in November 1976, more and more lads were talking about the need to get more organised. Everton came running out of the Gwladys Street end and across the pitch to attack Leeds. Fighting broke out and some Leeds hid in the refreshment area, which Everton set alight in an effort to smoke them out. Johnna decided he would have a go back at one lad who was being particularly cocky and when he went for a piss Johnna went too and hit him and nicked his scarf.

Silver organised a van from Bradford, in which he also took people to Wigan Casino after certain games. Later, around 1978/79, the Bradford lads would meet a second van in Leeds containing the likes of Freddie Walker and Steve M. These two little groups went together up till the early Eighties. Going in vans meant the lads were free to go where and when they wanted, unlike the hundreds of fans who went on the special trains and were herded around like sheep. As Leeds had such a big fan base around the country, someone nearly always knew the lay of the land whenever they visited a new town or city or had been told where to go by someone else. It was different for matches in the capital, as they would make their own way there, meet in a pub near Kings Cross and then discuss what the plan should be.

Home matches often involved ambushes near the train station. One good battle was with Nottingham Forest in 1977. The Bradford contingent had come in on the train, the likes of Benny, Neil and Johnna, who was with a new mate called Leggy from Pudsey who had a false leg. While they were there, one of the biggest specials yet arrived at the station. Many of the Forest wore donkey jackets and some had balaclavas. Among them was Cookie, one of their known lads, and others from the Newark area.

Johnna and a few others left and went to a nearby Army and Navy store to buy balaclavas themselves, while in the station Leeds and Forest weighed each other up briefly before Big China took the lead. He grabbed a broom off a guy sweeping up and ran down the platform towards them. Several followed, including Leggy and his cousin Beeky. They chased them under the old tunnel that went to the platforms and then up the stairs and onto the platforms proper. Johnna and friends were just getting back inside the station when they saw Forest going under a bridge. They put on their balaclavas to infiltrate the Forest special and got to the front and attacked.

Leggy and Beeky – or 'Big Nose' and 'Spastic' as they called each other – were two game lads. Leggy sold his aluminium false leg to get some cash to go to a game at Coventry one year. He then went to the hospital to try to get another but they didn't have any, so they sawed a crutch in half and strapped it to his stump and nailed the bottom to his boot, then gave him a stick to help him balance. About twenty Leeds went in Coventry's main pub and when the locals walked in, they ran them up the road. Coventry came back with greater numbers and it kicked off again outside the pub. Things were getting a bit difficult as more locals joined in but Leeds couldn't run off and leave Leggy, so they fought on until the police waded in.

Leggy hit one lad on the head with his stick and a copper grabbed him and said, 'What are you doing with that stick?'

'It's my leg,' replied Leggy.

'What leg?' said the copper.

'Exactly,' said Leggy. 'I haven't got one.' When he pointed down to the crutch job where his leg should have been, the copper laughed and let him go.

3

BLUE MURDER

MOST FIRMS CAN testify that Maine Road in the Seventies was a daunting place, with visitors regularly coming a cropper in the grids of terraced back streets. For a match on Boxing Day, 1975, most of the Leeds contingent went in the seats in the Platt Lane end but a few went in the Kippax. Towards the end of the game, City steamed into the Kippax, cornering Leeds, who backed off onto the pitch. It was a frightening experience for the younger lads. There were about 3-4,000 Leeds fans and only several hundred City but the fighting was intense and for those caught up in the melee, it seemed a long time before the police got in. On the way out Benny grabbed a City hat off a kid to wear to avoid detection. It was so violent that a man from Bradford was apparently found unconscious in a garden two days later.

City always turned out at Leeds. While still at school in about 1975, Benny saw several City casualties lying in the train station with their shoes missing. City robbed clothes off some Leeds lads after a match at Maine Road on Good Friday 1977, with the trouble reported in the papers. City rushed in near the end of the game through the lower exit and initially had the upper hand against Leeds at the front of the Platt Lane end, causing people to spill out onto the pitchside. People were trapped between rows of seats with bodies falling on top of each other. It was every man for himself and Scottie found himself being hit on the head by one lad while another was pulling him down from the side. As he tried to get up, a huge surge forward caused yet another lad to fall on top of him, and he trod on the lad's head as he tried to hold his ground. Finally he and two others stood and began pushing back from the main group of Leeds next to a line of police, which saw them get separated and end up on the City side. City went for them. The cops did nothing until one grabbed Scottie and pulled him out, dispatching him onto the track around the pitch. He got to his feet and blended back into the Leeds crowd. It was another scary experience, with one Leeds fan getting stabbed during the mayhem.

In November 1977, Leeds faced Man City again. Travelling in vans was becoming a trend, but for big away fixtures like City most now took the coaches, knowing there would be strength in numbers. On this occasion, they parked on a corner by some football pitches and went to a nearby pub. Johnna, Martin, Mick and Alan B fell behind and, realising they were late, set off to find the ground, hidden among the ominous back streets of Moss Side. When they arrived, only the Kippax was open, so they ventured in and stood at the back. They did their best to mingle, agreeing with Mancunian conversations about how good the previous week's exploits at Forest had been and that they were up for West Brom the following week. They managed to maintain their cover even as Leeds took a 3-1 lead, but with ten minutes to go the atmosphere was becoming more fraught so they said their goodbyes, slyly smiling about their impending victory as they headed back to their coach.

As they walked down a side street away from the ground, a guy in a donkey jacket, accompanied by several punk rockers, appeared and asked if they were Leeds. To defuse the situation, Johnna, a punk himself, claimed he had come all the way over from Bradford to see Man City, and yet here he was about to be attacked by his own fans. At the same time, Mick was walking up the road some way behind them and as Johnna glanced round to locate him, a guy on a motorbike deliberately ran over him before driving off, laughing. Johnna turned back to face the City lads, who apologised and moved on. Perhaps the punk connection had worked. But the man in the donkey jacket remained and asked if they would join him to 'get the Leeds fans'. Johnna told him they had to get back to where they were parked before the Leeds contingent arrived and finally he left them to it.

By now, people were split up and trying to make their way back to the coaches. Johnna could see Martin some way back being set upon by a gang of City fans. One slashed him across the face and he saw Martin pick a City scarf off the floor to use as a bandage to hold his face together. Johnna debated whether to go back but saw more City fans coming down towards him. He hoped they would walk past him so he could return to Martin but unfortunately it was 'the ugly git in the donkey jacket' and some of his mates. He obviously hadn't believed their earlier story and had gone for back-up.

They now quizzed Johnna again about what part of Bradford he was from. Not knowing that there was an area in Manchester called Bradford, he said, 'Little Horton Lane.' The name meant nothing to them and he was attacked, with one of them hitting him across the knee with a hammer and another one chucking a brick at him. Faced with ten angry City fans brandishing weapons, the lone Johnna backed off into a garden, while they hovered by the gate. Out of desperation, he knocked on the door of the house and asked to be let in. 'Fuck off, I'm having my tea,' said the man who answered, doing little to enhance the reputation of Manchester natives.

As he stood there wondering what to do, feeling a mixture of fear and confusion, Johnna began to get angry. He knew he was going to get battered, or worse, but going down fighting was better than hiding in a garden. He walked towards his tormentors just as a copper appeared, asking what was going on. Johnna said he was a Leeds fan and had been attacked, and the officer said he would escort him back to the coaches, telling the City group to move on. Johnna also said that his mate had also been attacked and possibly stabbed but he didn't know how bad it was. 'Well we haven't had any reports of knife injuries,' said the copper.

Further along the road, near the coaches, they had to walk past the gang of City fans that had attacked him and Martin. As Johnna approached them he hung back, then said to them as he passed, 'I hope you come to Leeds next month because we're going to destroy you.' They just smiled.

When he and the others got back to the coach, they swapped horror stories and discussion turned to what they should do next: retaliate or leave. Six people were still missing from their coach and a quick check with the coach behind revealed even more were missing in action. Someone went to find a phone box to ring

Manchester Royal Infirmary. He was told that it was full of Leeds fans and he had to ring back later, as it was chaos there and they were too busy to answer individual queries. When he reported back with their news, it unsurprisingly caused fury.

China arrived back at the coach with a professional boxer from Bradford called Pete. They realised that City were still about and mingling between the coaches. 'Right then, fuck this,' said China, after hearing what had happened to Martin. They reflexively jumped off the coach and attacked the nearest City fans, then gathered a small mob to look for more.

At the top of the road they spotted more City and set off towards them, with an injured Johnna hoping he would encounter the lads he'd met earlier. China and Pete were in work clothes and looked like a couple of labourers – China had on a pair of steel-cap Wellingtons. They reached a bus stop behind the City fans as Johnna shouted over to distract them. As one of the City fans turned round, he was kicked straight through the bus shelter window. Others came to his aid but Pete the boxer and China, who was built like the Honeymonster from the TV ad, dished out similar punishment. The City lads were taken aback by the ferocity of China's attack, but carrying blades and slashing people wasn't in the script for Leeds and he was livid about what had happened.

The police arrived and forced them back on their coaches, curbing their lust for revenge. They rang the hospital again later on and were told that thirty or forty Leeds fans had been hospitalised. When Martin had got on the coach, a policeman took him to one side and pulled away the scarf that was wrapped around his face. The flesh of his bloodied cheek fell forward.

'I'll go to hospital when I get back,' he said.

'You won't live if you don't get that fixed now,' replied the copper.

They took him to casualty in a police car and he returned home with twenty-eight stitches across his face. Johnna had an indentation in his knee from the hammer blow. Some weeks later, Martin went to Manchester with the CID, found the youth that slashed him and received £1,000 criminal injury compensation.

Johnna was even more enraged by that incident at City than when he was himself the victim of a severe knife attack later on in the Eighties. Looking back, he says it was probably a defining moment for him and many other Leeds fans regarding what could happen if they wanted to follow their team away from home. Whereas before they had indulged in relatively minor punch-ups, this changed people's attitudes. The City match was also seen as yet another example of Leeds hooligans not sticking together. Over the next few years they would unite and would take vast numbers to Manchester, turning the tables on City.

China and Pete were 'good lads' to have by your side at matches. Benny remembers a day at Forest when he was in a car with Pete and four others driving through Nottingham. They saw a few locals at a bus stop. 'Pete said to stop the car. He got out and went over to one of the kids and smacked him, demolishing his nose, then got back into the car and we drove off. The police caught up with us and took us to Nottingham police station. It sounds cruel but we couldn't stop laughing at the kid as he tried to say what had happened, because his nose was so badly smashed he just made a distorted nasal sound when he spoke. He kicked up such a fuss at the station, shouting and trying to get to Pete and have a go back, that the coppers had enough and told him to leave. Then they told us to get back in our car and get lost.'

Big China's size was often an asset. When Leeds played a night match at Bolton in the League Cup in November 1977, China, Benny and Johnna went for a walk around the ground to see what it was like, having not been there before. They walked down a dark, narrow alley, with a street lamp on the corner, leading towards the Bolton end. As they walked, they noticed the acoustics in the alley made every word echo loudly. They heard some Bolton fans around the corner and shouted 'Leeds!' as they neared them. Neither group could quite see the other but as the Leeds trio approached the street light China's huge figure was silhouetted by the lamplight, casting an even bigger shadow that grew with every step he took. Suddenly they heard a shout of 'Look at the size of them!' and heard footsteps running in the opposite direction. When they turned the corner, the Bolton lads had gone.

China is sorely missed, having died of a heart attack in 1999, at the age of forty. At his funeral, Pernod Harry, another well-known lad, told China's wife that he would never forget a day at Spurs when some lads pulled out blades on him and, despite the danger, China waded in to rescue him.

* * *

A month after the trouble at City, Leeds played them in the League. The police were expecting trouble and frustrated the Leeds fans all day, so very little happened, much to everyone's annoyance. However their prayers were answered when they drew City in the third round of the FA Cup in January 1978. Some recall not ever seeing Leeds in such a mood for revenge, even for Manchester United, universally know as 'the Scum'. Retribution was in the air.

Leeds fans invaded every part of the City end. There was trouble in the South Stand when the visitors were showered with beer after City scored, and when the visitors went 2-0 ahead fighting fans poured onto the pitch. With their Cup exit seeming imminent, many of the Leeds thugs felt if they could get the game abandoned, all the better. City goalkeeper Joe Corrigan was brought down at the Kop end for apparently sticking two fingers up at supporters; Scottie recalls seeing Steve M attacking Corrigan in the goalmouth and then a surge of Leeds fans come from the Kop. The goalie denied making gestures to fans and helped police arrest a fan.

The game was held up and police horses rode onto the pitch. Both teams were taken off but the rioting continued for a further sixteen minutes. Eight mounted police came on to the pitch, thirty-two people were arrested and thirty injured. Leeds tried to tear the fences down in the Lowfields that separated the away fans and ran across the pitch to get to City. They were kept at bay, just, by police.

Then someone said to open the gates ten minutes before the end of the game. A lot of Leeds fans went back on the terrace and out of the ground while the others kept the police inside. Those that went outside could see City coming out of the ground running for their lives to get away. Leeds attacked anybody and everybody coming out. Johnna saw Martin, standing in a daze with what looked like a Coke can ripped in half in his hand, swinging wildly in an attempt to stab the City fans around him and shouting, 'Bastards!' His view of City had been drastically tainted by the severe injury he had sustained at Maine Road.

Leeds then charged up into the Lowfields stand as the City fans tried to get out. Everyone was in a frenzy – until they heard a loud shout for help. A woman was trying to get her disabled father out of the ground and in a moment of gentlemanly conduct everyone seemed to stop what they were doing and move out of their way, with some helping him down the stairs. Then, as soon as they were gone, the Leeds mob steamed straight back into the City fans. City scrambled back into the ground and lads could spot the terrified looks on their faces. More were being attacked from the pitch and from the side in the Lowfields.

It wasn't all one-sided. Outside, Benny saw City's Cool Cats mob, led by Donald Francis, chasing Leeds. Benny ended up running away onto the motorway after stoning their coaches before being rounded up by the cops and carted off. Francis and the Cool Cats, who were prominent towards the end of the decade, were well dressed, smooth operators who were usually tooled up and always hovering around Maine Road and in the Kippax at home games. Eventually the trouble died down; the Leeds hooligans were exhausted and the City fans had been dealt with. Revenge, everyone agreed, was sweet. The penalty on the club was not. The FA banned Leeds from playing home cup ties for three years, though the ban was lifted after one season. Officials claimed Leeds fans were trying to get the game abandoned and fences were later erected inside the ground to keep them off the pitch.

Skiz, who was later part of the so-called Very Young Team that emerged in the 1980s, was barely into his teens but can still remember the buzz he got from watching it all unfold:

Joe Corrigan stuck two fingers at the cop and it all kicked off inside and outside. I was only twelve or thirteen but I remember being outside and it was total mayhem. I didn't know anyone then but the buzz I got from watching it was unreal. It was pure madness.

You had about two thousand Leeds, I won't say lads, as it was all sorts of people – punk rockers, Mods and a middle-aged father-of-three with his denim jacket on, all up on this hill waiting with bricks and sticks to get into the Mancunians. It was like a scene from the miners' strike. To see all these people on this hill must have been scary. It was wave after wave of Leeds steaming into the City escorts. The police didn't have a clue.

A Man City lad also recalled the events of that hectic day:

Leeds were good at home in those days. We got the service train in the morning, about fifty-handed. Got to Leeds about twelve, came out of the station down the approach and loads of Leeds came out of the pub opposite the staircase at the side of the station. We had it on the approach and chased them back into the pub.

Instead of going past the pub and heading to the ground, we turned left at the bottom of the approach and plotted up in a pub at the end of that road. Our numbers rose to about a hundred, there were loads on the train that day. We were all in the pub and outside because it was a decent day.

Then hundreds of Leeds were coming up the street. We cleared the pub of empty glasses and bottles and had it with Leeds again. If anyone has seen Agincourt, where the air is full of arrows, that's what it was like with glasses and bottles, everyone had armfuls of them and we ran Leeds all over. Then the Old Bill turned up and escorted us to the ground.

That was before the game. After the game it was a different matter. We were in the end opposite the Gelderd End. In the right hand corner at the side of our end was about two thousand Leeds. About fifteen minutes to go, the corner completely emptied. I never thought much about it at the time. We came out after the match and we must have had a mob of about two thousand, I kid not. We felt invincible, it was a top mob, all the main heads.

Leeds came behind us and I have to admit there were thousands of them, it was going off all the time, to-ing and fro-ing. Our numbers seemed to dwindle and we were getting split up, with fights breaking out all over the place and the Old Bill trying to control it. We managed to get about four hundred City to stick together but Leeds were coming from behind. This was at the time of the motorway flyover being built at Leeds.

We came around the corner to face this big hill and then we realised where the Leeds in the corner had gone. There were hundreds of them at the top of this hill in front of us and thousands behind us. The ones on the hill launched hundreds of bricks into City's mob. Loads of lads were going down with head wounds, it was a nightmare. They charged down the hill into us and the ones behind charged into us. It was carnage. At that point it was every man for himself.

I had it toe-to-toe for a couple of minutes, my head was split open and the blood was in my eyes. I saw a gap and ran like fuck. I got chased across a road where I nearly got run over, I didn't even wait for a gap in the traffic. They chased me for what seemed like hours but was probably only a few minutes. I hid in a derelict house. Then I saw the train lines and dropped fifteen feet down a wall onto the tracks and walked back into the station. On the way down the train tracks I met loads of other Blues who had the same idea. They were all carrying injuries as well.

About sixty were on the train back and it was like a hospital train. There were some horror stories. I am sure loads of older lads will remember that day. You won't ever see the likes of that again.

In the aftermath, someone was arrested for the attack on Joe Corrigan. Johnna found himself in court – in his case for trouble with Liverpool the previous October – on the same day the guy was convicted. Johnna had been in the Lowfields when Liverpool scored and he shouted 'Bastards!' to no one in particular. A copper grabbed him and tried to drag him out over the fence but the crowd started pulling him back into the Lowfields. After a lot of pain, Johnna shouted for someone to let him go, and the lads obliged. He was escorted round by the Gelderd End and almost the whole Kop started singing 'silly, silly cunt' at him because he was in his punk gear, which made him very much in the minority at Elland Road. He often saw football lads outside gigs in the city waiting to attack the punks and spent a lot time trying to prevent attacks and keeping the peace.

After a poor start to the 1977 season, victories against Manchester City and Forest provided a much needed boost for the team ahead of a clash with West Ham in the capital in November. Some went on Wallace Arnold coaches and Johnna went on one half full with lads from Halifax. The drivers pulled up near the ground but had to move on as no one fancied getting off next to fifteen loitering skinheads.

As soon as they neared the ground, Johnna saw a Bradford City fan he knew called Steve and started chatting. They made their way towards the ground so they wouldn't be seen near the Leeds coaches. Inside Upton Park, Johnna and Steve couldn't find any Leeds fans, as there was no segregation and people had again split up so they wouldn't be noticed. The pair stood in among West Ham, putting on their best Cockney accents. Luckily they were near some Irish blokes who couldn't tell the difference, plus Steve had a maroon silk City scarf on which might have helped. But they struggled to keep the accents up and fortuitously spotted some Leeds fans from Harrogate down the side, so they ran across the corner of the pitch by the flag to join up with them.

They were spotted cheering when Leeds scored and West Ham made a move for them. Johnna, Steve, six other lads and a couple of girls were by some steps when they saw the Hammers coming upstairs. In a matter of seconds the two groups seemed to swap places as West Ham easily despatched them down the stairs to the bottom of the stand. Things were looking pretty unpleasant until a steward opened a gate and pushed them outside, quickly shutting it behind them and saving them from a battering.

But now, outside and with no coaches in sight, they felt even more vulnerable – especially as a group of forty West Ham were nearby. The Harrogate lads decided to disappear and left to go back on the Tube, a costly mistake as they were later attacked and one was stabbed. Johnna and a couple of others sat on a wall by a row of shops, waiting desperately for their coaches to turn up. The West Ham lads tormented the trio with comments like 'Should we beat them up' or 'Nah, let 'em off,' just loud enough for them to hear. Johnna armed himself with a brick hidden behind his back, as every so often the group would pretend to come near, then say, 'Nah, leave 'em.' Eventually the coaches appeared and they escaped. They passed some Millwall in surgical masks and white doctors' coats and exchanged abuse as they headed out of the capital.

The following January brought an away game against Birmingham City. Johnna and his mate Chris, a Man U fan, were in the Leeds end when Birmingham came in and it kicked off. As Johnna grappled with a Brummie, he was arrested and taken down the tunnel just as the players came out onto the pitch. He was put in a cubicle inside a police van along with ten Blues lads until it got too full and was then deposited at a police station. He soon attracted the attention of a big black guy.

'You Leeds bastard,' he snarled. 'Normally I'd kill you but my wife is coming back from Liverpool tonight.'

So he just hit him instead. Johnna tried to have a go back but the others grabbed him. When he was eventually released, the cops told him what bus to catch back to 'the football ground'. They had the last laugh – the bus took him to Villa's ground, not City's. Fortunately Villa were not playing.

He had to hitchhike back. After a few lifts, he managed to get to the M62 with some Liverpool fans. He walked along the motorway and was soon picked up by the police and arrested again. They radioed through to Bradford to check his details before dropping him off in Manchester. As he began walking yet again, a girl approached him saying, bizarrely, she was interested in hitchhikers. They briefly chatted before she left – and told a gang of thirty lads that he was a Leeds fan. They promptly charged after him with planks of wood, shouting, 'Get the Leeds bastard.' Johnna managed to elude them and got back to the motorway again. He failed to get a lift at Birch Services and in the end encountered more police, who took him to a station to get a taxi, which his dad ended up paying for as he had no cash. He was back in Birmingham before the courts on the Monday and was slapped with a £100 fine.

4

THE MERSEY BEAT

TRIPS TO LIVERPOOL were always tasty. Like Maine Road, Anfield was a daunting ground to visit and their massive support and ruthless scallies saw numerous firms come a cropper over the years. Their police weren't friendly either. Liverpool won the majority of the games against Leeds in the Seventies – bar the 1971/72 season when Leeds were victorious against them in both League matches and beat them on their way to winning the FA Cup against Arsenal – but a trip to Anfield in 1973 holds particularly great memories for one lad. Sean is a well respected and original member of the Service Crew and went on to be a linchpin, with Griff and Ricky B, in helping the next phase of lads come through from about 1983.

I went to Liverpool as a kid in 1973 and jumped the train with a pal of mine. I told my parents that I'd be going to Scarborough with my pal and his aunt. Little did they know I was going to a place to be scared out of my wits but it was to stand me in good stead for the rest of my life.

We got to Lime Street and there was a lot of older lads with us who'd followed Leeds all over Europe so knew the score. Some of them were involved in the gang wars in town so were used to what was going to happen next and when we got out of the station and a mighty roar went up, it went off. The Scousers were here.

There were bodies flying in all over, Leeds were holding their own, then all of a sudden another mob of Liverpool came in from another side entrance. I got in the middle of the bunch but we got pushed back against the barriers, Liverpool seemed to get the better of us but the older guys were getting stuck in big time.

Then all of a sudden the coppers came in and started whacking anyone with these big sticks with brass on the end. One grabbed me by my coat and gave me a swipe across the head with his hand, fucking hell did this hurt. The only other person ever to crack me like that was my dad. They seemed to get it together and held us all against the barriers. They really were a bunch of nasty, miserable old bastards who obviously had experience of dealing with trouble in this city the only and most efficient way they knew, like the old Irish cops you saw on the Cagney films with their nightsticks.

One of the older lads said to me, 'Fair play kid, you didn't move there, but that was only the start of it.' I thought, what have I let myself in for? I had seen a bit of carrying on outside the Lowfields at our glorious Elland Road but this was now on their terms. Would I see the rest of the day out, would I get killed or would I be taken home by the police, or worse, be lost and stuck in Liverpool? The day had just begun.

We started to move out of the front of the station and to the right. I had never seen another city, other than Glasgow and Edinburgh due to my mum being Scottish. It was busy with buses going past and kids abusing us out of the windows, it seemed that every kid must have got off every bus passing, as Liverpool were both following us and were in front of us. I got talking to this big ginger-haired lad and he warned me to watch myself, don't stray out of the escort or I'd be picked off, chinned and robbed. This sent a shiver through me but I took note.

Then there was a commotion, some of the Liverpool in front had attacked the escort and it was going off, the coppers were backing the Scousers into and over the road. A big, black-haired lad in a denim shirt got past the law and smacked one of ours, this lad then booted another Leeds lad, then Leeds got stuck into him. The coppers then started battering him and a couple of the Leeds lads, I think one of our lot got nicked.

I remember going past blocks and blocks of flats, like the old Quarry Hill and Saxton Gardens in Leeds, and thinking, they look rough little kids, like us. They were playing football and lobbing bricks at us before the law chased them off, to a load of abuse. We just seemed to be walking for miles and I thought, I'm going to die if we don't get there soon. I asked an older lad how long left and he replied, 'Don't worry, you'll know when we're near, kid.' I thought that we'd see the tall floodlights, then he said, 'This is the famous Scottie Road, be careful.' We seemed to go past loads of pubs with big, horrible blokes hanging out of them. One Leeds fellow tried to go into one and they started fighting and yet again the Old Bill responded and battered and nicked a few but this time from both sides. I thought that Leeds bloke must've been mad.

We got held up at a crossroads and I saw one of the older skinheads from down our street, sadly he's dead now but he did love a carry-on. He was amazed to see me here. He was about eighteen then. He said, 'Come up here with a few more of us,' so we obliged. I asked why have we stopped and he informed me we weren't far.

Everton was to the left and Anfield was up a slight hill ahead but the law had to move a load of Liverpool on so we could pass. He said this is where they attack you – again – and he was right. A hail of bricks and bottles came into us and a big shout of 'Liverpool, Liverpool' could be heard but some of the Leeds at the front ran at the Scousers and started scrapping – fists, boots were going in from both sides.

The escort was now restless. Fights were breaking out behind us. It seemed all hell was let loose and the coppers seemed to lose it but then more came towards us down the hill and chased the Scousers everywhere, though they wouldn't follow them into the flats. The law were really pissed off by this time and huddled everyone together, making us walk quicker. It was really dodgy, all streets of terraced houses. This was the time to stick really close to the older lads from down our street.

We could see more and more Scousers walking towards the ground, with us on the opposite side of the street. Some had scarves on, some had the old plain red Umbro team shirts on and most had the fashion of the time, either skinheads in Harringtons and Dr Martens or long hair, stripy jumpers and flared jeans on. These were the ones making comments and up for a piece of the action, as a lot with us were. The adrenalin was pumping inside me by now, not that I knew what it was but I was excited. My pal Rob, who I had gone with, was shitting himself and close to tears I think, although he was bigger than me but the same age.

All of a sudden a massive roar went up and literally ten yards in front of me a load of Scousers ran into us. Everything was going mad all around us, at the side, the front, the back. They had steamed the escort from one of their dodgy side streets. I didn't know whether to laugh, cry, run off, stand and fight or just be rooted to the spot in fear but as it happened Leeds seemed to get the better of the immediate action. The Scousers were backing off. I ran and kicked this kid about fourteen years old, never forget him, he had a school jumper on.

The coppers came in and pushed us back onto the main road, what I now know as Anfield Road. This was leading us towards the ground and 'reinforcements'. We got to the ground and were queuing to get in and a couple of the older skinheads said, 'Hey, why don't you two try and get in for nowt, just get down and push in against our legs as we pay in?' Rob wasn't too sure but I just dropped down and pushed through with this kid and that was it, I was in for free and I had 50p extra for crisps and pop. Rob too made it but was nervous we'd be caught.

More and more Leeds were coming through the turnstiles. The coaches had arrived and some fellows were coming in with busted noses, cut lips and eyes. There had been some serious fighting where they were and they looked like they'd come off second best. One kid was talking to Big Brian from down our way, he was a big skin too. He said, 'Scouse bastards ambushed us as we were walking up the road, came out of the park and down the road near The Arkles.'

Brian replied, 'Oh yeah we've just had it with some of them. They attacked us as we got to the ground. We did all right I suppose. Backed them off, same old fucking story here, you know the score, always waiting for a chance to pick you off and the law are bastards too.' This skin said, 'They'll get a shock when that other special with the Harehills lot gets here, they'll knock fuck out of them.'

Brian told him the story of all the fighting from the station to the ground and mentioned how I'd booted the Scouser. He patted me on the head and praised me; I was chuffed to bits. He did inform me however, in a rather sinister tone, that it was only about a third of the way done.

We went up the steps into the ground and were in a corner section. FUCKING HELL I couldn't have ever visualised anything like it. There were Scousers on all sides of us, it was packed and people were still coming in our end. There was an orange tape separating Leeds from them and a few old coppers with those horrendous big sticks. As the ground filled up we were getting pushed towards the tape. I looked across at the Liverpool fans and one kid, who looked about seventeen, said, 'You're gonna get it kid, you're fucking dead.' I didn't know what to say but the older Leeds were just giving it back to them.

All of a sudden outside the ground a massive roar went up again, signalling that the other special with the Harehill lads on had arrived along with some other coaches. We could see some fighting outside our end over the wall in between our end and the long Liverpool end. It looked rough, bottles flying and bricks, bodies running in everywhere, police on horses and on foot.

A big roar of 'Liverpool, Liverpool' went up in the ground from every side. It was deafening. The big end opposite was swaying and it looked packed to the hilt. Leeds *responded with a shout of 'Super Leeds'. I shouted it too, fucking hell this was my pride and joy. I shouted it at Elland Road many times to my heroes and this time I was on their patch and it felt good.*

The tape got nearer and nearer and so did the Scousers and they looked horrible. Some of these looked like men, definitely older lads anyway and they wanted a fight. I was easy pickings to them. One old copper with grey hair tapped his stick and laughed at me. He meant, come near that tape kid and you're getting this across your legs. I took heed of the warning.

Lots of older Leeds were coming in the ground now, these were the ones who'd been at it outside. They were all laughing and joking about the fighting. They were a mix of skins and smart blokes. I found out this was the Harehills firm, there were lads and men from Seacroft, Gipton, Armley, Beeston, Bramley, York, Wakefield, Bradford, Selby, London, all over. I recognised a few from the home games but these were hard core and the coppers knew it too as they stiffened up.

Then as the teams came out, Leeds ran at the tape and started fighting with the Scousers and the coppers were taken aback. Liverpool were stunned too. There was a bit of a melee and the noise by now was deafening, just a noise, no words. The Scousers surged towards us, coppers' helmets flying, punches going in, sticks waved into everyone. More and more coppers were coming in to break it up. This was madness. They were dragging bodies out and taking them towards the pitch.

One Liverpool fan spat at the Leeds lads at the front and the law manhandled him round the side of the pitch. A few Leeds were taken out too. I picked up a Liverpool kid who had fallen down with some of the Leeds at the side of me. He looked at me as if to say thanks and then jumped back across the tape into his end. He had dropped his silk scarf and programme and I thought about going to give him it back when Big Brian said, 'No way, they'll drag you in and kill you Sean. Anyway, class it as a souvenir.' Taking scarves from fans with menaces was the 'in' thing then. I was lucky I didn't have to chin him and I'd add it to the Burnley scarf I'd removed from a kid at Elland Road. And if you're both reading this, I didn't mean it. You know the score, it was the fashion then and I'm sure you would've done it to me or many another Leeds fan if you could have.

I felt great. I'd paid nothing to get in the ground, nothing for a programme and taking that scarf was like taking the enemy's colours at Waterloo. I suppose it was no different at all, as I'm older now I realise that there's something in the British male that makes us so territorial, home or away, and it must be our history of war and being an island race.

Before the game kicked off the Liverpool Kop was amazing, singing, swaying, a mass with banners and scarves. To be honest this was what I'd come here for, to see my hero Allan Clarke score a winner, Lorimer to pound their goal with hotshots, Bremner and Giles to dictate the play, Eddie Gray to go on his mazy runs. These were the best two teams in Europe to me and they were about to do battle. I looked at Liverpool – Callaghan, Heighway, Keegan, Toshack, Hughes and Tommy Smith – they fucking scared me with that team but I just hope that the Scousers would feel like I did. I'm sure they did in a respectful way and I must admit I've never seen anything like that Kop or tasted the atmosphere like Anfield. I've been to every one of the grounds in Britain worth going and they've all had their moments for atmosphere, ours included, but that was something else.

The game was typical Liverpool v Leeds, big on rivalry, blood and guts, lots of free kicks, lots of Bremner winding them up, the big defenders getting involved, the wide men trying to carve openings, forwards going close. People don't remember but these games were the ultimate in the top division in those days and as I've said, maybe Europe, even bigger than the Leeds v Man United, and that includes outside the ground too.

We drew, I think, and when it was time to go Big Brian said, 'Stick with me and everyone on the train. They'll escort us back and it will be the same as on the way here, if not worse, but you'll be all right Sean, you did well coming here.' I was made up. One of the older lads had praised me. I had been scared but now it seemed to leave me.

Leeds seemed to have more on the way back to the station than coming to the ground. One Leeds kid outside the ground from Wortley had had a right whacking. He'd been thrown out and the coppers just watched him get it by all accounts, bastards. Any away fan will tell you that was the form in those days at Anfield. It was similar on the way back, little bits of fighting here and there, police involved, more nickings though and a lot more of them Leeds fans, but this lot walking back seemed different, hungrier, more experienced, harder and nastier, and the same could be said of the Scousers. My pal told me that a lot of the Scousers were dockers and hard as fuck plus, the regular scallies from the streets.

When we got down the long road we'd come up, towards town, there was a scuffle near some flats and I saw the same kid who I'd picked up in the ground, whose scarf I had in my pocket. He looked at me and ran over the road with his pals after having a row with the front of the escort. I felt better for nicking his scarf. As we approached the station, the law made us tighten up and warned us that if anyone retaliated when Liverpool attacked us we'd be battered and nicked. Jesus Christ, talk about British justice. He was right, they came at us near a town hall but these Leeds were different and got into them. There seemed to be thousands of Scousers but probably a couple of hundred in reality. As I'm older now I can judge things as a man, not a frightened, impressionable kid.

In the station, I was going to go get a can of pop and some crisps but one of the older lads grabbed me and warned me of the danger of all the Scousers on the corner watching to pick off stragglers. We got the train home and all the way back all the older lads were talking about the fighting all day. There were a few casualties and one Leeds kid had been stabbed in his leg outside the ground and they'd only patched him up, fucking hell this was the 1970s, not the Crimean War. There was something about all this talk I liked, I could tell Rob didn't but I loved it. I was a cheeky bastard anyway.

We got back to Leeds and went for the 23 bus home and all the older skins from Bramley, Armley, Pudsey and Farsley got on with us. They were all going drinking and meeting girls but they were sound with us. One of them said, 'Hey kid show ' em your scarf,' so I did and they were made up with me. One of them even bought the programme off me. I wish I'd kept that as it was my first ever away game and what an eventful day it was. It actually made one of the biggest impressions on my life and is probably still up there nowadays and I've got the memories forever.

I got home and my mum asked if I'd had a great day, was the weather all right, how was Rob and his aunt. I don't know about his aunt but Rob was in another world. He'd have fucking nightmares that night and this was a kid who went on to play rugby at a very high amateur standard and do the doors around Yorkshire, a big, hard lad, but that day changed him forever. Me, well I couldn't sleep at first due to the excitement, so I came downstairs and cuddled up to my mum. I think we watched The Two Ronnies together, her little angel and little did she know I was turning into her little monster because of that day. I then went to bed and slept like a log, God only knew what was to follow.

This was Rob's last time he went to Liverpool but it wasn't mine. I had many, many more to come and most the same as that first crazy, scary, eventful, wonderful, life-mapping day. I also had many a good 'do' at home with the Boys from the Mersey. I must say, I've got many friends in Liverpool now who are in their firm and I love going over for a drink with them now and then.

Liverpool undoubtedly led the way in football fashion and their impact was felt across the country, followed closely by the London mobs. Dressing started to become important for what became the Service Crew from about 1978 and lads would go on shopping trips to Manchester, with a couple of girls in tow for cover. There was always robbed gear up for sale, taken from shops in Leeds, usually Olivers, which was the first main clothes store along with Class.

In *The Liverpool Boys are in Town*, a book about the ever-changing trends in Merseyside, author Dave Hewitson says a 'defining moment' in their fashion history took place at Leeds in 1977. Liverpool's lads acknowledge that flares and scarves had been laid to rest after a fight in the car park at Elland Road. The old Kopite bootboys attacked a group of teenagers wearing straight jeans, cords and Adidas trainers. It was a few moments before lads on opposite sides recognised one another. When the Liverpool lads realised they were fighting their own, the brawling stopped and was replaced by laughter. That moment, the author concludes, meant that going to football for the hooligan lads was not just about 'having a bit of a scrap, it was now also about the clothes and the attitude. A whole new youth culture was about to emerge.'

When Liverpool won their first European Cup in Rome in 1977, few could have imagined that the pictures of fans in flares, draped in flags and scarves, were to soon become museum pieces. In 1976, Benny remembers being at a service station in Oxford bags and loafers when a Scouser in a denim jacket and jeans with a trim on the bottom said, 'If you come to Anfield looking like that you'll get murdered.' But by the time of a match at Liverpool in 1978, the Scousers were in tight jeans and Stanley parkas with flicked hair. 'As far as the eye could see there was a sea of Sambas,' recalled Benny. Between 200-300 of these strange creatures were outside the ground when Leeds arrived and it inevitably went off in Anfield Road. The Leeds skinheads also had a few 'wedge-heads' in amongst them, with some getting hit by their own side because they were mistaken for Scousers.

A Liverpool fanzine called *The End* later featured an article entitled 'Our trip to Leeds' which detailed their views on journeys to Elland Road and their not-so-fashion-savvy rivals. A sketch with a sarcastic punchline portrayed a Leeds fan as a huge, pie-munching cyclops with a scarf around his wrist. As well as some immaculate dressers, however, Liverpool also had their little urchins. At a night match at Anfield in 1979, Sean claims to have seen lads wearing old school blazers and the rip-off Post Office baseball boots that cost about £3. Thirty-four fans were ejected from the ground and sixteen arrested. Buses taking Leeds fans through Lower Breck Road to their train at Edge Hill were hit with bricks, iron bars and even a spiked railing bar. Leeds retaliated by ripping out seats and throwing them through the broken windows. Even worse was an incident before a Liverpool visit to Elland Road, when the top deck of a bus was set on fire, forcing seventy fans to smash windows to escape, with some clambering down a lamppost.

A night game at Anfield in March 1980 was yet another moody fixture. Some of the Bradford lot went over in a minibus, with others on coaches, and the police put them in a pub before they walked towards the ground and had a few scuffles on the way. They paid in, only to find the locals were all around them. It was scary. Liverpool were in the Leeds section, fighting at the bottom, and at half-time there was trouble by some steps near a refreshment stand. Stevie M went into a group of them but there were too many and the cops soon waded in and stopped it. Dean from Oldham and a few others were nicked and kept in a cell at the ground. They then had the unfortunate experience of being let out before the match finished. The urchins were lurking about. Dean and his mates were chased towards a copper, who merely said, 'Fuck off, you shouldn't have come.' Fortunately the gates were opened fifteen minutes before the end of the game and they ran inside, so their pursuers gave up.

Leeds got trounced 3-0, and when they looked outside the ground there seemed to be more fans out than in. Everyone said to stick together as they heard the usual, 'We're gonna kill yer Leeds' from all the skinheads and wedge-heads, or flickheads as they were called in Leeds, as everyone with that hairstyle would continually flick their heads back. They walked to the Arkles pub with Liverpool constantly trying to get into them, while the older lads told everyone to stay tight and keep them out. It was highly intimidating and by the coaches Liverpool eventually went for them in a mass charge. Every Leeds fan got stuck in, big blokes, straight fans and lads, and managed to back them off a bit. It was a dodgy night but Leeds felt they had stayed tight and performed well at one of the most menacing grounds at that time. Older lads congratulated the younger ones even though they had been petrified.

'Liverpool were an awesome firm and were having successes pretty much everywhere they went with their huge support,' said Benny. 'Another time at theirs in 1981, about five thousand Leeds left the ground and forty-odd of us peeled off from the escort on Scotland Road, thinking we could go and rejoin it if things got on top. Several hundred had gone over on the train that day and there'd been some trouble before the game. With Sean, Musky, Al P, Big China, Jonsey, Pele, Ricky, Zoz, John, Terry and some Seacroft lads, we went off to see what we could find.

'We walked for about twenty minutes before encountering some little urchins with the cuffs of their coats over their hands, who started chucking bricks at us from some flats. We chased them into the flats but when they pulled out knives, we thought, this isn't part of the script. Only one of our lads, a miner, had a knife on him. One Scouser in a corduroy box jacket pulled out a blade with a serrated edge, similar to what Rambo used.

'When we got back to Lime Street we had another scuffle by the Empire Theatre. Then at the station, as we got to an escalator, one Scouse lad took one look at the size of Big China and piped up to his mates, "It's not fair, we haven't got anyone his size!"'

When Liverpool came to Elland Road during the same season, two thirty-strong mobs fought each other for about mile, to-ing and fro-ing down the road after the game. The Scousers had knives and broken bottles wrapped in newspaper. About 100

Service Crew waiting nearby spotted what was going on and started chucking bricks. Liverpool ended up running through gardens to escape.

They were good battles and Sean feels the two firms have a certain respect for one another: 'Leeds versus Liverpool will never be the same as those days and if there are any of you lads in your mid-forties around, keep those memories forever, because I will.'

5

ONE NIGHT IN PARIS

AFTER LEADING LEEDS United to an enviable string of trophies, Don Revie was made England manager in the summer of 1974. Talk of his replacement dominated the headlines but when Brian Clough was announced as his successor, the news stunned players and fans alike. Though he had enjoyed great success at Derby County, Clough was a well-known critic of Leeds's uncompromising style and, shortly after his appointment, he famously told the players they should throw all their medals in the bin, since they had won them unfairly. His hamfisted attempt to change the dressing room climate failed. After only forty-four days and one win in seven games, his tenure came to an end. Until recent troubled times, he was the club's least successful manager.

Jimmy Armfield replaced him and steered the team to better times – eventually all the way to Paris for the European Cup Final, in May 1975. In the aftermath of the Three-Day Week, power cuts and open warfare between the government and the trade unions, football was a welcome distraction. The bleakness of the coal-mining communities was left behind for a balmy night in the French capital and what should have been Leeds United's finest hour.

A glimpse of what lay ahead that infamous night was evident a few days earlier when the Yorkshire masses crossed the Channel to purchase tickets for the game against Bayern Munich. Alan from Cow Close was one of many who hopped on a 'Wally' Arnold coach for the princely sum of £17.50. Recently made redundant and paid three weeks' wages, he told his young wife he was keeping one week's money to get tickets. He sat beside a youth from Scarborough who was with three mates, all passing round bottles of Pernod.

They arrived in Paris at 3am and there was already a huge queue at the ticket office. Some Leeds fans at the front had been there for two days, enjoying the contents of boxes of wine. At about 9am, a lot of French and German supporters got together and tried to push in at the front by the turnstiles. 'There was a no man's land near the front and some Leeds lads came running down to where I was, telling everyone what they were doing,' said Alan. 'We could hear a commotion but couldn't see anything, so me and several others left the queue and walked up to face them. They numbered about a hundred but we charged into them and ended up splitting them up, but only briefly as more got involved and the scuffles escalated into larger fights, with several coppers getting attacked.'

A well known lad in Leeds at the time, who was from the Kippax and used to wear a Celtic shirt, could speak French – which was a surprise to his mates – and said he would help sort things out. A dozen lads were posted in the no man's land area and rotated every ten minutes with different lads to keep order. When it was Alan's turn, one of the foreign supporters took a swipe at him. 'I grabbed his arm and brayed him, before letting him go and naively moving away slightly with my back to them,' said Alan. 'The guy grabbed his chance, picked up a nearby bottle and tried to hit me over the head with it.'

One of the Leeds fans 'on duty' next to him was the youth from Scarborough he had met on the coach. 'The Scarborough lad grabbed the other bloke's hand as he went for me, pulled him over to one side and kicked him that hard he went over a nearby fence,' he said. The French police mainly stood and watched, perhaps making mental notes about what they would face in ten days' time. It was certainly a clash of cultures. Alan couldn't understand what the woman at the ticket office was asking him, and he was so keen to get his hands on the coveted *billets* that he kept repeating, 'Give us me ticket, give us me ticket' – which was probably what she was trying to do. Meanwhile, fans at home were also having problems getting their hands on tickets, which all seemed to be going to players and supporters' clubs. Some Shipley lads managed to get some off a landlord who had got them off striker Joe Jordan.

Many Leeds arrived the night before the game and got pissed after raiding hypermarkets and indulging in fights with police. Up to 4,000 settled in a park beside a hypermarket near the ground, but the police got stuck into them with baton charges and then water cannons. The police were also armed, which was a shock to British fans who had never been abroad before – though after sufficient alcoholic lubrication few seemed to care.

Alan, Manny and several others walked around the ground past touts selling tickets. Some were stood next to police but that didn't stop a lad from walking up to one and hitting him. As the coppers didn't immediately reach for their weapons, that signalled they weren't keen to use them. More touts were hunted down and one took a few smacks before running into a garage and locking himself in a room.

The Shipley lads found some Algerian touts and watched one for a bit. He would walk up an alley to exchange money and tickets and then come out again. One young lad who needed a ticket was told to go over and ask for one and then they'd follow him up the alley. The lad went over and instead pulled out a knife, only for the tout to pull out a gun. The lad turned around expecting everyone to be behind him but no one was there once they had seen the gun. The next tout they found was jumped as soon as he went to his pocket. They took his tickets and his gun. It turned out to be a starting pistol and when it kicked off with the police later, someone fired the blanks at them, only for the police to respond with what some claim were live bullets.

The Germans did not arrive until the day of the game and some Leeds yobs picked fights pretty much as soon as they saw them. It was a volatile atmosphere but large groups travelling together for long periods of time made for good bonding experiences, with this the first time many had ventured out of the UK. Seeing Leeds playing in Europe was a great feeling and believing they could be coming home as European Cup winners meant the teenagers and young men felt even more invincible. Every Leeds fan that could go did go, making up an away support of about 30,000. At Barcelona a month earlier, a crowd of 110,000 had seen Peter Lorimer score against the home side, which included greats such as Johan Cruyff and Johan Neeskens, to secure a place in the final.

But once the game was under way at Parc des Princes things did not go to plan and will forever leave a bitter taste in every Leeds fan's mouth. A Beckenbauer foul on Allan Clarke for a penalty was discounted and Lorimer's volleyed goal in the second half was disallowed after Bremner was deemed offside. Bayern Munich's two goals from counter attacks ended any hopes of triumph for the Peacocks and ultimately signalled the end of an era at the club.

Enraged, the Leeds masses erupted. A moat ran all the way around the pitch, about six feet wide with spikes either side. One of Alan's mates, incensed at what was happening on the pitch, decided to get at the referee. He ran down the aisle between the seats and dived over the moat, landing in a heap on the other side, leading some to think he had impaled himself. But he rolled over as police went over to him and began tussling with them, before hitting the deck again. The crowd watched as some men in tracksuits ran over. Some suggested they were crack martial artists brought in to break up trouble. They feared the worst for the moat jumper but again he got up and had a go at a couple before they pulled him over a barrier and dragged him away, amid debris being flung onto the pitch. Stan went mad with rage watching what was happening to his mate and began kicking off the plastic seats and skimming them onto the pitch. Alan had a go too. He couldn't break them off in one go like the raging Stan but still managed to smash them and, as others joined in the smashing and throwing, it spread.

Soon the crowd were ripping out rows and rows of seats, venting their anger against the Germans who they felt had cheated their way to win the crown of European football. Dougie had managed to nab two crates of beer at half-time while Alan distracted the bar staff, so they also had plenty of empty plastic bottles to throw on the pitch. All sorts of things were chucked in the dying seconds of the game: coins, shoes, hats, scarves and more plastic bottles after the bars were ransacked. Hundreds of lads started scaling the fences around the pitch but were battered down by the police.

The events after the final whistle were inevitable. 'Every cheeky bastard German we saw got chinned,' said Alan. 'We were trying to tip the buses over that they were on. We were so angry.' However, the police response was ferocious, leaving numerous walking wounded. Their reaction was no doubt prompted by fans' behaviour the previous night as well as what had been going on inside the ground.

Alan went back the same night on a train full of French and abused as many as possible, while Manny and Co. stayed on, venturing into the city centre. Scottie and his mates were in the park next to Parc du Princes and his coaches were due to return to the UK straight after the game, but some dossed down in the park. When he did board the coach, it was only three-quarters full because of arrests and the missing. By the time they arrived at Calais, news had spread and freight workers showed their displeasure by holding up banners saying, 'English Scum.' A strike by ferry workers left thousands stranded at the port. Twenty-eight Shipley lads shared one hotel room while they waited to get back. It all exacerbated the foul mood. There was anger not only over the result and refereeing but at the ticket hassle and the club seemingly not serving the real fans.

Paris was a turning point. It put off some supporters from going to watch Leeds, a few permanently. Yet coverage of the rioting reached far and wide and hooked a generation of youths who heard about, read about or saw what happened. The French mayor described the trouble as worse than the storming of the Bastille and to the new breed of hooligans, that was exactly the point. It was not the first major outbreak of football violence by English fans in Europe – that had come two years earlier, when Spurs played Feyenoord in Rotterdam – but it had perhaps the greatest impact. From then on, the hooligans of Leeds United were tarred as some of the worst in the country, a reputation they would spend the next three decades doing their best to live up to.

* * *

By the mid-Seventies, soccer fans were moving around the county in larger numbers than ever, thanks to the special trains, although these were often old and clapped out, with passengers herded on and off. Policing in general was lax at matches and local forces were ill-prepared to handle the hundreds of rampaging fans who felt more and more invincible with each week, as they invaded towns and cities up and down the country. There was trouble abroad too, with Glasgow Rangers rioting in Barcelona, Spurs in Rotterdam and Leeds in Paris. In 1977, 5,000 England fans ran amok in Luxembourg.

Then came punk rock, and suddenly going to pubs, gigs, and matches were all that mattered. Johnna, the punk fan from Bradford, amassed a large collection of Vivienne Westwood gear, which he swapped and traded to live on for a couple of years while DJ-ing from time to time and hitching to gigs. He made friends from different towns through going to gigs and saw one as Leeds and Boro were about to do battle at Elland Road one time. Both groups fronted each other by the South Stand and Johnna was at the front when he recognised his punk mate Scrubber. They both opted out of the imminent fight and stood chatting at one side, saying, 'You don't need us.'

In Leeds, football lads from different areas developed their own social scene when they met up in the city centre. Little by little the circle got bigger and the numbers at matches began to swell. A turnout of 500 in one mob for big games by the early Eighties was not unheard of, although large numbers sometimes meant more 'idiots', the type who would do things that could embarrass or let others down in a tight situation. While the bitching and falling out among the neighbouring areas eventually petered out, it was never totally forgotten. In any event, the big numbers were vastly different to some of the paltry shows in previous years.

The first away match Dean from Oldham saw was at Rochdale in 1977 and thousands went. His next away game was Man City in September 1978 and this time he was in for a shock. 'I was expecting a similar turnout so I wasn't too bothered until I saw only 400-odd wary Leeds fans had made the journey,' he said. 'I soon realised this was a different league. There were about twelve Leeds lads in front of me in the ground and I overheard them talking about some trouble they'd been involved in in the city centre before the match. City kids were shouting across through a fence and some Leeds were in the seats in Platt Lane end singing and then fighting.

'At the end of the match, they opened the gates but Leeds didn't want to leave. Those on coaches had to go one way, trains the other, and the police put a bus on back to the station. There were about seventy Leeds walking with a light police escort. We could see guys lurking about in the alleyways trying their luck as we were taken to the bus to get back into the city. About fifty City hovered about but in the end nothing happened and once on the bus, glad to have got away unscathed, the lads started singing and wrecked the bus.'

Yet for West Brom at Maine Road that October, in the second replay in the second round of the League Cup, Leeds took thousands. West Brom brought only 500 supporters, there were some neutrals in the pen but the rest were Leeds, some 7,000 in a crowd of just over 8,000. Dean saw it as a defining moment, the first time they went to Manchester in numbers. He was expecting the same experience as before.

'After the match, as we walked by the coaches and a stretch of wasteland, there was a bonfire with some lads, who we assumed to be Cool Cats, floating about. We were walking to get a train and once past the coaches things seemed a bit moody and numbers had thinned out as some had already left but Leeds just ran across and into them. The chase went on to Princess Parkway. It felt great. A few kicks and punches were thrown but Leeds were mainly running after them.'

Friday nights in Leeds from around 1979 would be spent at the Adelphi in the city centre, where the sound was Roxy Music and electronic vibes. 'The place was buzzing and always full,' recalled John from south Leeds. 'Manchester said they were "doing it" at the time but Leeds were doing it too.' The New Romantic movement was on its way and at a match against Arsenal at Elland Road in 1980/81, many were dressed like Spandau Ballet, with checkered blankets over their shoulders and tucked into belts. Although some Arsenal commented, 'Look at Leeds, they look like Scousers,' the following year they were dressed the same.

The Precinct was the pub to drink in in Leeds throughout the Seventies and Eighties. Everyone went there and John and Scottie remember its sticky carpet and the dance floor ending up as a boxing ring, even for women on hen nights. Lads would get there for 8pm on a Friday and sometimes on a Saturday, then do a circuit of pubs in the city centre. From about 1982, it was the meeting place before everyone headed off to Jaccomellis, often known simply as Jac's. The casual fashion led to battles with bouncers over disagreements with their door policies on dress. It amounted to them not wanting football lads to come in, so Jac's changed their rules from week to week trying to catch them out. The first group of doormen were not popular and when they knocked back one football lad from Jac's, he returned wielding a saw. 'We treated the place as our own and they knew it,' said John.

The Black Lion was another key pub and the original home of the Service Crew. It was a den of iniquity, with all sorts of gear being sold inside, and was full of characters. A lad in a raincoat with a false arm would come in, unscrew the arm, put it on the table and open his coat, which was stuffed with clothes he had lifted from various shops. 'I'd finish work at 3pm on a Friday, go home, eat, change, then out to be in the Black Lion by 5.30,' said Sean. 'If you weren't there by 5.40 you got shit from the lads. There'd be as many as two hundred queuing at the bar, so it took ages to get served. My dad would shout, "See you Sunday," as I left each Friday evening. It'd be out with lads, drinking and wiring slots and earning as much as £150 extra a week – you can see why we were popular with the girls. But if you wanted to get into football you went to Jac's. In 1980/81, Boar Lane at 10.30pm on a Saturday night was as bad as any football match.'

The lads became established in the city centre and essentially became townies from then on. The Jubilee opposite the Town Hall was another good venue with the upstairs sometimes turning into a Wild West show. The Warehouse on Fridays was also a spot with good sounds in the early Eighties but went downhill later in the decade. As certain lads got things together in the city, the out-of-towners were also hooking up with them at matches and meeting the Service Crew off the trains at Birmingham New Street, Manchester or at grounds. They included the twins from Cheltenham, some skinheads from

Hereford, others from Stratford, Telford, the North East, Leicester, Uttoxeter and East Anglia, Dean and his brother from Oldham, Geordie Andy and others from Bolton and Bury. There was always a healthy contingent from York, Harrogate, Doncaster and Wakefield but support for Leeds spread much further than that, with other groups from across the country: Shrewsbury, Banbury, Oxford, Stockton, Hampshire, Whitby, Reading, Scarborough, Bedford, Kettering, Peterborough, Macclesfield and Blackpool, as well as Scotland, Wales, Ireland and even Norway, Denmark and Sweden.

Grounds like Derby or Coventry were okay to mooch about on your own but when it came to Anfield and Old Trafford, there was safety only in numbers. Going to those intimidating grounds, lads from outside Leeds could spot the types who were prepared for whatever lay ahead and could see who the main guys were. New Street Station became an important meeting place, as Leeds were often in the Midlands playing other Division One teams like Aston Villa, Birmingham City and West Brom. When their train pulled in, the usual suspects would appear on the platforms – Al P, Griff, Sean, Musky, Benny, Gaz Patrick, John, Ricky B – before everyone headed off to a pub where much banter would ensue.

They were exciting times. When Dean was back in Oldham, his mates would talk about buying the latest Clash or Jam record while he had stories of being chased through alien towns and cities and the thrill of being part of a mob. Leaflets did the rounds for a while calling for lads to get together. Dean read one in the toilets in the Kop once ahead of a clash with Everton, which said, 'We take good support to Liverpool but never turn up at Everton. Get the vans together and get the regulars together...' Johnna can remember seeing other leaflets around the pubs saying, 'Why do we go separately? Let's get together.' They were signed, 'Jack T Ripper.' When police were trying to catch the infamous Yorkshire serial killer, they played a tape of his voice to the crowds at Elland Road, to which the crowd chanted, 'You'll never catch the Ripper,' and, 'Twelve-nil,' in reference to the number of his victims.

71

If socialising in the city brought football lads together, there was one opponent that was guaranteed to unite the entire region. By the late Seventies, the rivalry between Leeds and Manchester United was one of the bitterest in British football.

6

THE AGE OF THE TRAIN

'ALL LEEDS TO Man United on the 9.20am train to Victoria.'

December 1979 was the first time a small group of teenage lads decided to bypass the specials and use a service train instead. A few lads who mixed with the National Front had mentioned it for a couple of weeks while they were leafleting and selling their newspapers, but Al P was behind the idea after suggesting it at a home match against Spurs a few weeks earlier. It was a fixture that had all the makings of a pivotal battle.

On the day, only a few went on the service train but it marked the start of something and the origins of the Service Crew name. A second wave of lads was emerging to represent Leeds United on the terraces and the casual scene was ushering in the next phase of football violence.

Sean picks up the tale:

We got to the ground and we were all bunched together.
Man United were on both sides of the road with us. It was
an eerie moment but we were confident. We had a good
mixed bunch of older lads and all us lot, who were fifteen or
sixteen years old then. The policing was minimal, as it was
at nearly every ground in the country in those days, but
Leeds didn't seem to bother about that, maybe fear took
over.

As we walked down Warwick Road, United tried getting
in with us but we had lads like Winnie, Ricky, Leeky,
Lumby, China – aka Honeymonster – and Johnna from
Bradford, who was dressed like Adam Ant in these fucking
big fourteen-eyelet boots and punk gear and must've looked
out of place with all us fashion freaks. The older Donny lot
like Big Tez, Ogger, Joe and a few more were there, then

you had some of the town lot, the lads who drank in the
Vine, Whip and Black Lion, so you could say we weren't
bothered, we were well up for it. The Wortley/Farnley lot,
Seacroft and a few younger ones from other areas like
Bramley, Beeston, East End Park, Harehills, Rothwell,
Kirkstall/Burley were all mixed together. We felt
unstoppable, in our Adidas cagoules, baseball jackets, Samba
or Kios boots, Stanley parkas and green flying jackets, with
big fringes, wedge haircuts or grown-out skinheads. All
cheeky, nasty, game little fuckers, yet we must have looked
an easy bunch to go for.

There was a big roar as we walked down the road and
Brummie, who was from the city his nickname suggests,
got a smack in the side of his head. That was it; our old lot
were straight into them. Stevie M had hold of this kid on
a wall, punching fuck out of him, and Leeky and Winnie
were fighting at the front of the escort. United were
mainly all scarfers and shirties but they did have a lot of
lads on that road, then the whole of the forecourt seemed
to run up towards us. By then about two minutes had
passed but it seemed like twenty. Us lot weren't bothered,
we had backed them off, wouldn't say done them but we
got a big psychological boost as we were all kids and I
could see some of these were hardened, experienced
hooligans.

Got to say there was hundreds at the ground and they
got on the forecourt. There were little pockets of scuffling as
we walked down and they were trying to get in a 'midget'
escort. There were about 150 of us tops and about ten
coppers, with two on horses. When they came at us it was
like a tidal wave, everyone was getting stuck in, every man
for himself. There were boots flying, punches landing, then
they started throwing things, a bottle came into us and a
brick or two, in fact they were hitting their own fans. We
did really well there, massively outnumbered but they
actually had too many bodies, I think, to do us any great
damage.

Me and this Manc in a black Adidas cagoule got fighting.
He had a black muzzy and a big fringe and we were giving
each other what for and hung onto each other like two
pitbulls, fair play to him. The coppers moved in to break it
up and seemed more bothered about the Manc fans than us.
A few of them got smacked about and truncheoned, though
one of the twins from the Vine got a right punch from a
copper. Then they gave us lot a bit of a roughing up, kicking
us and punching us but we weren't bothered, we'd just held
Man United on their manor.

Some of our older lot were stepping out of this makeshift
cordon and wanting a pop with their lot before being
thrown back in with us. Then the forecourt seemed to
empty and United went up the road over the bridge. Our
coach lot had arrived and we could tell it was going off with
them. The police were undermanned and some of them
holding us back had to leave to assist those up the road. This
gave people like Ronnie, Crabby, Slip, Pele, John, Viv,
Wayne Andrews, Ward, Shack, Hush, Billy Blackhead, Al,
Johnno, Binden, Benny, Gilly, Scully, Carl Williams, Foxy's,
Baz, Zorro, some of the Wakey and Ponte lads, a few of the
Cockney Whites, Selby/York lads and myself, of course, a
licence to have another go with them.

It kicked off again with the United that were left on the
forecourt but didn't last long. The law came into us again
and held us by where the United Megastore is now. They
had nicked a couple of us by this time, as they were pissed
off with us. One of the older lot, Spike, a mad Rangers fan
and teddy boy who used to drink in the Whip and the Vine,
got chinned by the law and I think Monkey from Ponte got
nicked. A lad from Barnsley called Crowey went up to them
and said 'Munich 58' to provoke them but they were just
having verbals. The law then decided to put us lot into the
ground as we were getting a bit cocky.

After the game, there was little to write home about, just
a few scuffles going up Warwick Road. We were with the
special train escort and they'd held us in for about an hour.

When we got near the eye hospital, us lot tried to break away down a side street but the law sent the horses after us and rounded us up. It was weird as some of us who'd gone on the service train wanted to get away but the special lot didn't.

As we got over the Mancunian Way we tried to get away near Deansgate, as we could see a load of United down a street near the shops. There was a little scuffle but they ran off and the law shepherded us back in again. We got to Victoria and United were waiting for us. We could see them but the law held us up and moved a few on before taking us up to the station. As we got in, some came in the side entrance and it kicked off, some of them were Man City as well. They were playing away somewhere down south, I think, so obviously Leeds in their own centre was too good to miss.

Al P cracked this big lad and his mate got into him. We ran out to the taxi ranks and got into them, with Al P chasing them round a bus stop. Pele and the Seacroft lads were having it too before we all chased them down the hill to the back side of the station. Needless to say the law weren't happy, fucking us off back into the station. Me, Ricky, Alan, Shack, Winnie, Stevie M, Pele, Baz, Zoz, Terry P and a few more lads tried getting out again as a mixed bunch of United and City came mouthing at us. They got all the old shit like 'We've just done you' and 'Come round the corner, nigger' to some of their black lads who were fronting us up. There was always a bunch of lads who hung round Victoria looking for Leeds and Scousers who went shopping. They got a few smacks and ran off, then we went into the rail bar and had a few drinks, with the older lot buying pints for us younger lot. A few of us were robbing crisps and chocolate for the train home.

We were a blinding little unit when I look back at things, all cheeky as fuck, game as fuck but deep down all tight when we were together and I think the older lot liked this about us. We got the train back to Leeds and all the talk *was about the forecourt, the day in general, who we played next at home and how we couldn't wait for our next away match.*

When that came around we had a load more on the service train. Things were starting to look up for Leeds going on the train and within two years no one went on the specials. We had amassed a load from the coaches too. Some of the older lads from the early and mid Seventies were starting to come back, as they had finished their jail sentences and had kids by then. Word had got round too that the only way to follow Leeds was by the service train, as you had the freedom of getting in other towns and a drink. We certainly had a mixed bunch. The older lot were starting to become trendy and we had the political element of the NF coming as well with all us 'fashion boys' who'd been going a couple of years by then. Leeds were starting to be taken seriously home and even more so away due to a certain somebody just saying, 'Let's go to Man United on the 9.20 service train,' in 1979. History in the making.

With Leeds and Manchester United both dominant forces in British football during the 1960s, it was perhaps inevitable a loathing of 'the Scum' would exist. No neighbouring teams matched Leeds' prowess on the pitch and as the reputation of United's Red Army increased, relations soured and were inflamed by the high-profile defections of players Joe Jordan and Gordon McQueen, who jumped ship over the Pennines as the club was starting to fade.

Their rivalry stretched back to the mid-Sixties when both were at the top of their game. They met in FA Cup semi-finals in 1965, 1970 and 1977, with the latter fixture a particularly tumultuous occasion at Hillsborough. Man United were out for revenge at that match after hectic scenes at Elland Road two years earlier. Indeed trouble was never far away when the teams met. Despite professing undying hatred towards all things Manchester, some Leeds lads admit a slight admiration for their hooligans, in that the Red Army has always 'kept it together' and 'brought it' to Elland Road. No one denies that. Sir Alex Ferguson is quoted as saying, 'Unless you have been to a City and United derby, that's rivalry – and as for Leeds United, deary, deary me.' Even the police would say to Leeds, 'We hate you, why do you come here?' But they would stop off in Manchester at any opportunity.

In 1971, both sets of fans arrived at Elland Road a while before the match, as was common in those days, with Man U in the Scratching Shed. Twenty minutes before kick-off, they raced across the pitch to attack Leeds who were mainly in the bars and refreshment area below the Kop stand. Someone shouted, 'They're coming across the pitch!' which prompted a mad rush back out onto the terraces. By the time Leeds were on the terraces, some 200-300 Reds were at the bottom of the Kop. The Leeds lads used the back stairs at each side of the Kop to charge down towards their rivals. Boys and dads were caught up in the scuffle and things got 'quite naughty' when the vastly outnumbered 'Scum' were pinned in at the bottom. Younger lads, like Scottie from Harehills, stood at the side watching it unfold and were enthralled. It was all over in a couple of minutes as the police regained order and returned Man U to the Shed.

The following year, again at Leeds, Man U were chased back to the city centre and their train was bricked as it left the station. After demotion in 1974, United were then promoted at the first time of asking and returned to Elland Road in October 1975 with nearly 10,000 supporters and the reputation of being the biggest and worst-behaved hooligan army in the world. Their huge away numbers were well known and they didn't disappoint on this occasion. With several hundred officers on duty, police manpower was stretched to its limit. Fighting broke out in the streets and went on until evening.

The M621 motorway was in the process of being built and an area of terraced houses had been flattened, leaving a large mound of rubble which provided an excellent vantage point and ambush spot. Leeds gathered on the hillside after the match, armed themselves with bricks and concrete and lay in wait. As Man U came within reach, they came under attack. Police were faced with trying to control running battles, smaller fights involving one or two people and much larger brawls with several hundred on each side throwing missiles. Sixty people were later hauled before the courts, where the prosecutor told magistrates, 'The battle of Leeds United was fought on the football ground, in the side streets and the broad main streets of the city as warring gangs went on the rampage. Frantic pedestrians had to scurry for safety as bricks whizzed about their ears. They heard the sickening thud of boot against body as those involved were either thrown or beaten to the ground and kicked mercilessly.'

One Service Crew lad called Dave met a 'Scum' fan years later who was there that day and said he was stabbed and badly beaten. A Bradford Red who drank in the same pub as some of the Bradford Whites said he was attacked four times coming back from Elland Road. The first time was when a group of Leeds turned on him. He lay still on the floor. Others came over and picked him up and asked if he was okay. When he said he was, they replied, 'Oh, you are are you? Well have some more,' and beat him up again. When they left, he got up and tried to make his way back to the city centre but was attacked again and had his scarf and jacket nicked. Then someone else attacked him with a shovel. He never went to watch Man United at Leeds again.

Man United took a beating that day but when the semi final of the FA Cup at Hillsborough came around they were out for vengeance. The difference in the size of support was embarrassing for Leeds. Out of a crowd of 55,000, they had just half the Kop, while the rest of the ground was taken by Man U. It was like playing at Old Trafford. Some claim half of Leeds' tickets ended up in the hands of their rivals, possibly down to the Yorkshire Reds buying them up. Two ten-foot steel fences had been erected inside Hillsborough and the police, anticipating trouble, put more than 1,000 officers on duty.

The first thing Johnna the Punk saw on arrival at the ground was a Leeds fan tipping a tray of hot tea over a Man U fan. The Red and his mate were about to get some drinks when the Leeds fan said, 'Have these,' and threw the tray over him, resulting in him screaming and shouting, 'I'm blind!' Others, like Alan and Dave Franks, didn't have tickets and tried to climb into the ground after a fight involving bottles and glasses outside a nearby pub. Dave managed to get in after getting a leg up off Alan and a few others but then police appeared and chased them off. They ended up in a park where a group of fifteen Hell's Angels were playing footie. They took their ball from them and a fight broke out, resulting in the lads throwing the Hell's Angels in a pond, soaking them in their leather jackets. Another group of Leeds fans were milling about by the turnstiles and every Man U fan that came through got attacked, causing the police to put officers there to protect them.

The Leeds end had a line of police down the middle separating the two sets of fans. After Man U scored their two goals, Leeds tried to break through and managed to back some of them off and during the second half a group repeatedly went into their half of the section and attacked them from behind. A *Times* journalist who witnessed the trouble wrote:

At one stage a fight broke out at the top of the terrace. Against the skyline it was possible to see a long weapon crashing down on somebody's head. Although I could not see who was hitting whom, the people around me seemed to know.

The fight created an almost hysterical atmosphere among the people outside and when the police arrived on the top terrace the group on the ground burst away, charging down the Penistone Road.

The explanation of academics and sociologists and even some sports ministers seemed difficult to accept as one watched the breaking of windows, the vandalising of parked cars, urinating in gardens, charging in hundreds down back streets of terraced houses and terrorising local residents.

Perhaps what I saw was unrepresentative but what took place was on a large enough scale to be very disturbing. It is not just the cost in policing and lost trade that a neutral city like Sheffield has to pay but the frightening tyranny of virtually uncontrollable youths.

After the game, which Man U won 2-1 to reach their second consecutive final, the two firms met on the same street and battle commenced. The 100-150 Leeds had the impetus and went in first against 300-400 United. The fighting lasted a good hour all the way to the train station, with the police trying to gain control in the middle. 'They claim they did us and we claim we got them – everyone has a different tale to tell but I felt we stood there,' said Scottie.

As Johnna and other Bradford lads walked down the street back to their coach, the road was littered with badly beaten Reds, some covered in blood. One was half in and half out of a shop window. He was covered in blood and his scarf looked as though someone had tried to cut it from around his neck. The police forced everyone on to the coaches and Johnna's was one of the last to leave. As they drove away they looked out of the back window and they saw a load of Man U fans running down the road towards them. They laughed and waved.

It has gone down in Leeds folklore that when they played at Derby County in 1979 a couple of weeks before another trip across the Pennines, everyone was in a pub singing: 'Fourteen days till we take the Scoreboard,' to the tune of 'Amazing Grace'. When it came to the December fixture that same year, the first time the lads had used the service trains, a couple decided to spice things up and take petrol bombs. Newcastle had recently thrown a petrol bomb at West Ham fans inside the ground, which gave them the idea. Ten bombs were made but they never left Leeds station, as the lads sensibly thought better of it and chucked them in a bin. After the match, Dean from Oldham was getting a local train home from Victoria Station when he saw a massive mob of 500 Man United walk into the concourse, looking for Leeds. Most were wearing cream, chain-lace fisherman jumpers, stripy tops, Pod shoes and Adidas cagoules with wedge haircuts. They looked very impressive.

At the return fixture in May, Leeds were waiting for their rivals to appear. It had been all they talked about at Wolves the previous week with chants like 'Oh Man United, you're gonna die next Saturday morning at half past nine.' The Red Devils had to beat Leeds to win the League and lads were out in the city centre by

9.30am, hanging about for their escort. Various small groups of Mancs came under attack until the 11am train arrived from Manchester with hundreds on board. They came charging down the station and a tidal wave of casuals ran Leeds at first down towards Jaccomellis, until Leeds regrouped and the to-ing and fro-ing began. It led to a day of non-stop fighting, brawling, running and chasing which lasted well into the evening.

Ranks of police flanked the visiting supporters on their way to the ground and they filled the road. Meanwhile hundreds of Leeds walked past the chip shop and the parked coaches near the ground, a natural ambush area where anyone was fair game. One mob spotted a minibus containing their enemies, who had got lost. They were engulfed by 200 Leeds who set about wrecking the vehicle.

Johnna the Punk sat this one out, as he was not in favour of such a large number attacking a much smaller contingent. He went to see a mate who sold programmes by the club shop and as they chatted, a coachload of Man U appeared and charged at him shouting, 'Come on Leeds.' He was swallowed up until some police waded in to break it up but ended up nicking him and no one else. As they chucked him in the back of their van, he asked why he was being arrested and they laughed and told him it was because it was easier than nicking all of the others.

Attacks on the Red Army continued all the way to the ground and those naïvely wearing scarves were picked off. Another group of about 100 was attacked as they sang 'We are the Reds of the West Country' round the back of the Kop. 'They obviously hadn't been before and went round the back of the Kop, and all the Leeds fans queuing up piled into them,' said Benny. 'There was a big fence behind the Kop where the British Road Transport depot used to be and they got battered at the fences as they climbed them to get away. It was typical Scum arrogance, thinking they could swarm the place with their numbers.' Inside the ground, Man United filled two-thirds of the bottom of the Lowfields. They watched Leeds win 2-0, ending their title hopes. Bricks went back and forth, with people being carried out with bloodied heads, and a big fight involving the old Harehills mob in the South Stand went on all through the match. Earlier in the season, one Leeds home game had seen a paltry crowd of only 16,000 or so, which prompted United to sing, 'Sixteen thousand, ha ha ha!' Leeds retaliated with, 'Munich, Munich, ha ha ha!'

There were so many Leeds fans waiting outside Elland Road at the finish that they kept the visitors inside. The police kept charging Leeds up the road to disperse them and eventually the lads knew they wouldn't let the Reds out until they had moved on, so they went up into Beeston but left a spotter behind. When the police finally brought them out they marched them towards the train station in front of Beeston Hill. Wave after wave of Leeds started running down towards them, prompting some to try to get back into the ground. One Leeds lad said it was reminiscent of that well known scene from the film *Zulu* when the British soldiers faced line after line of rampaging Zulus. The police waited until Man U got to the flat part of the hill at the bottom, then set the horses on Leeds, something they were known for. But it didn't deter anyone, the lads just bypassed the mounted officers, although not in great numbers, and still went for their rivals. One copper on a motorcycle was knocked off his bike. The ones that did get past the police either got nicked or found that, just as they closed on their foe, police reinforcements had arrived and backed the away fans towards the ground, putting a shield between them and Leeds. After about an hour Leeds began to tire and gave up.

A newspaper article reported how thirty fans were arrested before the match and one United fan had to sprint to safety after finding himself on his own.

Just before kick-off, several hundred Leeds were cleared from a stretch of Elland Road after a lone Manchester United fan was made to run a 'gauntlet'.

He was alone in the home supporters' end and faced a 50-yard sprint to a nearby police patrol.

Officers moved in only to find that two other groups had reached the Lowfields car park where United fans were waiting to get into the ground. Two fans were hurt and several arrests made.

Police were called to an incident at a Morley pub where they escorted a number of people out after two sets of fans clashed.

Inside the ground what appeared to be a red-haired punk rocker was led from the pitch. He returned a few minutes later minus the red colouring with several stitches in a head wound. His red hair had been blood.

A smoke bomb was thrown from the United pen which landed on the pitch.

United were kept in after the game awaiting an escort to coaches and to the station, but Leeds waited for them and when they appeared starting chucking bricks until mounted officers and others with dogs charged towards them, scattering them up the hill towards Wesley Street and Beeston. One Leeds fan came to a police van covered in blood, the victim of a barrage of stones from his own supporters. More arrests were made on the way to the station, where the fighting led to an elderly woman receiving cuts and bruises after being knocked over in a subway. 'A situation that could have been far worse was prevented,' said a police spokesman, although he admitted it was one of their busiest days of the year. The Red Army did not disgrace themselves in action that day but Leeds felt they did well.

In February 1981, Leeds again played at Old Trafford. The plan was to get an early train to Stalybridge, eight miles east of Manchester, and then take buses into the city to avoid the police. It didn't quite work out like that. The train was full and someone suggested they get off in Stalybridge for a drink. Hundreds promptly ran riot in the streets, robbing a Kwik Save and trashing cars, so it wasn't long before the police arrived and rounded them up. Another train full of lads pulled in but everyone was put back on and carried on to Manchester. The escort was massive, with sporadic scuffles en route and a bit of a crush in the Leeds end at one point. 'Looking back it was an episode of wanton vandalism,' one lad recalled.

According to the *Yorkshire Evening Post*:

Shipley Skins: skin girl Vicky, early skinhead Stewart Barber, who was stabbed by Chelsea in the early Seventies (and later died in a road accident), and Dave B, who was as hard as nails and refused to cut his long hair for anyone.

A bonehead is arrested at the Manchester City versus Leeds match in November 1969. Maine Road was the scene of some ferocious battles in the early days of modern soccer hooliganism.

The Cow Close lads drinking in Paris before the European Cup final in 1975: (from left) Billy, unidentified, Mick Steel, John Manual, unidentified, Jed, Jeff Keeton and Wally Newton.

The scene inside the Parc du Princes in Paris shortly before the outbreak of one of the most infamous riots in European football history, an episode that made Leeds United synonymous with disorder.

A bus driver dashes to safety as fire rages through the top deck of his wrecked soccer special taking fans to Elland Road for a match with Liverpool in September 1979. Some passengers escaped through windows. © *Mirrorpix*

Crushing at Old Trafford as Leeds beat Man United 1-0 in February 1981. Note the straight jeans of the lad on the left, between the police officers, and the huge flares of the youth jumping from the fence. © *Mirrorpix*

Young casuals on the pitch against Arsenal at Highbury in April 1981. The game was held up when inadequate segregation led to fighting. © *Mirrorpix*

The police drag out troublemakers at Leeds v Liverpool in February 1982. The Scousers had the best team in Europe in the early Eighties but also some of the most ruthless young scallies. © *Mirrorpix*

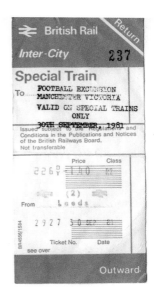

Two train tickets from the earliest days of the Service Crew. Their reputation was forged on hair-raising trips to grounds such as Anfield and Old Trafford.

Leeds United 3 Newcastle United 1 and it kicks off in the stands in a Division Two game in October 1982. Elland Road became one of the most intimidating grounds to visit.

Two scenes from Chelsea away in the 1984/85 season, a long-awaited confrontation between two of the biggest hitters among the casual firms. Above, one of the Leeds mobs out that day gathers in London before the match. Below, Chelsea fans pour onto the pitch at the end of the game, some to celebrate promotion, others to goad the Leeds fans, leading to mayhem.

Left to right: Tobin, Little Taff and Eddie Kelly, sporting a nice perm, outside Jaccomellis nightclub, aged fifteen.

The Service Crew hordes descend an Underground escalator on their way to the Den, the daunting home of Millwall FC, in 1985.

The Very Young Team shoplifting squad: (from left) Dag, Skiz, Farra, Gobby, Terry, Mason, Cheesey and Paul K. To a large extent the VYT took over from the Service Crew from the mid-Eighties.

A contingent of Leeds arriving at the train station for a highly-charged Scotland-England international in Glasgow in 1985.

More than 300 fans ran riot when they got off a Manchester-bound train in search of alcohol.

Police from four divisions were brought in to restore order leading to 16 arrests of which 12 were released due to a lack of evidence. Four, including one juvenile, were charged with breaches of the peace.

Shops, houses and private cars and one police vehicle were damaged but no one was injured.

Another article ran under the headline '40 fans on riot charges':

Nine people are to appear at Strangeways Magistrates Court including three all alleged to have kicked a youth unconscious in Selby Road, Stretford.

The youth was stood outside a phone box with his friend inside and a van pulled up and several lads jumped out and chased him. He was captured and kicked until he blacked out. His friend was also attacked.

A van was stopped by the M62 at Middleton and six men and one juvenile were later charged with assault.

Other fans were charged with assault, drunk and disorderly, police obstruction.

Police expected thirty coaches but forty-two turned up and some fans had to be moved to another section of the ground and motorcycle police were brought in as reinforcements at half-time.

The Bradford contingent had gone across in their van and went round Salford in a little group before meeting up with the main mob in Manchester. A copper went up to Al P and said, 'All right Al, how you doing?' Al punched him. When everyone asked why, he said he was an old schoolmate who was a Man United fan. Meanwhile, another group had got to one of United's main pubs, the Sawyers Arms, in the city centre. 'Hooligans smash up a pub in a fight between rivals,' declared one newspaper later.

Leeds fan were inside drinking quietly when Manchester United fans entered.

Glasses, chairs and tables were thrown at them as the fighting spilled outside and other drinkers ran for cover on Deansgate. Shoppers scattered as bricks from a nearby road repair site were thrown.

There were no arrests as police arrived after the trouble. However, police with dogs lined the route to Old Trafford as 1,000 fans were escorted to the ground.

Two hundred pensioners were drinking in the pub at the time the trouble kicked off.

Bryan Flynn scored for Leeds as they ended Man United's unbeaten run of league games at Old Trafford that season. There were 5,000 visitors among the crowd of 45,733.

The first time the two teams met in the 1981/82 season was a Wednesday night at Old Trafford, this time a victory on the pitch for the home team. 'We went over in the afternoon and ended up having a do with Scotty from Salford and his boys,' said Johnna. 'Me and Ricky stood on the bridge outside Old Trafford on our own and fought God knows how many of them. How we didn't get killed I don't know.'

Most lads stayed outside on the steps of the Scoreboard End and there was a lot of trouble during and after the match. Diddie, Shoot and Hush were in a group of thirty who got out of a big escort. As they approached a parade of shops they saw a good mob of Man U. They ran at them and an Asian lad punched Hush, putting him on his arse. In the confusion, Leeds split up and Diddie and several others got lost. They came out on a street and saw some lads walking up the road who said they were heading towards the Mancunian Way to go back to the train station. On a corner about a mile further on, fifty Man U charged out of a pub towards them and the lads thought they were in for a hammering. But with perfect timing, another mob of Leeds appeared by the corner at just the right moment and in the end they ran Man U down to the bottom of Mancunian Way by a subway.

In April, there were forty-five arrests 'as hundreds go mad in

Leeds after match with Manchester United at Elland Road,' according to one local paper. This would be the last time the two rivals met for almost a decade, as Leeds slipped down a division, although the hatred never subsided.

7

A WRECKING REPUTATION

AFTER TROUBLE AT three consecutive games in September 1979, the Leeds United directors were expected to announce the closure of half of the South Stand ahead of a home tie with Ipswich Town. A bus was set on fire at a match against Liverpool, fighting broke out at Bolton a week later and then again at a clash with Man City, when £5,000 worth of damage was caused when nearly 3,000 seats were ripped out. The club once again found itself before the FA for the mayhem at the City match and a three-year ban on home cup ties, imposed when Leeds fans invaded the pitch against Man City in 1978, had only recently been lifted after just one year.

This was nothing new for Leeds, in fact it was the fourth time in eight years they were brought before the FA – a trend that would continue throughout the Eighties. A pitch invasion at Elland Road after a controversial goal by Jeff Astle for West Brom in 1971 was one of the most memorable incidents, especially when Arsenal beat Leeds to the title by just one point that year. Referee Ray Tinkler needed a police escort from the pitch and never officiated at the ground again. The club was banned from hosting matches for four games and was forced to use neighbouring grounds.

Towards the end of the Seventies, there was disquiet amongst fans about the managerial skills of Jimmy Adamson, as well as more heat from the FA. A 7-0 drubbing by Arsenal, a loss to Bristol City and an early UEFA Cup exit saw several hundred protesting outside Elland Road over two consecutive weeks in November 1979. Another loss against Forest in January saw the Kop closed for two games after missiles were thrown and the club's smallest crowd for seventeen years, 15,000, attended the Coventry City game. Mounted police were needed to disperse disappointed supporters after a 0-0 draw. Adamson resigned a few months later and former striker Allan Clarke took over.

Off the pitch, Leeds were much more organised with large numbers going to fixtures. But it wasn't always about serious violence. One lad was fined £400 for throwing a peanut onto the pitch at Birmingham one year, and a trip to Ipswich in March 1980 saw the locals asking some Leeds lads if they wanted to be penpals. When they went in the Ipswich end at the end of the match, which Leeds lost 1-0 in the dying seconds, some lads came running over to them. They readied themselves but these lads weren't after a ruck. 'We stopped to chat a while and buzzed off the adulation these Ipswich guys were paying us and then we moved into another part of the ground, laughing our heads off after they had asked us to be penpals – and so did everybody else when we told them,' said Johnna. The police later escorted them out of town, though only after one of the lads had grabbed the mic off a band in a pub and belted out, 'There's only one Leeds United.'

For West Bromwich Albion, a good mob from Leeds and surrounding areas gathered on the station concourse led by Griff, with others from Featherstone and Pontefract. They were met by some of the 'out-of-towners' – the twins from Cheltenham, Dean from Oldham, the Stratford lads, ten or so from Brum including a black lad called Bailey, Brolly Chris, who unsurprisingly carried an umbrella, and a good crew from Telford, including Dawksy. About 100 went on a train to Smethwick, then walked towards the ground, chasing the odd group of locals. They got in the ground early, with Al P going in West Brom's section. After the match the police let everyone out together. The lads were in little groups of five and six in among the hundreds of West Brom fans and had a bit of a dodgy walk back to the train station, with a few punches thrown.

On the platform at Smethwick, the majority of West Brom were on the opposite side to Leeds but a few were waiting for the same train as them. Once on the train, it didn't go unnoticed that twenty West Brom were in the end carriage. They were sitting ducks. The lads waded down the train towards them and besieged them until they reached New Street, which must have seemed a very long way. The Baggies tried to defend themselves but with so many Leeds there was little they could do. As the lads went up the escalator at New Street, the West Brom lads rallied and had a go at some at the bottom until the police put a stop to it.

Another time at The Hawthorns, Sean saw Al P smack one of their main lads who 'looked like Billy Connolly'. Little scuffles broke out along the road after the game and they ended up in a park with equal numbers of about 150-a-side. 'Billy' was stood there in his steel toe cap boots when Al P steamed over and whacked him.

The 1980/81 season saw many violent clashes home and away, culminating in the death of a Leeds fan at Tottenham Hotspur in February. There was trouble away against Coventry, Villa, Everton, Palace, Arsenal, Birmingham City, a huge mob out at Man City and a memorable piss-up in Brighton. At Coventry, a tough city but one not noted for its football hooligans, Leeds encountered about forty lads, with one swinging a huge chain. They chased them off, but in another fight near the ticket office Coventry had the upper hand until the cops stepped it.

For Villa in November, a good Leeds firm walked around the ground before the game but afterwards on a train back to New Street containing both sets of fans, a mob of well dressed Villa lads charged a carriage containing about fifteen Leeds. They managed to hold the doors shut but they were in for more trouble at New Street. Villa got off first and went up the escalators. Leeds got off and did the same – their mob included Wayne, Dean, a couple of lads from Leicester and some from Wakefield – but they soon encountered about seventy Villa with their main guy, Danny, at the front. Villa chased them back down some escalators onto a platform and eventually down the tunnels. The fifteen did what they could and threw bricks forcing Villa back for a bit, but each time they ran out of ammunition Villa would charge them again and they had to dodge the trains coming in and out of the station. Wayne took a beating and at one stage saw a train going past him as he desperately ran, only to see his mate Musky sat inside, watching helplessly. Eventually the police stopped it and led the filthy, oil-stained lads out and they were eventually able to make it home.

At Maine Road that December, an 'incredible mob' landed at Victoria Station. A few City were milling about, sussing things out as Dean waited with others to meet the lads off the train. The next thing they heard was a booming chorus of 'Sieg heil, sieg heil, sieg heil.' It sounded evil and the City lads didn't hang about. The police marched them to the ground but there was little trouble, just a solid mob of about 400 of the worst hooligans in Britain.

On the same day that Leeds were away at Everton that March, Liverpool had West Ham in the League Cup Final. Two brothers, Paul and Brian, from Leicester, and two of their mates got to Lime Street early and some Scousers asked where they were from. They said they had heard about the shenanigans at Stalybridge in Manchester two weeks earlier and said they heard Man U had been done. One of the brothers went to the toilets downstairs in the station and a lad asked him if he had any 'odds' on him. Not having a clue what he meant – loose change – he replied, 'Err, yeah, I think Liverpool will beat West Ham 2-1.' He managed to get back with the others and just as Everton started to surround them the Leeds train pulled in.

Paul and Brian are two hilarious characters who hooked up with the Service Crew after first going to Leeds as teenagers in the mid-Seventies. They were brought up on the same estate that the Leicester Baby Squad are from and have known them since they were kids. They first travelled with their local Leeds Supporters' Club until the branch was booted out for a while because the organiser wasn't handing over the ticket money to Leeds. They would depart from Humberstone Gate, a main street in the city, with Man City and Man U's supporters' clubs just over the road. Travelling from Leicester, every game was an away game for them. They would usually go direct to Leeds or via Sheffield on the train, meeting other lads each week either before or after some trouble. Equally they would encounter rivals on their journeys, often Forest, and they used to get terrorised by the Man U supporters' branch at Chesterfield – there would often be four of them and forty Reds.

When it came to Crystal Palace in March, forty got the night train to London on the Friday and arrived about 4am, feeling groggy and looking for somewhere to kip. They headed to the sex cinemas in Soho. The bloke at the cinema wanted to charge them £10 each but they got him down to £3 and a few sneaked in for free.

It stank and was pretty grotty but it was somewhere warm and dry to sleep. When eventually they left and got to Euston, they encountered several hundred West Ham who chased them away. At St Pancras they saw Millwall on their way to Sheffield, who also had a go at them, forcing them back by the ticket office. Their bad luck continued when at Kings Cross they bumped into Chelsea, who were playing Newcastle United.

For Arsenal the following month, a few again headed down to London the night before, pissed up, which became a regular thing for some matches in the capital. About fifteen ended up killing time in all-night cafes before gathering in the Cockney Pride pub. Carried away with their growing reputation as wreckers, some of the lads set about smashing the place up, resulting in them being banned from going in again. Some were bemused as it was a perfectly good meeting place.

Meanwhile, the Leicester brothers and a couple of others got to St Pancras and walked to Kings Cross to wait for the main Leeds mob to get in. Millwall were also floating about the station, looking for West Ham. When Leeds came off the train with shouts of 'United', the Millwall Bushwhackers ran into them, thinking they were their hated East End enemies. Millwall seem to have got the better of the fighting, catching Leeds by surprise, but the police were soon there. Highbury later saw running battles all through the match due to inadequate segregation. Leeds had to walk past Arsenal to get to their section and everyone was mixed in and the trouble got the match held up for a time.

Certainly the match was much more eventful than when Arsenal had visited Elland Road earlier in the season. Football Against Racism was at the ground as part of a national tour and there were a lot of police about and also students, who were set upon in the streets. Arsenal's leading face, Dainton Connell, widely known as Denton, was there and one older Leeds neanderthal was right in his face, saying, 'You fucking nigger, you're gonna lick my boots.' Because of all the police, Denton couldn't retaliate. (Denton, who was also known as 'The Bear', died in October 2007 in a car crash in Moscow while working as a bodyguard for the Pet Shop Boys.)

An Arsenal account of that day in 1981 suggests they underestimated Leeds:

> It was a big day out for both firms in many ways. Leeds were a good firm, always up for it, but in all honesty never really caused us that many problems. The thing with Leeds was you knew they would turn up and I always looked forward to playing them.
>
> Arsenal at the time were getting a massive firm up and at Highbury only West Ham, Tottenham and Chelsea would turn up in numbers. Out of them, only West Ham would get the upper hand. Man United and Liverpool would bring good mobs down but always get turned over – if we could catch them. Same as Everton, Newcastle and Man City. At Highbury, when it came to any of the big northern crews, we didn't really worry about them.
>
> I think most of us felt the same when arriving at Highbury that day. We got to the ground late after a drink in the Plimsoll Arms. As we walked in to the Clock End, we could see the police running up into the crowd up the stairs into the west side of the end. We ran up after them, hearing the sounds of fighting going on, and ran straight into a fucking massive Leeds firm. I got punched a couple of times and then had to fight my way out of this mob, down to where a group of about 150 Arsenal were holding out against Leeds. We regrouped down along the West Stand standing area and spent the rest of the first half in running battles with Leeds and the Old Bill. We had been caught out and had underestimated Leeds.
>
> A big Arsenal mob in the right hand part of the Clock End got into the Leeds section in the away fans area in the middle of the Clock End and battered them. The Leeds got out from there and came into the west side of the Clock End,

making a bad situation even worse for myself and the small group of Arsenal trapped there. The second half kicked off late due to the fighting but the fighting where I was calmed down, as we were now surrounded by the OB and outnumbered by Leeds.

At the end of the game we joined up with the rest of the Clock End and headed off towards the coaches at Drayton Park. Any Leeds we came across got dealt with. We had been embarrassed in the ground so it was payback time. As per normal then, Arsenal split up into a few different mobs that went off on their own. Some went back to the coaches, some down to Highbury Corner. In those days train travel was easier and it looked like most of Leeds had come down on British Rail, so off to Kings Cross. We got to Holloway Road tube and ran down to the platform to get any Leeds travelling back to Kings Cross from Arsenal station. There were about 200 maybe more of us waiting.

The plan was to get on the train, pull the communication handles and kick it off on the platform. The train came in and we stormed onto the platform. Leeds stayed on the train but the OB fought us, proper toe-to-toe stuff, it was fucking amazing. I got clumped by a truncheon and went down. Some brave sod got me up and we all ran back up the steps away from the police. The train full of Leeds left and we jumped on to the next Tube.

We arrived at Kings Cross and attacked any Leeds lads who had strayed from the firm. It kicked off in the underground booking hall and Leeds got chased up into the main line station. We regrouped and steamed into King Cross Station, only to get run straight back out. This started about ten minutes of us running in and getting chased out of Kings Cross. Leeds were getting the upper hand and the OB started to get control of the fighting and chased us away from the station. A few of us went back but were so outnumbered that we didn't even bother going at them.

I'd got a couple of digs and a truncheon around the head and I was covered in dirt after hitting the floor at Holloway Road station, so thought I'd leave before getting nicked. We were fucked by splitting up into different firms after the game. The fighting at Kings Cross could have been different if we'd stuck together. No matter what is said about this game, Leeds turned us over and became the only northern firm to get a real result against us at home when I was active down at Highbury, between 1975 and 1991. They didn't humiliate us and plenty of them got done but fair play to them.

The following season was different. Arsenal were more than ready for Leeds and sorted them out pretty easily. We had been taught a lesson the year before and we had to make sure it didn't happen again. Maybe others saw it differently but that's the way I remember it happening on the day.

At Birmingham in April, the Zulus were waiting for Leeds at New Street after Bailey, a Brummie Leeds fan, had told them to expect a good mob. Embarrassingly, very few turned up. Dean met the Twins from Cheltenham and a few others but there was no big mob from Leeds, so they had to sneak about the station trying to find a way out without encountering Blues.

Brighton was the last away match of the season and a few decided to go down on a minibus to London on the Friday before the match. Dave Lee, Geordie Andy, Dean from Oldham and some other North East supporters met in Leeds along with a lad called Kenny, who resembled Lemmy from Motorhead and who brought his girlfriend and son. He spent practically the entire journey snogging his girlfriend with his son looking on, embarrassed. He and his little party left the lads to go off and do their own thing on arrival, with the others settling in one of the pubs. The lads later saw them at it again in the pub, with the son sat nearby looking awkward. Before the match, trouble erupted between the police and Leeds fans in a park by the ground. There in the middle of the argy-bargy, sat on a bench, was Kenny and partner in yet another passionate embrace, with his poor son looking thoroughly bored.

Later on, as a group of forty Leeds were mooching about on the beach, they heard the sounds of someone having sex in a boat on the shore. They surprised the couple, who turned out to be two blokes who jumped up and ran away after being disturbed.

Spurs and Leeds have had some memorable battles over the years and it is a fixture that many relish. Fourteen Leeds lads were chased down train tracks after a match at Spurs in 1979, and in February 1981, football violence took on a tragic dimension when a teenage Leeds fan lost his life. Many remember it as the first time a Leeds hooligan crew travelled to London in large numbers, armed with Persil tickets for discount travel. A firm of about 100 congregated at the Cockney Pride pub in Piccadilly Circus, where they gradually got pissed to random shouts of 'Sieg heil' to provoke any Spurs fans, who were believed to have a large Jewish contingent and hence were known as the Yids. They eventually departed for Liverpool Street Station to take an overground train to Tottenham High Road. Many wore distinctive Kios shoes with a red tag on the side. Al P surveyed them at the station in Leeds and, knowing how much they would stand out at Spurs, said, 'We're going to get murdered today. Just look at us in our Kios.' But Musky and Benny thought they looked pretty cool in safari jackets after a recent shopping trip to Manchester.

Al P had brought a nutty skinhead mate from Rothwell with him and when they got to White Hart Lane the lad roared, 'United!' This brought Spurs from everywhere. The nearby pubs seemed to empty and though Al P, Ricky B, Griff, the Donny, York and Bradford lads did what they could, they were overwhelmed. Some Spurs fans even left their wives to join in. Shopkeepers were hiding underneath their counters and the lads were getting legged everywhere. It was scary stuff and Spurs were clearly victorious. Once inside the ground, news also filtered through that a fan from Bradford had been taken to hospital after an incident near a pub.

Spurs fans were in the Leeds section and scuffles continually broke out during the game. Afterwards, everyone was on edge, thinking there was more to come and calling to each other to stay together. The gates opened and Spurs seemed to be everywhere. It was dark and cold. Sean, Ricky and another lad were stood together when the lad said, 'Fuck this. Let's walk with the coaches.' Fearing the worst, some sloped off on the coaches, leaving about 120 to make it back to the train station. They saw a lone copper and asked which way to go, hoping for a safe route out. He gave them two options: one way was a certain hammering from Spurs but he said they'd be okay if they carried straight on down the road.

They were reassured when they noticed a building site on one side, at about the same time as Al P spotted the enemy up ahead. 'There's loads of them,' he said, and with that everyone dashed into the building site to grab what they could. Everyone was told not to run or they would get it later. They set off walking, which soon turned into a trot, then a run, and when they got nearer started chucking missiles as instructions were shouted for people to hold onto the metal bars. Al P buoyed everyone at the right moment by shouting, 'Come on Leeds,' and they clashed in the road. The fierce tear-up lasted about a minute before Spurs 'had it on their toes'. The feeling of putting them on the back foot on their own territory was one to savour, especially after taking such a beating earlier in the day. Cops soon appeared, letting a dog loose among them, pushing Leeds off to one side against a wall and hitting them with their truncheons. No-one really cared though – they had got the result they had come for.

Tragically, it later emerged that Jeremy Burton, aged seventeen, from Bradford, had been with some friends near the ground when he was punched and fell backwards, fracturing his skull. He died of a brain haemorrhage four days later when his life support machine was turned off. A teenage Spurs fan was later charged with manslaughter. A friend of Jeremy's later testified that they were keeping quiet on the way to the ground, trying to hide their accents, when a big skinhead came over with an ice lolly. He ran past and the friend then heard someone being hit and turned around to see Jeremy on the floor. His death was all the more poignant as he had planned to go by car but ended up taking the coach instead. His attacker was jailed for three years.

When Tottenham came to Elland Road in December, some Leeds fans from Stockton recognised some Middlesbrough with them, an unlikely but potentially dangerous alliance. Word spread that a vanload were by an industrial estate near the ground, so a posse set off to find them, including Sean, Stevie M and Ricky. They found them and had a good fight in which Ricky was hit with a spanner and had his head split open. Though the fighting wasn't on the scale of the previous meeting, more was to come, as the two teams were to meet at Tottenham in January in the fourth round of the FA Cup.

Officials announced a ban on all banners, to avoid any provocative references to the fatality the previous season. Between 350 and 400 Service Crew headed to the capital and were on a real high because of the turnout. They headed to the ground but as they approached the main road from a ginnel by a pub, a copper on a horse cut them off. Only about seventy made it past him, with the rest trapped by the police. Some heavy hitters got through – Al P, Stevie M, Sean, Big China, Slip, Pele, Paul, Steve S and Jono – but they were still wishing they had the others with them. Stevie said to keep on walking and then Para Dave shouted, 'We are Leeds' announcing their arrival.

Stevie shouted for everyone to attack but he has a stammer and by the time he managed to say, 'G-g-get the b-b-bastards,' Spurs were all over them. Sean's head was split open and his nose broken and Al P and Stevie were nicked, which meant they lost two of their best lads straight away. There were hundreds of Spurs, big blokes fighting with youngish lads, and they overwhelmed them, although Sean was told later that it was a combined firm of 'London United'. At one point, China saved Pernod Harry in a doorway. He waded through a crowd of Spurs to get to him, some brandishing knives, the incident Harry later recounted to China's wife at his funeral. The Harehills lot steamed in across the road and made an impressive stand as a pub was hit and a café got wrecked.

In the end the cops sorted things out and kept Leeds to one side while they got the rest out of the ginnel and walked them to the ground, where Sean was patched up by the medics. Leeds lost the game 1-0, which further vexed their supporters. Everyone was ready to go mad. There were scuffles all the way back to the Tube and this time Leeds had the upper hand. One lad known for his far-right affiliations was going up to the Spurs lads and saying, 'Gaaas,' and cracking a few, clearly his idea of a good time. 'A battling mob brought terror to Tottenham High Road,' reported one paper later. Police cordoned off both ends of Dysons Road and fencing from nearby houses was used for weapons. Shops were trashed and bricks and bottles were hurled. 'I just went to the back of the shop and closed my eyes,' said one shopkeeper.

The trouble lasted for several hours, with one Leeds fan lying unconscious in a pool of blood after being hit by a Spurs yob who ran over from the other side of the road. 'All the lads by the gateway after the game sang "Chipmunks Are Go!", a Madness song at the time, and fired themselves up before piling out onto the street and running Tottenham up the road,' recalled Shoot. 'I saw a local paper the week after saying it was the worst trouble they'd had at Tottenham for years.'

Leeds were scheduled to play at White Hart Lane again that May. West Ham were at home to Man United on the same day and Leeds encountered the East Enders on a Tube after their match, with the Hammers thinking for a moment that Leeds were Mancs. Six Leeds were in the end carriage – Dave Lee, Musky, Dean, two Huddersfield lads and Geordie Andy – and as they pulled into Moorgate they heard a roar, their door opened and in came the ICF. A huge black lad stood in the doorway with a couple of dozen accomplices and the six thought it best to try to escape into the next carriage, but in panic they fumbled their attempts to open the connecting door. They eventually managed it but as Musky was the last man, someone took a swipe at his ear with a sovereign ring, causing a scar he bears to this day. They found more Leeds on the Tube and recruited some to return to the carriage. Scuffles spilled out onto a platform, holding up the train. They saw more West Ham on the opposite platform and a chorus of 'I'm Forever Blowing Bubbles' was heard as the police set about putting people back on the train again.

At Kings Cross, Leeds decided to walk to Euston to find Man U, who had exactly the same idea and were walking to Kings Cross. The police had cottoned on to it and went along as well. The two firms met on Euston Road, with Leeds on the north side and Man U on the south. The 200-strong Leeds mob was dwarfed by an impressive 600-700 Man U but the cops made sure they kept them apart. It was a striking sight: two great firms in the capital at the height of football hooliganism, prevented from getting to one another and just standing and checking each other out.

8

TAKING IT AWAY

THE 1981/82 SEASON got off to a violent start with mayhem at Swansea City on a hot Saturday in August, despite an atrocious result for Leeds, who lost 5-1. Some on the train breached the mail carriage and started going through the bags, chucking letters out of the window and nicking cash out of birthday cards. Wayne walked down to the buffet carriage only to find a couple of lads cooking breakfast for everyone. It was anarchy.

One of those involved was Johnna the Punk:

Swansea had just been promoted and everyone was into going to new grounds. We filled our van with cans of lager and the old playing cards and set off. Halfway down, we stopped at the service station. After we had been to the toilet we went in the café and queued to get some food. I was feeling a bit dodgy as I had been out all day the day before.

Suddenly we heard someone behind us say, 'They're fucking Leeds twats.' I looked around and there were about twenty big lads staring at us. There were only three of us as everyone else was downstairs, so we were hoping it didn't kick off because it didn't look too good for us. If it had, we would have stood but didn't fancy it that much, feeling crap.

There was a big queue and it seemed to take forever. We could hear from what they were saying that they were Burnley fans. They kept on slagging off Leeds and I thought I would buy a hot pie and a hot cup of tea with no milk – if it kicked off, whoever came at me was going to get it in their face. We finally got served and turned around to leave, expecting it any minute, then China walked in, saying, 'What the fuck is taking all the time?' I think he sussed something was going on as he immediately looked over to where these Burnley fans were sitting. These guys were big but China was an imposing figure: we didn't call him Honeymonster for nothing.

He walked straight over to them and said, 'What team do you knobheads support?'

One of them said 'Burnley' and China just laughed and said, 'Come on to us? We don't bother with knobheads like Burnley.'

We all walked out laughing. The Burnley fans just sat there and said nothing.

We got back in the van and set off to Swansea. When we got there we parked up, then asked someone where the ground was. As we walked towards it, we passed a bus station and it was full of Leeds vans. This lad asked us if we wanted to buy any clothes, as a new shopping centre had just opened in Swansea and the Leeds fans had ransacked it. We declined but asked him where everyone was and he said all the pubs round the corner were full of Leeds. He was right. Everyone came running over, saying, 'It's great here, we've already wrecked their new shopping centre. We've been walking round Swansea all morning and we have seen nothing.' We stopped in the pub for a bit and found out that the ground was just up the road.

It was getting a bit boring, so me and Karl W said we were going for a walk. We walked round for a while and we didn't see any Swansea fans so we decided to go in this pub for a pint. We went up to the bar and the barman came over and said he wouldn't serve me because of how I was dressed – I had on Vivienne Westwood's latest Worlds End Pirate collection. I was just about to say something when Karl grabbed the barman by the nose and started pulling him towards him, saying, 'I want a pint of nazi' – he always said that – 'and he wants a pint of lager.' But the guy said he couldn't serve us. He was English and Karl said, 'What are you saying? You would rather serve all these sheep-shagging Welsh bastards than us?' The guy said he'd lose his job, so we just walked out.

We went back down towards the ground as everyone else started making their way there. Finally some Swansea fans started giving it the big one, so the lads ran at them and they legged it. Unfortunately for them they were running in the direction of a load more Leeds. They had to deviate towards the prison at the back of the away end and the Swansea fans were banging on the prison door to be let in, surrounded by Leeds fans. Everyone started laughing at them and left them alone.

We turned round the corner to where we had to pay in and I couldn't believe it: the copper, the first one we had seen that day, outside the away end was sitting on a wall having a cup of tea and some biscuits and talking to a woman in her garden.

'Hello lads,' he said. 'Hope you have a nice time down here.'

You wouldn't think there was a game on, he was like one of those bobbies in the sticks. I thought, they can't have much of a mob down here if this is what the police are like. He can't have known about what had happened to their new shopping centre, either that or they didn't trust him with a radio.

Everyone went in the away end but Karl and I decided to go in their section down the side. We ended up in the middle. We could see all the Leeds fans carrying on in the away end and the Swansea fans singing back at them. We got a beer and watched the Leeds fans for a while. They looked good trying to get over the fence into the Swansea. The teams then came out and they had that twat Latchford playing for them. He had scored a hat-trick against us for 'Neverton' a couple of seasons before. Leeds got off to a bad start and were a goal down in no time, quickly followed by another and another. We then saw some Leeds fans breaking out of the away end and trying to get into Swansea's end but the police stopped them. When it got to four goals down, me and Karl started walking up towards the end where the Leeds fans were, and their lads if they had any, and me and Karl started shouting,

'Leeds,' hoping something was going to happen, but the stewards and police copped hold of us, dragged us out and put us in the Leeds end.

We ended up losing 5-1. We were totally embarrassed. As we left the ground the police had blocked the road off to our right to stop Leeds getting towards Swansea. We were all dejected and feared for the rest of the season, in which we would end up getting relegated. As we got by the bus station, some Swansea fans were leaning out of a window taking the piss, so they got some abuse back. Then some of them shouted, 'Hang on Leeds, we're gonna do you.' Some of the lads turned round and headed for the bus and were trying to open the emergency door but it wouldn't open. These Swansea fans were still giving it the big one, so in the end Leeds tried to tip the bus over. It was rocking from side to side and it was very close to going over when the cops turned up on horses and moved Leeds away. We walked back to the van and set off home feeling depressed.

On our away days we always stopped off somewhere for a drink. We drove for a while and everyone was gagging for a drink so we decided to stop further up the motorway. Somehow we ended up in this big pub up by West Brom's ground. We walked in and it was full of people in West Brom shirts. We ordered drinks and sat down. There was an uneasy atmosphere at first but we realised they were all normal supporters. A lot of them drank up and left while we sat there mulling over the day's events. Slowly, as we got drunk, we felt a bit better. We got talking to some lads at the bar and they told us this was the main West Brom pub. We had quite a good night, playing darts and talking about old games between us, especially the infamous Ray Tinkler game at Leeds which cost us the league title.

After a few hours, Silver decided it was time for us to set off back home. The West Brom fans seemed okay. If they were pissed off we had been in their pub they had the last laugh as they relegated us at the end of the season. Mind you, Leeds wrecked their ground.

A couple of other Leeds v. West Brom stories. One year in the Seventies, this twelve-year-old kid went up to Big China and offered him out. China was really embarrassed because he couldn't hit him or anything. When we started taking the piss out of China for bottling it, the little kid said to us, 'I don't know what you lot are laughing at because I am coming back for you lot when I have finished with him.' What bottle, or just a tad mad.

I also remember when fifty Leeds went in their end. They swept up the middle entrance onto the terrace and West Brom legged it. There was a big gap and you could see them charging into the Baggies. The police rounded them up and brought them round the pitch and put them in the Leeds end. Maybe WBA should have had that young kid fronting them.

Coventry City in September meant a trip to the country's first all-seater away end, which Leeds felt obliged to wreck. Coventry scored three in quick succession, prompting everyone to leave and head to a nearby park, as Shoot recalled:

Leeds got walloped 4-0. Coventry scored three really quickly – Steve Whitton got a couple – and everybody left and was sunbathing on the park at the bottom of Highfield Road. We had all been in Coventry before the game, with maybe 150 at the Penny Black pub. There had been a lot of arrests at the station as Leeds burst through police lines, and a bit of an off before the game outside the ground, with Coventry lads giving it, 'We'll see you on the park after.' It was the first all-seated away end and Jimmy Hill was chairman and it was an extortionate £5 in!

Anyway, about twenty-five of us were sunbathing when about 100 Coventry enter the park at the far side. We ran at them, backing them off to the toilet block at the far side of the park. Two police officers got between the two groups but Pernod Harry tells them, 'That's what we're here for.' The coppers shrugged their shoulders and told everybody to get on with it.

One lad came up to Ricky B and asked for his trainer back that had been nicked during the first skirmish. They surrounded us and it went off again with us under big pressure, as they had big numbers by the trees, until more police arrived.

Those arrested at the train station were not let out of the cells until Monday morning after being issued with hefty fines. On the train home they did the buffet section over again and helped themselves to cans and sandwiches by way of consolation.

West Ham United at home in November was a fixture everyone was looking forward to. The night before the game, a load of Leeds were in Brannigans, a live music venue with a club upstairs called Primo's. The skinhead band Fourskins were playing. They arrived in two furniture vans with some West Ham lads and it wasn't long before a big fight broke out on the stairs and spilled outside. Everyone had a pop, Leeds, the West Ham fans, the road crew and even the band, before the cops calmed things down.

The next day, about 300 Cockneys turned up in Leeds at about 11am, in brown leather hunting jackets and diamond Pringle jumpers. It was acknowledged as a 'good mob' which got into the South Stand early, with a line of police separating them and Leeds during the game. Afterwards at the train station, about sixty surrounded a couple of lads and asked if they were Leeds. They denied it, and when asked why, they said, 'Because you will do us, that's why, so just get it over with.'

'Nah, you wouldn't think any more of us if we took the liberty,' came the reply.

The pair thought fair enough and then they got chatting. The usual who-do-you-rate topic cropped up. The two lads said they thought Spurs were pretty handy but the brazen Cockneys said they only rated themselves and slagged off other firms. They asked if Leeds were coming to theirs later in the season and the lads confirmed that about 200 would be on the train. 'What! You won't get past Mile End,' they said – but they were to be proved wrong. After the same match, a Leeds fan was jailed for beating up an off-duty police officer. The officer, in civilian clothes, was walking along Dewsbury Road when a van pulled up and his assailant jumped out. He was nutted, kicked, had his hat taken off him and was kicked again. That attacker later confessed, 'It just happened. He was a West Ham fan.'

Before Leeds and the Hammers met again, there was trouble at Wolves and a battle with Forest when they came to Leeds. For Wolves, the coach carrying Benny, Flare Gun Foxy, Neil from Bradford and mostly straight fans was the last to arrive for the night game at the Molineaux, and they found themselves left behind. Others had parked further up by the ground and had had a good go with Wolves already. The lads knew they had to go for it when they encountered fifty locals lurking by their infamous subway. 'We had to run at them and hope that would back them off,' said Foxy. 'I pulled the hood of my yellow top over my head and we charged. It worked. The locals scattered and we got to the game unscathed.'

When Forest came to Elland Road in March, most were gathered in the Scarborough Taps pub by the station, where Al P had a habit of coming in on match days and shouting, 'They're here!' Everyone would run out only to find that no one actually was there. Neil, Brendon and a couple of others from Bradford arrived at the station and turned left to go to the Taps. Forest had also just arrived and one, in a cagoule with a Millwall top underneath, shouted at them. They started coming over a wall to go after Neil and Brendon, and Al P, who was by the Taps, started shouting, 'They're here, they're here!' again, but this time no one seemed to believe him. Nevertheless, they locked the pub doors, leaving the pair stranded outside to bear the brunt when Forest caught up with them. They got brayed two or three times before Neil sprinted off down Boar Lane. 'Where did you learn to run like that?' one spectator asked him later.

Others were drinking in the Whip pub in Leeds with Flare Gun Foxy's dad. He went to the loo and when he came back he said it was like the *Marie Celeste*, with pints left on tables, fags burning in ashtrays and no one there. The call had gone out that Forest had arrived and everyone had scrambled to the station. 'All credit to Forest,' said one of the lads, 'they came into the city, which was fairly unheard of at that time, and did really well and held their own. About eighty of them also stood their ground on Holbeck Park, with one of their lot, a six-foot-odd bloke with a huge beard who we nicknamed Sasquatch, holding them together.' He could well be the same guy that Diddie encountered one year and who he rates as the hardest he's come across. 'He was big, with a beard, and Al P hit him and he just laughed and I hit him and still he just laughed. Definitely the hardest lad I've seen.'

Notts County away a week later was seen as the ideal chance to find Forest again. A stabbing at the Precinct in the days before the match meant the police were out searching the 100-strong firm at the station as they arrived for the 8am train. A few were tooled up and one lad hid his knife in the chocolate bars in a newsagent's but was arrested, along with two others. The police were taking names and addresses, which threw up a few surprises when it came to occupations: a teacher, a trainee accountant and a university lecturer. Once in Nottingham, the lads walked round the city but found little bother, though they were welcomed with the words, 'It's the Service Crew, they're here,' when they entered the ground. There was much relief to see them, as a lot of Leeds fans had been smacked or chased earlier on.

Dean from Oldham remembers when Forest were at Elland Road for an FA Cup match that Leeds lost 4-1. 'A lot were wearing flying jackets and had done quite well in a battle before the game,' he recalled. 'They didn't have a huge support with them in the Lowfields paddock and they were kept in after the game. They eventually started throwing things and belted out an impressive rendition of The Stranglers anthem "No More Heroes."'

* * *

Everyone was looking forward to taking on the Cockneys on their manor that April. The Friday night before the trip to West Ham saw large numbers in the Smiths Arms by 5.30pm, then out in town, before forty caught the 1.15am train to Euston, with the rest coming down on the 8.10am on the Saturday. Arriving at Kings Cross at about 5am, the early visitors trudged down to Soho to blag their way into the sex cinemas for a kip. The preferred venue was nicknamed 'Sin Cinema', next to the Pink Flamingo, and cost £3. After breakfast in Piccadilly, they had a look around and headed back to Kings Cross for 10am to meet the rest. But instead they got off the Tube at Euston, where they encountered a load of Arsenal on their way up north. The Gooners chased them back down to the Underground shouting, 'Scouse bastards', thinking they were Liverpool fans.

When they did get to Kings Cross, they met several hundred more Leeds and all set off together for Euston, only to find Arsenal were still around. A fight kicked off around the double doors of the station. No-one could get in or out, until the cops broke it up. There followed small arguments about whose fault it was that they got stuck in the doors. They then squashed into a packed Tube train for the journey to Upton Park. Some got separated and when they emerged they saw a road filled with West Ham, all brightly dressed in Tacchini, Pringle and Fila. They walked down towards them, the West Ham came forward and stopped, and for a few brief seconds nobody moved.

'Come on Leeds.'

The two hordes clashed in the busy street, with passers-by and traffic forced to give way. West Ham backed Leeds off down into a market as vegetables and brushes flew through the air. Silver picked up a crate of cabbages and launched it at West Ham, backing them off, then Leeds got it back together. About two minutes later, a second mob of mainly Pontefract lads came roaring out of the Tube. A huge cheer went up. To West Ham it must have seemed planned, but it wasn't. The ICF waded back in but Leeds now had the upper hand and pushed them back towards the ground. Someone was wielding a broom, all sorts of wood and debris was being chucked and a flare gun went off in the melee.

The police appeared and tried to regain order. They managed to contain West Ham on one side of the street with Leeds on the other, smiling and fronting the mighty ICF, knowing they'd had the result.

'Who do you think you are?' said one shocked Cockney to Flare Gun Foxy. 'No one does this at West Ham.'

After the game, the Tube back to Kings Cross pulled in to one station a couple of stops from Upton Park, and West Ham were on the platform. Police kept the doors shut and the ICF banged on the windows with their fists. Some were waving sticks and bats and a policeman in one carriage remarked, 'It's been a long time since they got the wood out.' West Ham's version of events, as told in at least one book, is different, but Leeds insist this is the accurate account.

Everton away in May was another dodgy fixture. Shoot recalls thirty Leeds being followed by what seemed like half of Liverpool, along with some lads from a local boxing club, and scuffling constantly all the way to Goodison. Some of the Service Crew lads were walked through Everton's end, to rapturous applause from the other lads.

After the game, about twenty-five of them were put on a normal service double-decker bus back to Lime Street. Leeds were upstairs and Everton were downstairs. When it pulled in to stop about 300 yards from the train station and some Leeds went to get off, they could see Scousers hanging off the doors with craft knives in their mouths. The Scousers tried pulling them off and a tug-of-war went on over several of the lads. Eventually a St John Ambulance bloke on the bus decided to step in and had a go at the locals, even punching one of them. The bus drove half a mile or so until John from south Leeds said to everyone, 'Right, c'mon then.' They got off and he started running back towards the Everton fans on his own. The lads followed him and eventually made it back to Lime Street, where the Scousers were trying to get at any ones and twos. They gradually melted away and the lads headed for a train home.

Before another game at Everton in the early Eighties, the lads were set upon as soon as they came out of the station by the Walker Art Gallery. The police broke it up. A dozen later broke from the escort to call for one of their lads, who was at his sister's house on Anfield Road. As they walked, Alan threw a stone at one pub they passed and alerted the locals to their presence.

'We ended up at Anfield trying to find her house and in the end started shouting for our mate,' said Zoz. 'When we looked down the road we saw a group of lads on the corner who came running into us and chased us straight across Stanley Park towards Everton's ground. When we were by the main gates we saw some more Everton sat nearby. Assuming we'd been sussed, we decided to make out there were far more of us than there was. Someone said, loudly, "Come on Leeds, they're here," and set off towards them. They seemed to fall for it and were off up the road as we got nearer. When they saw how small our numbers were, they were pissed off and hurled some cider bottles at us as we walked past them, laughing.'

With performances on the pitch not going Leeds' way, their chances of avoiding the drop came down to the last match of the season at West Brom. Leeds needed to win. Around 400-500 lads went on the train, dressed in a mix of frayed Lois jeans, Stan Smiths, Pringles and Adidas Samba. As Flare Gun Foxy says, the fixture was destined to be troublesome as relegation beckoned. 'It could have been anyone,' he says. 'We were going down and it was just going to happen. Leeds were all around the ground. I remember Al P running across the pitch and the police were trying to hit people's hands on the fence to get them to stop pulling it down. Newspapers made us out to be bad, so we thought, right then, you think we're like that, we'll show you. We dug our heels in, as we felt singled out.'

The trouble mainly started about five minutes from the end of the match, with West Brom 2-0 up. The *Yorkshire Evening Post* reported, '8,000 Leeds surged forward and police stood in groups of 20 watching them trying to rip the fence down.' The iron safety fence ran the length of the enclosed goal area at the Smethwick end and the fans pulled it down, chanting, 'We'll support you ever more.' The advertising hoardings went, then the fence, and then two mounted officers rode onto the pitch. West Brom fans ran on towards their team from two unfenced main stands as police were pelted by missiles.

Outside the ground, teams of officers with dogs lined the streets but one group of fans overturned a car in the club car park and others smashed windows in nearby homes. A hotdog stand was thrown down the road. West Midlands Police said about 2,500 were 'completely out of control' and added that they would have been killed if the fans had got to them. About half of the 100 officers on duty were injured, along with thirteen fans. Twenty-three were arrested on the way to the train station and were to appear in court the next day, with others arrested during the evening and due in court on the Monday.

Superintendent John Mellor, in charge of policing at the ground, told the media that they were tipped off about trouble before the match and if they had not acted promptly then there would have been deaths. Newspapers said he was also a victim as he suffered facial injuries – and later went on sick leave – when his spectacles were broken during the riot. A week earlier, Leeds manager Allan Clarke had described his fans as 'the best in the country'. After the match, he was quoted as saying, 'Riot? I didn't see any riot.'

Leeds fans had been told ahead of the match that no stand tickets were available, as West Brom had not sent any. The club claimed West Brom said they hadn't received a request from them and when asked on the Monday before the game, they said it was too late. Any Leeds fans arrested would be expelled if they were found to be supporters' club members. Both clubs were later cleared of responsibility but Leeds had to print a warning to fans in every programme that season advising them of the consequences of their behaviour.

A couple of vans from Donny and South Elmsall stopped for a drink after the game in Smethwick. They got into some bother when the sieg heils started and the locals turned on them. They just about made it back to their vans and drove off, only to realise they had left someone behind. They had to go back but one of the vans had other ideas and carried on driving. They discovered their mate had been attacked and stripped of his clothes, and ended up in hospital needing eighteen stitches for a head wound. The coppers gave him some shoes and clothes and let him go home but some from the van were arrested and kept in the cells overnight. They had bags of ten pences on them from raids on pub fruit machines and handfuls of miniatures from breaking open the buffet section on previous train journeys. They also all had fairly long criminal records and feared the worst. They had to go back to the court two or three times, which with time off work cost them about £100 for each trip. In the end they were fined £10. They went to a pub next door to the court, turned over another fruit machine and paid their fine in ten pence pieces.

Leeds United could still have survived had Stoke City beaten West Brom two days later, but instead they lost 3-0, sealing Leeds' fate and ending eighteen consecutive years of top flight football.

9

YORKSHIRE WHITES
AND LOCAL RIVALS

THE CITY OF Bradford is divided by those who support Leeds
United and those in the Bradford City camp. The success of Leeds
in the Sixties and Seventies galvanised support up and down the
country and it was no different in Bradford, much to the chagrin of
the Bantams' own legion of fans. The first set of lads to start
knocking about together and going to watch Leeds were well
aware that their fellow townsmen classed them as glory hunters.
Silver, Bamber, Big China and Benny were all around the same age.
They started going across to Leeds for games and got to know other
lads. Some Leeds lads wouldn't talk to the Bradford contingent at
first but Sean and Benny got on well and helped bring things
together. Silver was a good character who bought and sold away
programmes outside Elland Road for a time. He would buy them at
grounds, then sell them on for an extra 20p. He would also sell
lottery tickets for Leeds and somehow got complimentary Kop
tickets. He amassed quite a pile and would sell them for 90p, which
was 10p cheaper than the official entrance fee. He would entice his
customers by telling them they could buy some soup with the 10p
they'd save.

By the time the Service Crew came into being in the late
Seventies, there were two firms from Bradford involved, separated
only by a slight difference in age, and numbering between seventy
and 100. The younger lads came on the scene from around 1979
and included Neil, Flare Gun Foxy, Johnna, Bob, Gilly, Taggy, Carl,
Bennett, Skully from Eccleshill on the Leeds side of Bradford and
the Shipley and Keighley lads. They were joined by lads from
Allerton like Bobby Gunning, Broth, Flynny, Ricky Bowers, Soffo,
Mick Robbo, Paul Army, Andy Raistrick, Jock and Andy Brown.

Those catching the train from Leeds to London on a match day would usually get the 7am service, stopping at Wakefield and Doncaster, where more would get on. They spent their time socialising in both Bradford and Leeds as well as heading off to Manchester on shopping trips. In their own town they seemed to prefer the wine bars, while their Bradford rivals, later known as the Ointment mob, usually favoured the pubs. Come the weekend the lads would follow a familiar circuit of bars in the city: the Smithy, Jaspers and Dukes, ending up in Bensons nightclub.

At first, the two firms got on. The older City and Leeds lads knew each other from Northern Soul all-nighters in Wigan in the late Seventies and would sometimes go together. Ever the entrepreneur, Silver would take a van to a match on a Saturday packed with lads and then return to Bradford at night to drive to Wigan with the help of a bit of whiz. The problems started with the younger Ointment lads.

When it came to fashion, it seemed the Leeds fans in Bradford were ahead of their neighbours, who took longer to adopt the casual look. Generally football lads stood out in the city but the dressers even more so. Their Slazenger labels and wedge haircuts initially didn't go down well with the City fans, giving them even more reason to pick fights. When they did adopt the casual fashion, they would often buy the booty from robbing sprees in Austin Reed from the Service Crew lads. Some removed Lacoste labels from garments and attached them to other unwanted items and sold them on to the unsuspecting locals. 'They lapped it up,' recalled one of the instigators.

As black lads joined the Ointment, the aggro that had always existed between the two firms increased, with Gazelles and flick haircuts equalling neo-nazi affiliations in City's eyes. Bradford, nestled on the edge of West Yorkshire's moors, was not the diverse conurbation it is now. In the late Seventies and early Eighties, Friday nights routinely ended up in fights in the early hours at 'kebab time'. Sieg heiling was a Leeds trademark, adopted by the masses in the heyday of football violence in a climate of identity politics, with Margaret Thatcher dividing the country. Whereas in other cities black and white youths were overcoming racism, the

115

same could not be said for this part of England. Some were heavily involved in the National Front, with the Eccleshill area flippantly referred to as the 'Fascist Republic of', while others just got caught up in it as impressionable youths. Many remember lads in the Smithy singing 'Sieg, sieg, sieg, sieg, heil' to the tune of 'Jingle Bells' in a bar one Christmas. To the lads it was just another thing to shout at the opposition. Birmingham had their Zulu chant and Man United shouted 'War!' The football scene meant following certain fashions and walking and behaving in a certain way. Many admit now that if you had asked them back then what the National Front was about or its background and policies, they wouldn't have known.

Wayne, a former miner from Featherstone, can recall a black lad telling him that loads of his mates from the predominantly black Chapeltown area of Leeds would love to join up with the Service Crew and go to matches but knew they weren't welcome. However, there were some black lads who went with the firm, the likes of Sugar and Jacko, who would come up from London, and Eric who lived in Bradford.

At Middlesbrough around 1983 – a fixture Boro claim Leeds didn't show up for – Paul M, Neil, a couple of Cockney Whites and three black lads were walking to the ground when they heard, 'Never mind the white lads, get the nigger,' something rarely heard in reference to Leeds fans. One of the black lads, Sugar, said: 'It's rough here isn't it?' to which Neil replied, 'It is for you.' A copper on a horse also heard it, grabbed the Boro lad responsible for the 'nigger' remark and made him apologise, and Sugar, Eric and Jacko carried on up the road laughing. Another time, some Man United lads shouted at Jacko, 'Why are you with them? They're all racist and Nazis. Come with us.' Jacko's response was, 'Fuck off, you mugs.' Several pubs became known as NF haunts, and some lads attended their marches. The younger Gilly, from Bradford, was about fifteen when he went to one in Halifax in the early 1980s. He was bombarded with missiles by the Anti-Nazi League and halfway through thought, fuck this, and switched sides. 'I thought I'd have a better laugh with the other side,' he said. 'I was fifteen so I would have followed anything.'

In December 1982, the tensions between black and white in Bradford culminated in a weekend of violence in the city. On a Friday night, one of the Service Crew was mugged by a black lad and had his wages taken, as he had gone out straight after work. The lads felt the police weren't interested in chasing it up and, as it was just one of several incidents over a number of weeks, decided to take matters into their own hands. At a match against Rotherham, it was agreed that the following Friday everyone would meet up and go to Jasper's, the bar where the black lads congregated, and have it out with them. For all their blustering about how hard they were, the Ointment, in the eyes of the Service Crew lads, were unable to sort out the problem so they took it upon themselves. At that time, the black lads had the run of the town, whereas today it is dominated by the Asian youth.

Thirty or forty met at the Lord Clyde pub, many of them tooled up, and then headed off to Jasper's. Most went in down the stairs and spotted about the same number drinking in an area off to the left. Others branched off to guard the fire exits. Without hesitation, they waded into the startled group and a mass brawl kicked off. Out came hammers, knives and the like, while the few women in there scrambled to safety. One was slashed across the breast by someone wielding an axe and to this day no one knows who was responsible. It was extremely violent and some admit they may have gone over the top, but at the time they were angry at another group of lads 'taking liberties' in their town. The fighting spilled outside before the lads disappeared into the night ahead of the police arriving.

Trouble flared in the Westgate area of the city on the Saturday evening when the black lads set out for revenge. Newspapers reported 'A Night of Terror in the City', with a pub landlord quoted as saying the city 'resembled a scene from the *Zulu* film'. The boss of the Market Tavern said he saw about 200 black and white youths, some singing football songs and 'Zulu' chants, and stopped them from coming in after hearing about the trouble. He saw people running around outside and heard screaming as well as lads shouting, 'Sieg heil.' The manageress of Jasper's, the scene of the trouble the previous night, said a group of black guys came in and went for a white youth at one side of the bar. She had to lead customers to safety out of a back door. It was reported that those involved in the Friday night trouble were also involved in this latest outbreak, with football hooligans, who had met at the Interchange and were picking on people at random between 10am and midnight, the main offenders.

Eventually, about a dozen Service Crew lads were traced and brought before the courts for the trouble on the Friday and subsequently given community service, suspended sentences and fines. The court was told the injured woman needed twenty-five stitches, two police officers were put on sick leave and two civilians were hurt. Six defendants pleaded not guilty to affray for the Saturday night violence.

After that weekend the feud ceased, much to the relief of the authorities, and the focus of any rivalry was less black versus white than Service Crew versus Ointment. The two gangs would fight many times over the years. On one occasion in the mid-Eighties, a large group of Leeds came through to Bradford looking for them, with the older Gilly leading the charge and taking them around the pubs. Benny, from Bradford, was in the Queens with his ex-wife and another couple when Leeds lads came pouring in. They knew what was in store and beat a hasty retreat with partners in tow before the mayhem started. It was a busy night, with lads from Huddersfield, who were out drinking in the city purely by chance, getting involved in trouble and a Bradford lad being stabbed.

Any lingering pleasantries between the two deteriorated over the years, especially when both teams were in the same division in the 1985/86 season. Newly promoted Bradford City travelled to Elland Road that September and hundreds of Leeds were out in anticipation. The Service Crew met in a pub in Bradford called the Smithy and turnout was good, with big contingents from Keighley, Shipley and Eccleshill. They walked through town up to the Queens pub near the station, where the Ointment came out with glasses and bottles and faced them. 'If you came with us we'd have a right mob from Bradford,' said one of the Ointment. That was never going to happen, though despite the highly charged atmosphere nothing occurred on this occasion, as most of the protagonists knew each other.

When the two teams met later that season it was a different story, as Johnna was set upon and repeatedly stabbed by an Ointment lad ahead of the game. Johnna had become a punk after a mate from Bradford played him some music at a Butlins holiday camp one year. He went home, chucked out all his old clothes and never looked back. He was one of only about thirty punks in Bradford back in the late Seventies and eventually moved to London to join like-minded friends. His passion for Leeds remained over the years, although he missed a season around 1978 due to absorption in his new-found musical anarchy.

Like other Bradford lads, he knew some of the Ointment and even went to Millwall with them one year after they saw him walking along the Old Kent Road wearing his Leeds hat as they drove past in a coach. But there was no love lost ahead of the City v. Leeds fixture in April 1986. It was a midweek game and Johnna was with about forty Bradford Service Crew lads, the likes of Muffy, Benny, Big China, Ashley and Gilly, who met in the Oddfellows Arms in the city. They assumed City would gather at the Marshfield pub, one of their usual haunts, just off the Manchester Road leading to the M606 motorway.

The lads got a bus to the Craven Heifer pub and it wasn't long before they saw Bradford running up the road, prompting Leeds to run towards them. City had bigger numbers but they backed off and dispersed and Leeds began walking along a long, straight road. Johnna was at the back, falling behind the main mob, when he heard a shout of 'Get the Leeds bastard' and a crowd of City jumped him. He was battered with bricks and planks of wood and went down on the floor, where he rolled up and took a beating. One City lad called Mick Jack helped him up after the others had left, along with a little black kid who must have seen the commotion. Johnna was then aware of someone shouting at him to stay where he was. He said he didn't want to miss the game but the bloke identified himself as a policeman and said that Johnna had been stabbed. He turned around and looked at the floor and saw a trail of blood. As he tried to walk he felt faint and had to lean against a lamppost.

Mick carried on to the game but the young lad stayed and when an ambulance arrived, ended up going with Johnna to hospital. He could not have an anaesthetic because he was told the wound was too wide and it wouldn't heal properly. Doctors said they thought he had been cut with a wide, cut-throat razor or two blades taped together with a block in between to make a bigger gash. He needed sixty stitches in his back and had also been stabbed on his arm and the side of his head. While he was being stitched, the nurse told him Aspin had scored, later winning the match for Leeds.

He went back to recuperate at Sean's house and had to apologise to his mum for bleeding on her sheets, but two days later, despite feeling numb, he was waiting for Millwall to turn up at Elland Road. He never knew who the kid was that helped him or got a chance to say thanks and despite him knowing some of Bradford's lads, it never got back to him who was responsible. He only heard from the ones who claimed they were helping to pull his attackers off him.

'My life changed forever that day and I was fortunate not to have died,' he says. 'I was stabbed and repeatedly hit on the head with planks of wood by a group of about fifty people and kept passing out then regaining consciousness and then passing out again. From that day on I started having panic attacks and suffering from depression.' He recovered but when the rave scene kicked in, over-indulgence in narcotics brought back the depression.

* * *

Other groups from towns like York, Wakefield and Harrogate have all played an integral part in the Leeds hooligan scene over the years. Prominent among them have been the Donny Whites, who at their peak numbered about 150 and pulled in lads predominantly from Doncaster but also from nearby Mexborough, Derne Valley, Retford, South Elmsall and other areas within a ten or twelve mile radius. Doncaster has always had a fairly rough and rowdy reputation and was often favoured by fans as a place to stop off for a few beers on match days, with the A1 just a few miles away. The likes of Newcastle, Middlesbrough, Chelsea and smaller firms like Peterborough have all passed through and encountered the locals, and the Nag's Head, Cleveland, White Bear and Gatehouse pubs have been the starting points of many a battle.

Lads would meet up in the pubs from about 5pm on a Saturday and by 7pm they would often be scuffling. After one fight in Donny, Griff ditched a machete on the roof of the markets when the cops were about. A young kid who had seen him do it promptly brought it to him – in front of cops – saying, 'You forgot this.' Cardiff stopped off in Donny one year and a pub filled up with their formidable docks lads. By 6.30pm the locals had gathered too. A Chelsea fan from Donny had some Chelsea mates with him and in a break from tradition they ended up joining in to take on the Welsh visitors. The fighting went on for a good fifteen minutes, with about 300 lads getting involved, until the police broke it up.

When Huddersfield Town were playing Doncaster Rovers in the Cup one year, some rookie cops were trying to pick people out in the crowds in the Nag's Head pub but the lads turned on them and gave them a hammering near the Frenchgate Shopping Centre. Distress flares were let off in the melee and everyone stopped after the bangs, wondering what they were, then carried on brawling.

The St Leger at Doncaster Racecourse every September also draws in thousands and often provided another opportunity for mayhem with visitors. In the Seventies and Eighties the event attracted numerous gypsies and travellers and was the scene of some fierce bareknuckle fights and brawls. The town centre would shut while the races were on, with the exception of a couple of pubs that the lads frequented. The town's unruly reputation led to it being the first in the country to have CCTV cameras installed in its streets.

For most lads growing up in the area, the Revie era cemented their support for Leeds as opposed to Doncaster Rovers, although relations between the two sets of fans has remained fairly amicable. Billy Bremner started and finished his career in football management with Rovers and some Donny Whites would watch some of their bigger games or FA Cup matches over the years. The area also had a fairly lively Manchester United fan base in the Eighties but that was kicked into touch first by the lads of the Service Crew era and later by their younger successors.

Older lads like Slaney, Shortie, Ada Jones and Pop were the main faces who became casuals first after the skinhead phase. They would return from matches and sit in the pubs clad in Tacchini and Adidas and tell an eager audience about their adventures around the country. Some of the local girls got into it all as well and thought nothing of getting into brawls while out with the lads. Neil and Pete from Goole, about thirty miles away to the north, whose little mob was nicknamed the Gooligans, were part of the older crowd and came from a notoriously rough area, while the South Elmsall lads always met at a café in the bus station in Doncaster. For trips to London, they would catch a 6am bus to Doncaster, arriving at 7am, then the 8.20am train to Kings Cross. The fare was £10.08 with a Student Railcard and the Persil two-for-one offer was a massive help – so long as you didn't lose your mate who had the ticket.

The casuals – the Donny Dressers – stuck together and would head over to Leeds and hook up with the Service Crew lads at weekends. When that era of the firm faded from around 1984/85, numbers seemed to diminish though pockets of forty or fifty continued going from different areas and would give the nod to each other. When the miners' strike started in 1984, the Doncaster lads joined the picket lines along with South Elmsall and others from the resilient mining communities. Many of the older lads were miners, as were their fathers, but many younger lads didn't realise the significance of the situation and just went along with it to enjoy the weekly or even daily tussles.

Gaz, one of the younger Donny lads, was one of the few Leeds hooligans to get involved in the England scene, and excelled at getting his hands on much sought after clothes. He began buying Stone Island clobber from Shop 70 in London in 1989 and managed to keep his source a secret. When Leeds played in Stuttgart in 1992, he and a mate went via Copenhagen and Stockholm just to rob some shops. One sold loads of CP, Boneville and Stone Island jackets and they came away with armfuls. The jackets cost only about £50 and some they paid for but as there was just one guy working in the shop it was easy to nick them. When Gaz got to Stockholm he found an even bigger shop to target, so he filled a bag and then emptied it out on the pavement and started selling. The lads with more readies, usually Cockneys, were buying in bulk but he managed to bring back twenty-two jackets, eighteen jumpers and three T-shirts. He went to the shop again and both bought and stole more clothes, but the third time he went it had shut down. By then, lads from Oldham, Mansfield, Everton, Portsmouth and Oxford were all aware of it. Gaz later had an opportunity to set up a clothes shop himself and now sells full time as well as running a bar.

When it came to linking up with Leeds lads on match days, Gaz and Co. would tag onto those who were good at sniffing out a bit of action, such as Sean, Griff, Dave S or Keith B from Seacroft. They started in the South Stand at Elland Road and progressed to the Lowfields. For away matches they always aimed to get in the town centre by 11am. Later in the Eighties, when a Leeds lad formed a band called the Bridewell Taxis, the Playground Chairs from Donny supported them and Griff managed another Wakefield-based band.

* * *

Of course, Leeds have their share of local enemies as well as local allies. With so many nearby clubs, many of them often in the same division as Leeds, it was inevitable that derby matches would be the scene of numerous battles, scuffles and large-scale policing operations. The authorities were foolish to think that so many high-tension fixtures, so closely packed together in the mid-Eighties, would pass off peacefully. In the 1984/85 season, Leeds had consecutive games against neighbours or near-neighbours Oldham Athletic, Sheffield United, Barnsley, Huddersfield Town and Middlesbrough, a pattern that was repeated the following season, with Grimsby Town thrown into the mix as well. Local pre-season friendlies would also erupt into violence, with several arrests at Bradford at the start of August 1984.

The West Riding Cup was held at the start of each season between Huddersfield, Halifax Town, Leeds and Bradford City. The others could not compete with the sheer numbers of Leeds and when they did claim victories they were in small-scale fights. In one battle with Bradford, Leeds lad Si Summers was slashed across his back when he got separated from the crowd. Word spread about what had happened and one of Bradford's lads, Priestly, was later jailed. To get at Bradford in the ground, Leeds jumped through their toilet block to reach their end and run them.

One Friday tea-time, during the time when Bradford City had to play games at Elland Road because of the 1985 fire at their ground, some of their lads came in for a match, possibly against Crewe. Derek, Dutton, Dave G, Jimmo and Little Crad, all from a new Leeds mob called the Very Young Team, were in the Prince of Wales pub, saw thirty of them come in off the train and chased them. One big guy, called Bernie, stood until the police broke it up. They then took Bradford home before the game had even started. A couple of years later, when the pubs were shutting in the late afternoon, they saw some more of Bradford's lads shopping in the city, so they went back to the station to wait and attacked them when they appeared. Derek was fighting with Bernie again and got arrested. A decade later, when Derek was serving a jail term, he saw Bernie, who came over and asked him what he was in for. When he told him it was for football, Bernie said, 'Haven't you grown up yet?'

The first time Leeds played at Barnsley in the early Eighties, about twenty opted to stay outside the ground. They arrived at about 11am and walked around the town centre looking for the local opposition – the so-called Five-O. Some Barnsley heard that Leeds were causing trouble and went to see them – big, boozy, 'proper Yorkshire' miner-types, not soccer casuals. They met on a bridge, with just a few police trying to keep them apart. One officer suffered a heart attack during the incident and later died.

After another rowdy game at Barnsley in October 1984, a police officer was quoted as saying, 'These people make miners' pickets seem like gentlemen.' They constantly had to break up the almost non-stop fighting, and during the game fencing was ripped down and flag posts were chucked like spears. Thousands stormed onto the pitch when the game finished as the players ran for the tunnel. Coins were thrown and bricks and stones hit the glassed section where disabled fans sat. The police were below and the missiles were aimed at them but the media later reported it as a direct attack on the sixty or so fans in wheelchairs, something that would tarnish Leeds' reputation for years to come. As the 'rolling riot' headed towards Barnsley's fans, the police waded in with their batons, while some Leeds fans turned their attention to the goalposts. Barnsley fans ran for cover and, as Leeds left the ground, they smashed the TV lounge windows and damaged offices. More than sixty people were arrested and club officials later met to discuss banning Leeds fans. Yet when asked for his thoughts, Eddie Gray said he didn't see any trouble.

A week later, Huddersfield had five times the normal amount of police on duty and staff at the Leeds Road ground were kept busy clearing away any loose stones and rubble that could be used as missiles. However, the fencing was still pulled down and seats ripped out and the second half was held up after a barrage of missiles were flung onto the pitch. Home fans were hit with lumps of metal and ball bearings, windows were smashed, doors battered and a toilet destroyed. Pleas from a Leeds director were heeded until Huddersfield scored the winner and another flurry of missiles landed on the pitch, followed by a further volley when an equalizer was disallowed. A paramedic was knocked over trying to get to the injured, several cars were trashed outside the ground and sixty-five fans were arrested.

This time Eddie Gray saw it. He said afterwards that his family would no longer go to away matches. 'I don't blame anyone for staying away from matches when you have trouble such as we experienced on Saturday,' he said. 'I feel sorry for genuine supporters but there is no way you could say that the trouble on Saturday was being caused by a minority.' Peter Lorimer said that match and the one at Barnsley was the worst violence he had ever seen.

The new club secretary at Leeds organised a meeting with police and the supporters' club, who agreed that away tickets would be sold only to members of the official supporters' club and season ticket holders. Lines of police would be positioned inside the ground to break up large groups of fans and seek out troublemakers. Officials were also considering appealing to Margaret Thatcher for a second time for help in banning the hooligan element. They had first approached her after the Derby riot in 1983. They wanted stiffer penalties for troublemakers and hoped that, after Thatcher's experiences in the Brighton bombing, her attitude towards violence may have hardened.

Yet there was more trouble at Huddersfield when they hosted Chelsea, with Leeds deciding to go across instead of attending their own game. Tobin, Tony, Johnny, Jimmo and Gav Derbyshire were in the Black Lion pub when they heard a noise outside and saw 150 Chelsea running from the station and down towards them. They went out to greet them and it kicked off in the road. 'There was more trouble in Huddersfield town centre and on Leeds Road as several hundred Chelsea were in the escort,' said Tobin. 'Near the ground, Al P warned everyone not to run but in the end the Old Bill sussed us. In the ground, Huddersfield were trying to get to us in the Cowshed end and there was trouble during and after the match.' There were so many Leeds there that one lad said it was the first time he had seen three full sets of supporters at the same game.

Another time at Huddersfield, fans were fined more than £3,000 after trouble at the bus and train stations, as well as in the ground, after a mob of Leeds gave nazi salutes in their escort to the ground. In October 1985, again at Huddersfield, Eddie Kelly was at the Cowshed side of the ground and did a few of their boys outside, but ended up talking to a few of them through a fence in their end. Afterwards Eddie told Watty, one of their scooter lads, 'We've had you again.'

'Yeah,' came the reply, 'you always do.'

After trouble at Barnsley not long after, Eddie saw the fighting he had been involved in on the news and had to jump up in front of the TV and distract his parents, as he was in the middle of it all in a highly visible striped jumper.

One Sunday a year later, it was Barnsley's turn to get one over on Leeds. Eddie and fifty VYT were walking around Barnsley town centre after making the trip in the back of an articulated lorry, when a pub emptied and out came a crew of Barnsley Man U fans. They chased Leeds and 'tanned us arse', according to Eddie, who heard one of them say scornfully, 'These aren't a First Division team.'

The Blades Business Crew of Sheffield United were, in theory at least, the one rival local mob who could give Leeds a run for their money. Before the advent of the BBC, an out-and-out casual gang, their fans had had a few run-ins with Leeds. 'The year after Leeds won the league in 1974, I was at a night match at theirs and there was fighting all through the game,' recalled Benny from Bradford. 'Leeds were singing "We've took the Shoreham" and Sheffield replied with, "You took the Kop at five o'clock again." Then Leeds chanted back, "Why don't you try and take it back again." I saw some eighteen- or nineteen-year-old Leeds lads fighting with some of a similar age and I remember thinking they looked like proper men.

'A year or so later, me and some pals again went to Sheffield United via Leeds and joined a huge mob on the train. This time the police were more alert and wouldn't let everyone in the Shoreham. They blocked it off to stop any getting near. On the way to the ground I was with Bootsy and the older firm from Bradford when an old man piped up, "Don't go down there, there's a load of United," to which every lad just set off sprinting up the road to catch them and chased them all the way down to the ground.'

March 1985 was the first visit by Leeds to Sheffield United since the late 1970s and the Blades Business Crew were waiting. A good 600 of their lads were out, numbers apparently swelled by a leaflet drop in and around the pubs. Griff put on four coaches from the Smiths Arms and many others went on the train. Griff told the coach company they were going to a Style Council concert, a ruse that worked a few times, as the drivers would just drop them off in the town centre.

As soon as they arrived, Leeds went walking around town looking for the BBC, hitting any random 'lads' en route. They eventually found some of their rivals in a square and Sheffield didn't hang about – they scarpered pretty much as soon as they saw Leeds. There was more trouble during the game and it escalated in the city centre afterwards, with Sheffield later admitting Leeds had the upper hand. From the ground to the bus station, Leeds claim to have run their rivals continuously, confirming Eddie Kelly's dismissive comment, 'They're not worth a wank.' It was, according to Leeds, a case of their numbers overwhelming the opposition. 'We've never had any bother with them,' says Eddie. 'They've only recently got things together and whenever we play them we always have loads in their end and all over their ground. It's something they have never done at Elland Road which is a reason why Leeds don't rate them.'

10

PLATFORM FOUR
AND OTHER BATTLES

BY 1981/82, THE firm was peaking. The Service Crew's reputation preceded them wherever they went and had also spread within Leeds in non-footballing circles. When out drinking on Friday and Saturday nights, the traditional rugby league types would ask, 'Where's this famous Service Crew then?' Benny can recall a moment when he realised how they were seen by others. He and some mates walked up the road from Leeds station one day and some youths spotted them and shouted, 'These are the Service Crew!'

Those that had gone in the Boys' Pen at Elland Road in the Seventies – a chaotic little corner between the Kop and the Lowfields where friendships and connections were made – had now graduated into a heavyweight mob. As children, they would pay to go in the Pen but then would run the stewards ragged as they continually attempted to sneak into the Lowfields during matches. The stewards then were rough, invariably boozed-up blokes rounded up from some hostel, or so it seemed, but they suited the times – the rowdiness from a sea of people clamouring to watch the matches mixed with beery breath and the smell of pipe tobacco and cigarette smoke.

Now the skinhead-and-scarf era had had its day. The firm was organised and could pull huge numbers. The Persil two-for-one train ticket offer was being put to good use, especially through one lad who was a binman and used to fish out discarded Persil boxes. He amassed quite a collection of vouchers. Then there was the Student Railcard scam, or the lads who would simply jump the trains or go round asking for £1 or 50p off everyone to pay for their ticket.

Stevie M, Mad Harry *aka* Pernod Harry, Freddie W, Ricky and Al P were just some of the older lads who had played a vital role in shaping things in the early years, and now the likes of Jono, Stonesy, Andy D, Sean and Griff had emerged too. Even though it was the heyday of football violence, some heard grumbles from older lads about how big the firm was getting and there being too many hangers on. The older lads had led the way, the Service Crew followed in their footsteps and soon there would be another generation coming through, the Very Young Team, led by Eddie Kelly and Skiz.

'We have been done at grounds but we were respected because of the older, pre-1978 lot,' said Sean from the Service Crew. 'Al P and Ricky were older and respected by the younger lads in the Service Crew. They were good at organising – and crazy. Ricky was a crossover between the two groups. He was the old head who showed our lot the ropes.' Diddie, from the Service Crew, was with Ricky and a mob of about forty Leeds at a home game when 150 Manchester United came at them one night in the early Eighties. Ricky often hit people with a hairbrush he carried with him and during the ensuing fight he lost it and decided to go back for it after things had calmed down and the police had moved Leeds on. He and Johnna went back into the Scum and the others waiting nearby were killing themselves laughing when they saw Ricky pop up in the middle with his hairbrush and start hitting them.

Another lad recalled the first time he was made aware of Ricky, at a friendly at Sheffield on a Friday night in the early Eighties:

Hardly any Leeds went but I remember this kid on the train saying: 'That's Ricky B, he's the main man at the moment.' We went to the game and got off at Sheffield and there were literally thirty of us with about 100 police to escort us to the ground. Some Kippax lads had gone in Sheffield's end and got bounced out and I remember Ricky laughing. He walked out of the Leeds end and went in their section and kicked it off himself. On the way back, with about fifty in an escort, Sheffield came at us and he was telling everyone what to do and when to stand. I was impressed.

*Then, maybe the next time you saw him or he saw you,
you'd get the nod of recognition and then you knew you
were part of something.*

One guy who everyone seems to have a tale about is Eddie C.
He was one of the notorious Harehills lads and was around from
the Seventies. There are stories of him and others going to
Liverpool in a hearse one year, pulling out a machete at Chelsea,
running a wing when he was in Strangeways Prison and crazy
antics at Millwall. His kamikaze attitude set him up as a Leeds
legend whether he wanted to be or not. He was later convicted of
killing his best friend, uttering the chilling words, 'This is a present
from Lucifer,' as he stabbed him. Afterwards he sat calmly in a
local pub and had a drink while waiting for the police to arrive.
Everyone has a story about Eddie C:

*Ricky was without doubt one of the leading figures in the
Eighties, but from the Seventies to mid-Eighties Eddie was
the man. Remember at Millwall, the cops on the Old Kent
Road asking, 'Who the fuck are you lot?' and when he was
told Leeds, he says, 'You can't be, we just walked a mob of
yours down.' Eddie says, 'That was the B Team, this is the A
Team.' Everyone was pissing themselves. Must say, when he
was with you as a young ' un, you felt invincible.*

*At Everton away in the mid-Seventies about six of us stood
at that intersection just over Stanley Park from Goodison. A
big mob of them charged but Eddie pulls a starting pistol out
from under his jacket. You've never seen people fuck off as
quick. The Old Bill chased us down some shitty back street
and held us for questioning and all their radios were going
on about Leeds with a gun.*

*When he and others were at court after the Birmingham
City riot in 1985, he went up to a Blues lad and started
break-dancing around him. The lad just looked at him, then
joined in. As someone said, it had to be seen to be believed.*

Remember playing Newcastle at home in the mid-Seventies? I was stood outside before the game and the biggest Geordie I've ever seen starts mouthing off. He must have been six foot four and twenty stone, with this great mop of black hair. He had about ten mates with him all giving it the big come-on. We outnumbered them but no one wanted to be first because of this fucking giant. Eddie says, 'What you waiting for?' and just steams in and this big fucker gets a smack off him right on the nose. I thought the big soft cunt was going to burst into tears. We all got stuck into them and ended up getting pulled by the police.

I went with Eddie and a load of lads from Harehills in a Tranny van to Scum. Once we got to Manchester, it seemed strange that the driver put on a crash helmet. He said, 'Ready when you are lads,' and pulls up and one of the lads opens the doors and they pile out straight into a mob of Scum and proceed to kick the shit out of them, then pile back into the van. The same thing happened two more times before the Old Bill stopped us and we spent the rest of the afternoon parked in a car park with half a dozen old bill babysitting us and missed the match. Driving back, one of the lads asked me if I fancied going with them next time. I thought, bugger that, I want to see the game. But I said, 'I'll see.' Often wish I'd said yes, but head ruled heart.

I was sat in the pub with Eddie the day he had stabbed his best mate and killed him. He was already at the stage of laughing a lot to himself. I finished work and walked into the Fforde Green pub in Harehills and Eddie was sat there. I went to the bar and got him half a lager and sat with him. About twenty minutes passed and then some plain clothes and uniformed officers appeared and said, 'You know what we're here for Eddie.' He stood up laughing and went with them. I didn't know what he'd done but found out about half an hour later.

An anxious-looking police officer leads a fan around the pitch during trouble at Coventry City in 1983. Leeds followers partially wrecked Highfield Road, the country's first all-seater stadium. © *Mirrorpix*

A vast Leeds mob marches through the streets of Manchester, from Victoria Station to Piccadilly, on their way to the long awaited end-of-season clash with Birmingham City in 1985. City's hooligans would later say it was the biggest rival mob ever to land en masse at New Street Station.

A sea of casuals inside St Andrews as tension mounts for the game. While many were expecting trouble, no-one could have foreseen what would happen.

Leeds fans threaten to invade the pitch as disturbances start inside the ground. Some say the trouble began when police truncheoned a fan on the fence.

Police line the full width of the pitch to keep Leeds and Birmingham City fans apart after the visitors came onto the pitch at the Tilton End.

Leeds fans in the goalmouth. They invaded the playing surface after Birmingham scored, although some of their fellow supporters derided them by singing, 'You're the scum of Elland Road.'

Riot police charge in to clear the Leeds supporters. More than 100 officers were injured that day as they fought with yobs at both ends of the pitch.

Another charge, this time by mounted officers backed up by colleagues on foot. The disturbances went on for at least an hour after the game and one young fan died when a wall collapsed outside the ground.

Leeds fans at Barnsley in 1986. The windowed building at the back is the disabled section that was apparently smashed up by the visiting contingent

Griff with Angie, one of the girls who followed Leeds and would get stuck in like any bloke, at an international at Hampden Park.

Someone sets fire to scrub at a game against Bradford City in September 1986, at the Odsal stadium, just a year after the deadly blaze at Valley Parade that killed 56 people.

A burger van at Bradford goes up in flames and people panic because of the risk of a gas explosion. The two staff inside had to jump out and flee for their lives.

Silhouetted against the sky, smoke and fans mix in an infernal image at Odsal. 'A pack of animals,' was how one newspaper described the Leeds followers.

Leeds run across the pitch in an attempt to attack the Bradford City fans. More than 60 people were arrested before, during and after the match. Two police officers and nine supporters were treated in hospital.

Up to about 1985, the scene was constantly growing, for better or worse. As one lad said, 'It's the uniqueness of our lot and how they bickered and mercilessly took the mickey out of each other from the different areas that made us special. The first time I heard the name Service Crew mentioned properly was at New Street when we were coming back from Swansea in 1981 and we saw some Cockney Reds. There was a bit of to-ing and fro-ing across two platforms and they shouted across, "Who the fuck are you?" and I remember Sean shouting the name back. We used to have a lad called Lumsden who had a nose a bit like Jimmy Durante, and they used to mimic him the way he said Service Crew in a deep voice. Most of the lads used to laugh about it, nobody really used the term to each other. "Our lot" or "lads" was a more familiar term. I suppose the Mafia don't use their name either. They were always up to scams, wiring slot machines or hitting the M&S returns and in the Templar pub at 5.30 every Saturday night where everybody and everything was deemed fair game to rip the mick out of. Yet every Saturday they went together to the match.'

The 'M&S returns' ruse came about when people learned that Marks and Spencer would give cash returns for any item costing under £15 without a receipt. Lads would simply go into the store, lift items off the racks, take them to the Returns Desk, claim they had bought them the day before and get 'their' money back. Another little scam the Seacroft lads in the Service Crew had going was getting clothes out of Olivers in the city centre. They'd go in and decide what they wanted for the next game and put whatever it was back on the rack near the door. They'd then meet when the shops were shut and put a car aerial with a hook on the end through the letterbox and retrieve the clothes.

* * *

Life in Division Two got off to a lively start with Grimsby away the first game of the season. 'Beirut? No Cleethorpes,' was one headline after hundreds of Leeds fans 'went on a looting, boozing, fighting orgy, turning the holiday resort into a town of terror.' Many went over on the Friday night and wreaked havoc. Others that arrived on Saturday could see mobs of Leeds dotted all over the place and knew what lay ahead. Cars were smashed, shops trashed and two pubs attacked, prompting police to impose a curfew. Twenty-four people were arrested overnight and brought before a special court the next day. The manager of the Dolphin Hotel said 'the whole town was under siege' and he had to turf out 200 lads when he shut at 9pm. The crowds then moved on to the Toby Inn at High Cliff; at least pubs did report 'incredible' sales of cider. Several hundred were rounded up in the early hours and penned in a seafront promenade shelter until daylight.

After a Saturday of drinking and taking the piss, the trouble continued when fans damaged a bandstand and wrecked a tea stall in a park. About twenty paid into Grimsby's end and ran them before being thrown out. Others went in and did the same or sneaked into the home seats. Afterwards, one group of sixty went round the back streets looking for the locals and they eventually came across 150 armed with bricks. Leeds spread out and started to walk towards them as the missiles came through the air. Dutton shouted, 'Now!' when they were twenty yards away and they charged. The Grimsby turned and sped off. One lad stood for a few seconds before realising he was alone and, as he too scarpered, he lost a training shoe but didn't stop to retrieve it. They were chased up the street and any that got caught were set upon. One lad hid in a shop and as some went in after him, someone else went for the till. When the police appeared, anyone that had a £5 or £10 note on them was arrested on suspicion of theft.

About fifty Leeds lads were put in two police cells and not let out until 1am. The next train home wasn't until 7am so they had a few hours to kill and walked around the town centre. It was kicking out time from the nightclubs and the locals seemed to be in a bad mood. They mobbed up and went for Leeds, who were debating whether to fight or leave to avoid more unwanted attention from the law. As Grimsby got closer, a lad called Smarty picked up a large tree branch and hit one on the head. Everyone again got stuck in until the police arrived. This time they were left alone after a taxi pulled up and the driver told the police it was Leeds who were attacked.

They headed towards the train station down a long, dark road with no street lights and as they walked two lads appeared to be looking for them, saying, 'Fucking Leeds cunts' – not realising they were in the shadows. Leeds stepped out of the darkness and they heard one of the duo say 'Oh fuck' as he started to run. A bottle hit the back of his head, his legs buckled but he carried on, much to the amusement of the lads. The police appeared once again and this time they let the lads sleep in the foyer of the station, mainly to keep them out of any more trouble until the train left. One newspaper said fifteen lads slept on deck chairs in Cleethorpes nick and *The Sun* wrongly claimed they were 'terrified' Leeds fans hiding for their own safety. Twelve people were later fined a total of £4,000 for criminal damage and breach of the peace.

Leeds were already under scrutiny after the mayhem at West Brom and, after Grimsby, manager Eddie Gray called the violence 'sickening'. Up to £5,000-worth of damage was caused to the ground and Grimsby called for Leeds to be banned from all away matches and demanded they pay for repairs, while threatening to withhold their gate money. The FA was also watching. 'Future of Leeds Depends on Fans,' headlined one newspaper.

At home to Wolves a week later, six loudspeakers played warnings to fans, messages flashed up on the electronic scoreboard and pleas for calm were made in the programme. Chairman Manny Cussins said a ban or a heavy fine could 'doom' the club, which reportedly had debts of £2 million. Closing the ground, he said, could cost as much as £500,000. Eventually no action was taken against Leeds for the Grimsby match, which, the FA said, was down to no mention of trouble being included in the referee's match report. Grimsby were told to pay the £11,000 in gate money or be in breach of Football League regulations. The media made much of it and one feature talked about 'an aroma' about the club that put people off:

The football league's most unloved club, Leeds United
Since promotion to the First Division under Don Revie in 1964, to the drop to the Second, they have hardly been a shining advertisement for the game.

Their football over the years has been seedy, boring, questionable tactics and many of their players possessed an honours degree in gamesmanship.

There's an aroma about Leeds that makes us keep our distance.

While they have striven to contain their hooligan minority, it's difficult to escape the conclusion that the club attracts the support it deserves.

The club is right to fear FA punishment and if pushed towards the brink of liquidation the nation will not grieve.

Little happened before the match at Fulham in September, though many expected to run into Chelsea at some point. As the match ended, people arranged to meet in central London. Skiz, from a fledgling firm called the Very Young Team, and ten others were walking from the ground when they heard a commotion and saw a bloke in a leather jacket and a hat in the middle of the road hitting anybody resembling a Yorkshireman. It didn't matter how many hit him back, he wouldn't go down. To make things worse, Chelsea then turned up, forcing them to scatter. Skiz and several others were chased a long way down a road when one of Skiz's mates said that a bloke in a Rolls Royce was shouting his name. Amazingly it was his uncle Roy, who lived in Surrey, asking if he wanted a lift. They couldn't believe their luck and jumped in. Uncle Roy was oblivious to what was going on and they drove past all the Chelsea lads in the Roller with his uncle asking him how his mum and dad were.

The October meeting with Chelsea at Stamford Bridge was hardly going to be a quiet affair. There is little love lost between the two clubs, with rivalry stretching back to the mid-Sixties. Ahead of the game, five of the lads went to Hampden Park for the Scotland-England game. It was largely unknown territory, as Leeds did not have a big presence on the England scene, but Griff, Dean and another lad from Oldham, Tom and Musky decided to go for the adventure. They chatted on the train to some Scousers and Chelsea hooligans who said they were relishing the imminent fixture and expected it to be a biggie. At Glasgow, about 100 of them joined the masses gravitating towards the ground, mixed in with the natives who looked distinctly scruffy compared to the English casuals. A chorus of 'Maybe It's Because I'm A Londoner' started up and the crowd of Scots parted to let them through. Inside the ground, the five Leeds lads hooked up with some Bradford they recognised and enjoyed seeing England win 1-0, although only a small section of the crowd cheered when the goal was scored.

Others were hearing how Chelsea would be waiting for them. On the Friday before the Chelsea game, a lad called Wayne went down and stayed with a Leeds lad who lived in Hounslow. Out in the bars, screwing fruit machines for pocket money, they encountered plenty of Cockneys saying they were 'going to get Leeds'. The following day, they tried to get to Kings Cross to let everyone know what they were up against, but they only managed one stop before they were chased off by Chelsea, so instead they made straight for the ground.

Everyone was on a high after coming to London as a proper mob in January to take on Spurs in the Cup, followed by the victory over West Ham in the markets in April. Now all eyes were on Chelsea. Leeds felt that no one had ever come into the capital to take them on in their regular haunt of Piccadilly before now. Arsenal were only two stops away from Kings Cross, the station that Leeds always came into, and there were certainly times when a few were milling about waiting for them, but never a huge mob.

Leeds took the decision to walk to Piccadilly because numbers were too great to go together on the Tube. Benny, Flare Gun and Stevie Li jumped up on a wall to survey the mob making its way down the road. It was a remarkable sight. They reckoned there were about 500 lads – a sea of Pringle jumpers bobbing up and down as they marched. At Piccadilly, nicknamed by some Cockneys the 'Piccadilly Tea Party' as it was usually the chosen venue for out-of-town football lads, the huge firm split up into different pubs, with the Cockney Pride and Snows next door being favourites.

Some Chelsea were about but when Diddie and around thirty-five others fronted some, they didn't seem to want it. Another group of Leeds chased some around Trafalgar Square. But thirty others, including Benny, Flare Gun, Silver and Shoot, were in a pub on the square when they were outnumbered by Chelsea congregating outside. It kicked off by the door, with some reluctant to go all the way out because of Chelsea's superior numbers. Chelsea pushed Leeds back inside, forcing them to react. Vinegar bottles were swiped off tables and chucked, with Silver clocking one lad right on his head, but with sirens in the distance Chelsea dispersed and the lads filtered back to Piccadilly. Another mob of Chelsea came over from Leicester Square and Leeds gave chase but the police rounded people up and began to separate them into three groups by the tube station. China from the Very Young Team, not to be confused with Big China, had just turned thirteen and was in one group when some American students came over and asked if they were part of a protest. 'No, we're Leeds United football hooligans,' came the reply as they continued on their way.

Plenty of lads were still dotted about the pubs. The police took about 150 to Charing Cross and, crucially, allowed only another 150 to go down the escalators at Piccadilly, keeping another large group at the top. Many good, reliable lads didn't make it down, leading to a sense of unease among those that did. Unbeknown to them, there was about to be a momentous battle between two of the true hooligan heavyweights on platform four.

A tunnel linked the two platforms and at the bottom of the escalators Para Dave started handing out leaflets, later found by the police and subsequently used in court as evidence that the fight was organised. They read, 'It was the Service Crew who stood at Upton Park and in the market…the Yids have to admit we are the hardest. We fear no one in England, the Service Crew always stand together. Today we will show Chelsea what we think of them…' It was signed, 'Dave, Leeds United Service Crew National Front.' In truth, while a few may have seen it as a rallying call, others dismissed it as a stunt. There wasn't much time to read it anyway, as Chelsea pulled in on a train and what seemed like hundreds came swarming off. Most were in their mid-twenties or thirties, big lads and 'proper men', with one at the front holding a walking stick. Events moved quickly as one of the older lads shouted, 'Leeds fans, Stanleys out...charge!' A few pulled out blades as everyone launched themselves forwards.

Silver and Flare Gun grabbed scaffolding off the floor where some repair work was being done. Silver had a pole about four feet in length and stood by a wall at the exit of the tunnel, felling any Chelsea that ran past. He floored one lad with a blow to the head and saw the same person at QPR a few months later, still bearing the scar. Knives came out on both sides and John W, who went down under a hail of boots, was about to be cut up until someone managed to drag him clear. Foxy had both a carpet knife and a lock knife and brandished both at Chelsea. 'It was kill or be killed that day,' he recalled.

Pieces of piping and metal came down on to Leeds but they got it back together after the initial wave of Chelsea. Leeds were now backing them off among bewildered members of the public. After five minutes of chaotic fighting, with honours roughly even, the police started appearing in numbers, some with dogs. The few officers there during the height of the bedlam had been powerless to stop it, with one even being spotted hiding. Dave M from Bradford was therefore amazed to see him on television one Saturday morning a few months later being praised for his bravery during the trouble.

A mob of enterprising Chelsea lads hopped on one of the Tube trains, having clearly enjoyed the ruck, and came back round a few minutes later to see Leeds being rounded up against a wall, to the clanging of weapons hitting the floor. Leeds estimated about 150 of them took on 200-plus Chelsea, and were gutted that more of their mob had not been there. 'If it was a boxing match, it would have been a points victory to Chelsea, but we got set up,' was Flare Gun Foxy's assessment. As for his penchant for carrying knives, Foxy says he isn't proud of it but producing a blade has sometimes stopped an aggressive situation. 'I've done some things I am ashamed of now but I was prepared to use knives, they were my equalizer. It was a last resort, if it's twenty against twenty there's no need. You would pretend you had one on you – hand on trousers sort of thing – but I kept it to myself when I did, as did others.'

As more and more police appeared, they took the lads upstairs and into the vans two by two as Japanese tourists stopped to take photos of them. One copper asked Dave M to pass him a knife that was lying on the floor, but he refused. A lad near him did pick it up and hand it over and the copper thanked him and said, 'Now I've got your fingerprints.'

Meanwhile, the mob that had been taken to Charing Cross encountered sixty-odd Chelsea after one stop, at Embankment. Leeds chased them along Villiers Street before the police again got them together and put them on a Tube to Chelsea. This time they got off at South Kensington and went back to Piccadilly, only to find the place crawling with police after the fight. The Met kept everyone in the cells till about 10-11pm. When he got around to taking China's details, one bobby was amazed at his age and called his colleagues over, saying, 'Can you believe he's only thirteen?' He was in a cell with twenty lads and other juveniles but the coppers said he was too young to be released and rang his dad – every kid's worst nightmare. As his dad couldn't get away from work, they eventually released him into the custody of a couple of the older lads. When he got back home and faced the wrath of his dad, he denied things as best he could but 'got it' all the same and had to sneak out for the next few matches.

Those arrested were taken in prison vans to Kings Cross and walked onto a train that had two extra carriages for them all. Either the last train to Leeds was kept waiting or a special was put on, and even those who had come in cars had no choice but to return on the train. As they pulled into Leeds, they heard on police radios that the British Transport Police were waiting to arrest anybody without tickets. This prompted a few to dive off early or steam through the police line at the station.

The older firm was already together but for the younger lads – the teenagers – the day helped consolidate them. Though when the names of those charged were in the newspapers, one lad's teacher saw it and pulled him up on it at school. As well as the Bradford and Leeds lads who ended up in court, there were others from Uttoxeter in Staffordshire, Leamington Spa in Warwickshire, Halifax, York, Lincolnshire and Scunthorpe. Most, if not all, were charged with using threatening words and behaviour and were subsequently bound over for £250 each to keep the peace. Seven had all charges against them dropped.

The *News of the World* called it 'The Bloody Battle of Platform Four'. Magistrates were told that several hundred fans were involved, with 145 arrested after the police started ushering a large group of Leeds fans down into the station because they were causing considerable congestion at ground level. The court heard that Leeds were told to make their way to Stamford Bridge but encountered Chelsea on the platform. One police dog handler managed to separate the two firms but then Leeds started chucking missiles, including scaffolding, at him and the Chelsea mob while apparently chanting, 'Kill the Chelsea scum.' A large amount of weapons were also recovered.

* * *

Later that month, there was trouble at Blackburn Rovers away and two Leeds fans were fined £400 after rival supporters clashed at Ewood Park. One twenty-year-old was said to have frightened an elderly couple and two young children when he banged on their moving car with his fist. He was ordered to pay £250. The second lad, a teenager, was fined for punching another youth in the face.

A crowd of 26,570 – the largest home attendance so far that season – came to Elland Road for the clash with Newcastle a week later. Three days earlier, the teams had met in a League Cup replay, with Leeds winning 4-1 at St James's Park. The home fans had chucked coins at the visitors and Skiz managed to collect about £15. At Elland Road, Benny remembers Newcastle 'looking like divs' in black and white kilts and scarves with feathered haircuts, amusingly out of touch for the times. It seemed to be a north-east trait. When going to Sunderland once in 1982, Leeds changed trains at Newcastle just as the Geordies were getting on a special and they still had donkey jackets and shoulder-length hair, while the young Leeds lads arrived with wedges, sports gear and trainers. 'You're fucking gay,' shouted the bemused Geordies. When they got to Sunderland they received the same response, looking like aliens as they overran the place. Dave M claims the coppers asked them nicely to not take the piss out of the locals because there wasn't much work up there. Discretion was sometimes the better part of vallour, however. When they came back and stopped off at Yates's in Newcastle for a drink the police came in and said, 'Right, in twelve minutes' time at the train station there will be fifteen hundred Geordies getting off and their first port of call is here. You can stay or you can go.' They decided to go, went to York instead and ran riot there.

Almost as soon as the Newcastle match kicked off at Elland Road, both sets of fans threw missiles and fireworks. Leeds fans in the South Stand were hit and the plastic seats were thrown on to the pitch. An appeal over the public address system for Newcastle fans to move towards the halfway line failed to bring calm, and the game was stopped for six minutes in the first half after Kevin Keegan was felled by an object apparently thrown by Leeds from the Spion Kop – others said it was thrown by Newcastle fans – and John Anderson was hit by his own fans. They were struck by either coins or ball bearings but the referee said the match would continue no matter what.

By half-time, twenty-two people had been arrested. Fireworks and broken seats continued to fly through the air during the second half. Three police officers were hurt and forty-five people were arrested, mostly Geordies. The words 'Please Behave' flashed up on the electronic scoreboard but had little impact. Extra police were brought in and about forty seats were damaged before Newcastle were forced out of the South Stand to the Lowfields by a bombardment from Leeds lads above. Some were terrified by the onslaught and climbing over each other to get out. The visitors were kept in the ground until Leeds dispersed but afterwards three coppers were attacked, one getting a brick in his face. Keegan later told *The Sun* that he thought he had been shot as he was about to take the corner for Newcastle. Four Newcastle fans and two Leeds fans were later jailed for between four weeks and three months.

A home match against Charlton Athletic a week later was considerably calmer, with fans behaving 'like choirboys' according to police, but the threat of having to close the ground still loomed as the FA investigation progressed. 'The future of the Leeds United Association Football Club hangs in the balance,' said the match programme. 'This in no way exaggerates the position and must not be taken as an idle threat...' It went on to appeal to 'true supporters' to help rid the club of the 'scab element' who had caused so many problems and put the club in jeopardy. The trouble at Grimsby and Chelsea earlier in the season had also not been forgotten and with the club in debt, chairman Manny Cussins said that a heavy fine would be the death of the club.

The FA inquiry eventually concluded that the terraces should be shut for the two homes games: QPR and Shrewsbury. This was actually a blessing in disguise, as the club stood to collect £10,000 more from each game if fans went in the seats rather than on the terraces. In 1982, the cost to stand on the terraces at Elland Road was just £2, while seats prices ranged from £3 to £5. Newcastle United were reprimanded for the behaviour of their fans but overall, the media labelled the FA's decision 'the Great Escape' for Leeds.

The FA's judgement came ahead of a derby match at Barnsley in November. Leeds officials said the match was a 'potential volcano' and 400 police were on duty. There were numerous arrests, seventy-nine people thrown out of the ground and a court was specially convened to deal with offenders. 'It's rightly believed that Leeds have the worst supporters in the land,' said the chief superintendent of Barnsley police. It was also the first time Leeds idol Norman Hunter faced his old club as Barnsley manager.

Leeds took thousands and everyone hit the pubs ahead of the game – the sheer number of Leeds forced town officials to cancel a Santa Claus parade, according to one local paper. Running battles broke out before the game, and inside the ground Leeds filled one end, with smaller mobs dotted about elsewhere. Dave M was with Flare Gun Foxy in the top tier of the side stand and when half-time came they decided to visit the toilets. As they walked in, Dave spotted a big miner-type pointing them out and before long they attracted the attention of other Barnsley fans. They managed to get away unscathed and bumped into about twenty other Leeds lads, who were then all confronted by what seemed like Scargill's Army, a mob of nearly 100.

As both groups faced each other, one big Barnsley bloke stepped forward and said in his thick South Yorkshire accent, 'Come on Leeds, if tha' wants a knuckle sandwich, step for'ard.'

Stonesy had slipped behind him and launched a flying kung fu kick to his back. As the man lurched forward, Para Dave ran in and hit him with an uppercut Mike Tyson would have been proud of. It knocked him clean out. Leeds then piled in and Barnsley, taken aback by seeing one of their big lumps face down on the floor, decided to leg it back to their seats. A 'flying nick' – a mobile van with fifteen cells – was kept busy ferrying people to court and one lad was jailed for six weeks for pushing a police officer into the crowd. Five others were fined from between £5 and £200.

Rotherham United away the following month was a rare victory on the pitch, the first since Newcastle. Skiz, John and Kev found themselves together before the match and when they encountered some locals, Kev, for some reason wearing one white glove, pulled out a knife and started slashing at them. Boxing Day at Oldham saw seven players booked and another sent off as fighting broke out in the terraces and nine fans were arrested and charged with public order offences. The notoriety of the Service Crew was growing match by match.

Leeds again captured the headlines at Derby County towards the end of January, when more than £20,000-worth of damage was caused to the Baseball Ground. Derby said the trouble started in the upper tier of the Osmaston end, where Leeds supporters were. About 400 seats were ripped up during battles with police before, during and after the game. Shorty, from the mining village of South Elmsall, was with a few who met some Derby by a hotel by the railway station. In the ensuing fight, someone was stabbed in the leg, which caused everyone to disperse.

Outraged by the trouble, County chairman Mike Watterson said, 'What happened today is not only a disgrace to football but a disgrace to humanity...these people are worse than animals.' He called for a complete ban on away supporters after forty-seven arrests – thirty-two of them Leeds fans – and eighteen injured, ten of them police. Derby manager Peter Taylor went on to suggest that the SAS and anti-terrorist and riot squads be used to deal with hooligans. Yet the club was criticised for letting both sets of fans buy tickets for the same part of the ground. Newspapers reported women and children getting caught up in the violence, with one woman being led away with a large cut on her forehead, dripping in blood. A Football Association disciplinary commission met to discuss the trouble, prompting the FA's secretary to say he 'feared for the future of Leeds, as they seem to create a record that cannot be allowed to go on indefinitely'. The two clubs were later told they were guilty of failing to take reasonable precautions to control the fans but were let off with a warning of a harsher penalty should there be further trouble.

On the same day that Leeds were to play the first of what would be three FA Cup matches against Arsenal, in January 1983, the *Yorkshire Evening Post* published an anonymous letter it had received from an alleged former Service Crew member, condemning their antics. The disillusioned twenty-year-old author explained how he had got involved with the firm in 1979 and witnessed the small group of lads 'dressed in fashionable sports gear with similar haircuts' mushroom to between 150-200 by 1980/81. He told of several days out and how their reputation grew as trouble at matches escalated with the police powerless to control it – using Swansea City away in 1981 as an example of how nearly 800 fans, 'none wearing scarves', ran amok.

He said that the lads, some who chose to carry knives at matches, met in pubs, discussed tactics and sometimes distributed leaflets. They were ultimately led by about ten 'top boys'. He warned that while he had finally come to his senses the violence would get worse. 'These people are the future dangerous criminals of our cities. I have seen them attack and I am amazed that there have been so few deaths at games,' he wrote. 'I write this letter because I am bitterly disgraced and disgusted at football violence. I have finally come to my senses and grown up.'

The letter was shown to Leeds chairman Manny Cussins, which prompted him to ask for the lad to consider giving evidence in person at the impending FA inquiry into the trouble at Derby. Among Leeds hooligans, past and present, speaking to the media was not uncommon. They had created a notorious reputation and it was inevitable the media would want to know more. Several articles about them appeared in national newspapers in the early Eighties, including the *News of the World* dedicating two pages and a picture of the lads at their regular watering hole, the Black Lion.

Just a couple of weeks before the *YEP* article, several national papers carried an interview with a 'swaggering thug called ET who is exposed as the general of Britain's most brutal army of soccer louts'. Twenty-three-year-old Steve Brooks, aka 'Evil Tiger', and two other lads, Andy Wells and Paul Jones, spoke of their exploits with the Service Crew and how they were planning to celebrate the imminent release from prison of another main lad. They candidly spoke of the camaraderie that existed among the lads. 'A Service Crew lad knows he is somebody to be respected. He might be unemployed but he can hold his head up,' said Andy, who had a Leeds tattoo on the inside of his lip.

Paul criticised players for caring only about money and fast cars and spoke of a 'revolution on the terraces', adding, 'A lot of lads are out of work with no prospects. The Service Crew is all they have.' ET was even more forthright, showing battle scars and boasting of only going to matches to fight, something the authorities would never be able to stop, he said. 'Money is no problem,' he bragged. 'I make £400 a week robbing fruit machines. The last brawl we had was good. I bit half this bloke's ear off and half his chin. We're the heroes of Leeds, not the scum. We might get done but we never run.'

Any hooligan talking to the media at the height of the terrace troubles was not going to be viewed with sympathy, although the lads saw that article as a bit of a joke. Several were also interviewed for a New Zealand television programme and tried to explain the scene and were frank about their adventures and hatred for 'the Scum'. It was amusing to see how the presenter informed viewers how firms behave: 'When Leeds go on holiday, they go to Blackpool...'

The Sun also ran a piece on the 'Savage Soccer Tribes' and described the ICF, Newcastle's Kenton Bar Boys, Millwall's Treatment, the Chelsea Boys and the Red Army as the 'terror gangs killing football'. Bizarrely, they called Leeds 'the City Service Chain Gang' and said members thought they were the hardest and wore deerstalkers reinforced with wood, metal and razor blades. 'If cornered, they whip off their hats and slash anything in sight,' asserted the over-excited author. The Treatment were said to wear sweatshirts and steel-capped boots and have fountain pens filled with ammonia in their pockets, while Newcastle's firm apparently chose to dress in kilts and scruffy tops and, inside grounds, would pull stockings over their heads and sprout 'deely-bopper' antennae which 'should be farcical but it terrifies even the hardest battle veterans'. The so-called Chelsea Boys were described as the most sophisticated thugs, still maintaining their Kings Road image, while the Red Army 'are friends of no one' and had snatched gems worth £40,000 from a London jeweller.

After the trouble at Derby, another newspaper reported that at least three 'highly organised groups dedicated to spreading soccer anarchy are believed to be operating in the north of England, with Leeds ∴ top.' Club officials said they believed they were picking matches to attack rivals and unless the culprits were removed the club would be put out of the business. Vice-chairman Leslie Silver said the names and addresses of gang members had been passed on to the police, who were following them up. Life bans had already been issued to twenty-four fans convicted of hooliganism and they were considering introducing identity passes and storing information on the 'bovver boys' on computer. The police were asked to investigate whether the trouble at the game was carried out by politically inspired neo-nazis. Plans were also being debated about whether to issue 10,000 leaflets ahead of the next home match against Sheffield Wednesday, inviting supporters to meet the board and manager Eddie Gray for discussions.

When it came to the fourth round cup tie against Arsenal, Leeds decided to ban the sale of tickets, although some 400 had already been sold and remained valid. About 1,200 were returned. Arsenal said they understood why but knew that ticketless fans would now try to get into the home end. Most went down to London on the Friday night and again kipped in the cinemas in Soho. The Leicester brothers caught the 2am train and headed over to Soho with twenty or thirty other Leicester lads. They knew which cinema to go in and as they walked into the pitch blackness they could see vague outlines of lads dotted about. But nobody was really sure who anyone else was and there were whispers that Man U were in, as they were playing Watford. It was a bit tense but everyone got some sleep. When the lights came on in the morning, everyone jumped up ready to have it – except the men in the dirty macs – only to discover that everyone was Leeds.

On the same day, Chelsea were travelling to the Baseball Ground, which had been wrecked by Leeds a week earlier. 'Battle-weary police are mounting one of the biggest ever anti-thug operations to combat the two most notorious groups of supporters in the land,' reported one paper. The cost of policing the FA Cup tie was expected to set taxpayers and the club back £22,000 as 450 officers – fifty per cent more than usual – were on duty. British Transport Police's Euston division had eighty of its 110 officers at work to cope with the other Saturday games played nearby. A spokesman admitted that each week they discussed which games were most likely to involve trouble and, based on fans' behaviour, Leeds and Chelsea were joint top of their league table. Club officials said they were concerned that a 'hardcore of about sixty' would travel to London on the eve of the tie to seek revenge on Spurs fans, after the manslaughter of Jeremy Burton two seasons earlier.

Even without those who had gone down the previous night, a huge firm arrived at Victoria on the morning of the game. There was trouble almost immediately, with a police dog jumping up at one lad at the top of some escalators. He grabbed it and the dog went flying down the stairs, while his mate chinned the officer holding the dog as he went careering past. They were both arrested. One lad remembers an article by a reporter who witnessed Leeds appearing in the capital. He wrote words to the effect that 'these lads in their smart clothes and long fringes could have been a load of Hitler Youth attending a Nazi war rally.'

One mob of about sixty came out of the Tube and walked up the road to see a crew of West Ham coming down, chanting: 'ICF, ICF.' Arsenal were also appearing and, thinking they were going to get boxed in, Leeds turned and went for West Ham first, ignoring mounted police nearby. Dutton, a trendy lad with a wedge haircut, ran over and kung-fu kicked one opponent in the road and another stood on a corner. Some saw it on the news later; an ITN cameraman was there and had trouble staying on his feet as he filmed the mayhem.

Shorty, from South Elmsall, grabbed a dustbin and flung it over the nearest rival but took a punch to the face that left him with two black eyes. He was then arrested by a man in plain clothes, who turned out to be a police officer – the German Shepherd dog with him should have been a giveaway. Shorty was handcuffed and carted off down the road, nodding on the way to Stonesy, who was bringing another mob up from the direction of the Tube station. Shorty was one of twenty arrested before the game and was later jailed for several weeks. Fighting continued in the ground and all in all it was a lively occasion.

Johnna was in the directors' box having his own battle with the suit and tie he had to wear. He was with his girlfriend at the time, whose dad was the club's accountant, and his full-on support for Leeds wasn't going down too well:

Before the game, I was told I had to wear a suit and tie, so I wasn't pleased about that, but for the sake of Leeds United I thought, okay then. It was all champers and fine cuisine before the game and when we took our seats I was quite pissed, well, hammered really. When Leeds came on the pitch I stood up and shouted, 'Come on Leeds, stuff 'em,' and my girlfriend's dad was looking quite embarrassed. I said, 'What's wrong with you lot? This is how you support your team.'

Every time the Leeds fans started singing I joined in, much to the disgust of everyone around me. When Leeds scored, I celebrated with the decorum of a man who had just won the lottery and just seen Leeds beating Man U in the European Cup final. I was dancing in the aisles singing at the top of my voice. Then the Arsenal fans outside the directors' box all stood up and were complaining to their directors to throw me out.

In the end, one of them told me to behave, so like a spoilt little child I took my jacket and tie off and threw them on the back of the seat. I had to sit for the rest of the game with my own steward watching me. We left at full-time instead of going back for a drink. My girlfriend and her dad weren't pleased because I had, in their eyes, shown them up and on top of that he had lent me the suit, which I had managed to get sauce on. I told him to bung it in the washing machine, it will be fine, to which he said, 'We don't do washing machines down here. I'll have to have it dry cleaned.' I love a cultural encounter.

When the second game at Leeds ended in a draw with a jammy Rix late equalizer, my girlfriend and her dad looked in horror at the prospect of another day out at Highbury with me. I promised to behave but he said he couldn't risk it because he'd got a lot of grief the last time. He did get us tickets close to the directors' box and when Leeds scored I jumped up, turned round and waved to my girlfriend's father's mates in the box in defiance. However, we lost and so they had the last laugh. I had to sit in the back of the car all the way home listening to those two being happy, with the occasional outburst from me like, 'We were robbed at Leeds.'

The much-anticipated clash with Chelsea at Elland Road in February saw thousands of Blues supporters fill the Lowfields but a huge police presence kept the fans apart. The club revealed it had been sent a picture before the game of a badly beaten football fan, with a message referring to Chelsea's recent exploits at Wolves and Derby and threatening, 'Leeds – you're next.' It was signed, 'Chelsea National Front.' About forty arrests were made and police said some Chelsea tried to escape their clutches by switching trains at Wakefield and mingling in with Leeds. The result was a 3-3 draw, one of many from recent matches that boosted hopes of possible promotion despite more players moving on and younger ones being introduced.

Leeds were also victorious at Burnley, which saw Skiz and Chalky, a little worse for wear, playing cards behind the goal. As they got louder and more abusive as the game went on, the police eventually gave Chalky an ultimatum — get nicked or take a beating. He went for the beating and was carted off, only to return and join up with the lads afterwards.

In the event, Leeds finished a disappointing eighth in their first season in Division Two but for the lads it had been mayhem all the way, with plenty more to come.

11

THE VERY YOUNG TEAM

THE FIRST SERIOUS encounter of the 1983/84 season came when Leeds faced Portsmouth at Elland Road in October. Hundreds of Leeds swarmed about the station and nearby pubs when about 300 of Pompey's 6.57 Crew arrived, but they were safely contained by the police. Griff went in for a quick chat with some he knew from England matches. After the game, a victory for Leeds, Pompey stormed down the steps of the Lowfields Road stand and kicked open an unlocked gate to confront Leeds. What happened next challenges the account in their book *Rolling With The 6.57 Crew*. Pompey jumped up and down and made a show but didn't come out through the gate and 'run everyone' as they claim. The police were soon on the scene to prevent a major disturbance.

The Service Crew took a decent mob down to Portsmouth the following February. They walked around Pompey's end and chased any they saw, prompting the home support to 'leg it' over the turnstiles into their ground to get away. Stonesy had some teeth knocked out that day and when Leeds were at Pompey for another momentous battle in the Cup in 1999, the lads pointed out the spot where it happened and ribbed him, saying they wondered if they were still there. Silver from Bradford, still wearing his donkey jacket, was arrested and stopped attending away games after that. Years later, Benny got chatting to some Pompey lads at the England v. Colombia game in the 1998 World Cup and they remembered the 1984 encounter and the 'loony in the donkey jacket who was nicked'. They had ended up in the police van and cells with him and said he was frightening everyone. In 1985 at Fratton Park, Pompey author Rob Silvester has said that Leeds went right to their turnstiles, a rare feat.

A game at Oldham usually meant a clash with Man City and Little Benny with his mob of Young Guvnors, City's younger firm. The lads used to call Benny 'Duck Feet' because he seemed to waddle like a duck and they derided the Guvnors for not being blessed in the looks department, however good they were as a mob. When Leeds went to the mill town in December, Eddie, China, Mason, Farrah and a couple of others were walking up a hill near the ground when about forty Man City appeared.

The six ran at them, grabbing what they could as weapons, with someone finding a broken tennis racket to brandish. City backed off and then dispersed, much to the amusement of the small Leeds group.

On the journey to Huddersfield that April, someone pulled the emergency cord and brought the train to a stop as they passed the old Leeds Road ground. A mob jumped off and charged down the hill towards it. Eddie, China, Little Terry and Tubby went straight to Huddersfield with about thirty others. As fifty Huddersfield Young Casuals approached, Eddie spotted a regular face in their firm, a black guy in a green beret, who told his boys to leave them alone, saying they were 'only kids'. Seconds later, someone picked up some loose stones and threw them in Huddersfield's direction and they scattered, to laughter from Leeds.

About 100 of Leeds' Bradford contingent met before the match. Realising there were too many to go together and avoid detection, they split up and caught two service buses to Brighouse. As it was a warm day, they then decided to walk the remaining three or four miles into Huddersfield. They started up a steep hill and Big China seemed to be struggling in the heat. Although a disadvantage on a day like that, China's size obviously intimidated rivals, which meant he often didn't even need to fight them. On one occasion in Oldham, China was in a convoy of cars that was attacked and booted by a mob at a traffic island. China got out and when they saw the size of him it put them all off and they had it on their toes.

The Bradford lads cut through the back streets and paid into the home end. They went into the far side of the Cowshed, where they met up with a few other Leeds who'd had the same idea. Fifteen minutes before kick-off, they bunched together, then turned and charged at the home fans, emptying the massive end as Huddersfield spilled down the terracing. The police turned up, unimpressed, and chased Leeds back to their end.

Chelsea away later that month ended up an embarrassing 5-0 defeat for Leeds, who had to witness their London rival's celebrations after gaining promotion to Division One. It was also the first time the lads saw one of their main guys appear with Chelsea. For whatever reason, a main figure in the Service Crew in the Eighties decided to run with Chelsea for a time, surprising everyone. It seemed he was sick of being singled out as a ringleader of Leeds and wanted to change things. He had got to know a lot of Chelsea over the years and 'defected' for a while. Needless to say it didn't go down well with the rest of Leeds and resulted in someone putting through the windows at his home.

When Chelsea had visited Elland Road, the previous November, a train bringing many of their fans was petrol bombed as it crossed a viaduct near Wakefield station. Five lads from 'Wakey' had made about a dozen bombs in milk bottles and lay in wait by an embankment with one lad in a car nearby. A policeman saw a 'ball of flames' go over the side of the viaduct. Some hit the carriage and exploded and passengers reportedly saw flames on the windows and the burning petrol running down the side of the train. In court, the group admitted that bombing the train had been openly discussed beforehand and they had planned the attack for two months. 'It's all part of the football scene,' said one. 'We expect aggro. We get it down there when we go. They expect it when they come here.'

One little trick Chelsea used to pull from time to time in Leeds was going 'offside' somewhere after a match, then coming back into town later on and ambushing a pub. One time the lads got wind of it and the Service Crew were ready and waiting for them in Jaccomellis. When the fifty or so Cockneys appeared, their plan backfired spectacularly and many of them took a serious hiding. Surprisingly, Pudsey is home to a group of Chelsea fans and some of the Bradford lads had a run-in with them one year after the infamous Piccadilly battle. Chelsea had been playing another Yorkshire team and were in the area and some of the Service Crew were drinking in the Junction Inn when a nervous local came in and said, 'You Service Crew think you're hard, well there's some Chelsea up the road.' Dave M, Carl W, Jed, Gilly, G. Bennett, Milly,

Robbo, and a few others went up the road to have a look and found them in a pub. The Leeds lads were outnumbered but offered them out while arguing about the Tube fight in Piccadilly. Chelsea didn't want to know. Carl W offered out Hicky, their leader, in a one-on-one and could see some Chelsea start to sneak out. Two Chelsea did follow a mixed-race lad called Manny into the toilet and threaten to slash his face, but when Dave M and G. Bennett followed them in they bottled it, despite having knives. The Headhunters didn't fancy it that night, despite their superior numbers.

For the trip to Stamford Bridge, about 400-500 met at Kings Cross and spent the best part of the afternoon deciding on a plan. With kick-off fast approaching, most set off and stormed out of Fulham Broadway station, attacking the pub across the road. Leeds were still on the streets when the game kicked off, chasing any pockets of locals that they saw. Outside the Shed they found a bigger mob, who looked shocked when the lads ran into them, scattering them amid shouts of, 'Come on Chelsea, we're here, where are you?' A couple of other groups did front Leeds but they were well on top. A Boro fan even turned up from nowhere asking if he could join in, to which everyone said, 'Help yourself.' The road seemed to empty and then the police turned up and escorted Leeds to their end, at which point a Chelsea lad went over to say fair play and that they would see them after the match. He was told Leeds would be waiting at Kings Cross.

Eddie and the fifteen he was with didn't get to the ground until late and when they heard that the score was already 3-0, they didn't bother going in. As they stood outside, about fifty Chelsea loitered around them, but when Leeds went towards them they backed off, which was a surprise considering the numbers. The police intervened and one grappled on the floor with a young Eddie Kelly, saying, 'If I get hurt, you get fucking hurt.' On the pitch it was a different story. Chelsea were all over Leeds, and every time they scored they went on the pitch to celebrate. By the time the fifth goal went, everyone jointly thought, fuck this, and retaliated. Some started ripping up the already old and crumbling terracing. They managed to use one big chunk to ram into the fence so they could get onto the pitch as others clambered on it or tried kicking in the gates. One lad picked up a kerbstone from the front of the terrace and chucked it through the scoreboard, which smashed. Bits of it were then thrown on the pitch. Some say they have never seen the lads as aggressive as that day.

At the final whistle, thousands of Chelsea fans poured onto the pitch, most to celebrate promotion but some to goad the Yorkshire fans. Leeds were doing their utmost to get at them and seemed more determined than Chelsea, who were shouting back at others to come and help them. A few came over the fences to the left of the visiting support and Leeds ran them out. Then Leeds started finally to break through the fence and the Chelsea at the front realised they would soon be on the pitch with them. That was when a few started backing off. Mounted police started clearing the remaining Chelsea away but when Leeds got through the fence they still tried to get over to their rivals. Several police officers were injured, including a couple hit by bricks, and the referee was knocked over. Almost an hour after the game had finished, an ambulance had to drive onto the pitch to get to one injured officer. Even Ken Bates tried to calm things down via a loudspeaker but failed. Afterwards he said the Chelsea fans were 'loud and boisterous' but wouldn't condemn them.

The mayhem seemed to go on for ages but the police eventually forced all the Leeds fans back in their end and brought in reinforcements to block the hole in the fence. Eventually it calmed down and Leeds were let out. Chelsea were waiting across the street but Leeds were laughing at them. They knew it was their day, although the Chelsea shouted that they would be coming up to Kings Cross. Everyone stayed on high alert, especially as they passed though Earls Court station, a known ambush spot, but nothing happened. They reached Kings Cross without incident and waited again, leaving a spotter near the station, but the Headhunters didn't show.

At least twenty-five fans were arrested in the ground and Chelsea had to investigate claims that their stewards were seen goading Leeds from the pitch.

* * *

From about 1983 onwards, a new generation of lads were starting to make their mark. The Very Young Team (VYT) was made up of about twenty youths from Seacroft, thirty from East End Park, sometimes referred to as 'the Liverpool of Leeds' for the criminal tendencies of its residents, twenty from Hunslet and Bell Isle, ten from Burley and Kirkstall and thirty from Doncaster. On a good day, they could pull in more and see numbers top 200. Eddie Kelly and Skiz were seen as the main two lads and led the way. The hardcore included China, Tobin, Jimmo and Dave Granger, Ashley, Tubby, Chalky and Sinbad, O'Neil, Farrah and the Twinnies, Simon, Gav, Buggles, Carrot, Lockie, Ricky Gott plus others from Harehills. Derek and Andy D lived near Bradford and were slightly older but knocked about with the VYT lads and always got stuck in with them over the years.

Although there had been fallouts between neighbourhoods in the past – East End Park and Seacroft were two areas that did not always get on – the VYT stuck together. From about 1981, while they were still at school and too young to enter pubs, they hung about in the cafes dotted around the city. China, Skiz, Derek and Andy D were big for their age and found it wasn't long before they could get in the pubs with the older lads.

The VYT quickly built up a reputation for 'slotting' in amusement arcades, shoplifting and other 'earners' and were often seen around the city centre with Head bags filled with stolen goods. They would head off to Manchester on shopping trips, in particular to a stall in the underground market where Trimm Trabb, Tacchini, Lacoste and straight-legged cords were in plentiful supply. 'Where are you lot from, Little Leeds?' the stallholder would jokingly ask. Skiz in particular was known for his 'little earners' over the years, the proceeds of which seem to have supported his gambling habit. He started going to matches with his parents, as many lads did, and had his fifteen minutes of fame at Elland Road in the Seventies.

I was about eleven years old and me and my mum and dad had a season ticket in the West Stand. After every match we'd stay behind for a drink. I used to take a tennis ball with me and play football. I'd done it for years and I used to kick it up and down and get egged on by all the half-cut adults. 'Go on lad,' they'd say, 'You'll play for Leeds one day.'

On this occasion I was being Eddie Gray. I dribbled past one, then another, only the defence to beat, nearly there. 'Shoot!' shouted a woman merry on a G and T. Not yet, I say, just a bit further, now's the time. I kicked the ball with all the strength I had and the crowd cheered, but I'd missed and CRASH, I'd smashed a window. Everyone went silent and then the stewards arrived with a member of the Elland Road staff. Well, they banned me from playing football and my dad had to pay for the window. Can you believe being banned from playing football at a football ground?

My dad was friends with a bloke called Pete Gumby who was in charge of the youth set-up and he told me to go down to the reserve games and be a ball boy. I did it quite a lot. One of the first times was when Leeds were playing Villa, I think. I was in the South Stand and there were no seats then, just standing, and Leeds had a shot and it went into the stands behind me. I was excited and I panicked a bit, as there was John 'Budgie' Burridge shouting at me to get the ball. I spun around and bang, that was it. The next thing I remember is John Burridge carrying me across Elland Road and into the changing rooms. When I had spun around, I'd run into the standing rail and knocked myself out. When I came back out I got a standing ovation from the fans and all the players. It was my claim to fame, my fifteen minutes of stardom.

One of Skiz's money-making schemes in the late Eighties involving Gordon Strachan's new book saw him meet the man himself who then ended up stopping a fight in a bar.

It was a couple of weeks before Christmas and late-night shopping in Leeds on a Thursday was a good time to make money shoplifting. I know any kind of stealing is wrong but *it was my livelihood, I didn't know anything else. I had always wanted to get a job and do something honest, make my mum and dad proud, but I always seemed to get in trouble, nothing major but being in the wrong place at the wrong time. Then again, it could have been the people I was hanging around with. They weren't just footie lads. They were all different sorts of lads hanging around in town day and night, seven days a week. You're bound to meet some dishonest folk and our group did that for sure.*

Gordon Strachan had brought a book out about Leeds so I decided that I'd be able to make a few quid, as Leeds were becoming popular again, for all the right reasons. I went out and got as many copies as I could to sell. I think I got about twenty and thought I could get a fiver a book. It was retailing at £15, so £100 for a couple of hours' graft wasn't bad in 1989/90.

Well, we were all in the Conservatory, a kind of trendy bar in the heart of the city one night when guess who came in? Gordon Strachan, and about six other players all in fancy dress. I couldn't believe it but I went up to the players and started getting them to autograph the books. People were seeing this and offering me a tenner a book so I had just doubled my profit.

We were outside when these lads came out and one of them had one of my books but had not paid for it. I asked for my money but he wouldn't part with the cash. At the same time the players were coming out of the bar. It kicked off with these kids and the next thing we had seven Leeds players in fancy dress trying to stop a fight. They succeeded. I think everybody saw the funny side of it, even the police. I even got a tenner off Strachan for a drink, but as usual the next day I blew all my money on the horses so I had to start again.

Although they respected the older Service Crew, the VYT believed they surpassed them in their hunger for trouble and were more organised, things they were happy to prove on match days.

They were also aware, as had been the Service Crew before them, that they had to maintain the reputation their predecessors had built up. Griff and Sean were crossovers from the older lot who helped them through from about 1984, using family railcards to get them to games and generally taking the VYT under their wing. When they did get into the pubs, they joined the lads in the Jubilee, the Templar, Oscars, the Boar's Head, Stallone's, Spencers and the Smith's Arms, with the Sunset Vine usually the last stop.

Crucially, when some of the older lads stopped going so often in the mid-Eighties, it enabled the VYT to stamp their authority. 'That made us,' said Eddie. 'They would be out drinking in the pubs and only really came out for the biggies but once they started to hear about our exploits, more came back out again. We'd see the older lot by the pubs before matches and some lads had older brothers who were part of that. We'd be outside the arcades on Mill Hill, as most were too young to get into the pubs. The more you were seen with the older lot, the more the bouncers were okay with you. They were well aware of the Service Crew but we always felt they were critical of us.'

Eddie went on to be *the* main face on the Leeds hooligan scene. He had been going to Elland Road since childhood and had lived in different areas of the city before later settling in Rothwell. He watched 'the Scum' flooding the Lowfields stand in the early Eighties and witnessed the battle with Man U that kicked off afterwards and liked what he saw. His reputation spread as someone who 'didn't give a shit' and was straight in when it came to fighting, and he quickly became notorious. Interviewees for this book said repeatedly that, while Eddie is unique and does only what he wants to do, he will never leave anyone behind. Some are wary of him, but he sets the pace and others follow. He did and said things few others would have, which set him apart from the rest and led to him rising through the ranks. Word spreads when someone excels in a fight and talking about the violence was common currency then: who stood, who performed and who could have done better. Whenever Leeds went anywhere, the police were waiting, the newspapers were writing about them and they had the attention of the authorities, which unconsciously added to the excitement of it all. The fights may often have been brief but the whole ride was an adventure.

One battle that helped make the VYT's name was against a gang of black youths in the city centre in the mid-Eighties. They were of a similar age to the VYT and would congregate around the Merrion Centre. The VYT and others had made it clear to this gang that they shouldn't stray too far from that area, while the lads had the run of the pubs and bars. There had been racially motivated fights between the black and white lads in the city in the past but some got on from having mixed at 2Tone nights at Tiffany's nightclub in the early Eighties. Now tensions were simmering.

On a Saturday afternoon in the summer, the bored teenagers of the VYT came across some of the black lads in the city centre. About forty VYT had earlier been at Headingley cricket ground, where England were playing the West Indies at cricket, and scuffles had broken out in the ground with some black lads from Hull. Now, as they neared the Farmhouse Kitchen Cafe, they saw these lads hanging about and challenged them. About an equal number came charging towards them, some armed with hammers, others with cutlery swiped off the tables. 'They tried spooning us to death,' recalled Tobin. They brawled on the street and downstairs in the cafe and the absence of any police meant the fighting lasted several minutes. But the cops soon got to find out who was involved – possibly with the help of a snitch, and it wasn't long before the lads were getting knocks on their doors. Fifteen were later charged with affray and some were jailed, while others got community service. It was after this fight that the VYT took their name. A policeman was heard talking about the Service Crew and said something like, 'If you think they were trouble, then watch out for this young team coming through.' They had jokey T-shirts made up with the name on and over the years it stuck.

The 1984/85 season was when they really emerged. The older faces were not sure about them at first and not everyone welcomed the young pretenders. According to Stevie Li from Chapeltown:

We teamed up with Eddie and the younger lads – six or seven years younger than me – in the mid-Eighties but we had a few lads that were older than me who weren't happy about that. I vividly remember Mad Harry, a main Service Crew lad, wanting to have a scrap with two younger lads from Bradford. The Service Crew was theirs, or they thought it was theirs, and they didn't show the respect the younger lot deserved.

Every firm had a young firm but not like ours. Our young firm would take on the old firm, mob-handed, whatever, and some of the older ones weren't happy about it and they wanted to sort it. It came down to sorting it in town one night. A place was arranged, outside Jac's. They didn't turn up, not one of them, but we did. Maybe they had the mentality of being generals in an army and the army was deserting them, as the younger lot did what they wanted and went where they wanted.

Mad Harry, who is from south Leeds, had a bit of a reputation, and some of his cronies agreed with him about the younger lot. But within a year they'd stopped going as the younger lot came through, they didn't have the pulling power any more. They didn't realise people my age were with the younger lads and that the young lads were eventually worth more than they were. You could never slag them off, they had led and had done their bit over the years but you have to let the new generation in. After that episode, Harry had a go at a few of the younger ones but got done over, so that was that. The confidence of the younger lot grew.

Scunthorpe United in the FA Cup at the start of 1984 turned into a big day out with a lot of trouble, and quite a few younger lads got to know one another after that. Eddie, Tubby and Little Terry met up in Scunthorpe and joined a good sixty or seventy who paid into the home end and it kicked off during the match and afterwards. Fighting also spread to rugby matches, usually involving Hunslet (an area within walking distance of Elland Road), Hull or Wigan, as the rivalries from Bank Holiday trips to Blackpool carried on back home. Leeds was a rugby league town where football came second, especially before the Don Revie era. For a time in the mid-Eighties, the soccer mob would watch football on Saturdays and rugby on Sundays, although the rugby lads hated the Service Crew and the VYT going to the matches. Indeed, when the half-time football scores were known at the rugby matches, the rugby diehards would often cheer if Leeds United were losing. Equally, the football lads would be bemused to see Leeds RL and Man United stickers on the same cars. A *Daily Mail* article in 1983 said that while Leeds United were the pariahs of their sport, the city's rugby team were pioneers with their excellent supporters.

When Leeds played at Derby in November of that year, most of the VYT were at Elland Road watching Hunslet play Wigan at rugby. They rated Wigan's Goon Squad quite highly and they had a good leader called Russ, who the lads nicknamed 'Scabby Lips'. He managed to deck Scottie from the VYT on the steps in the South Stand. There was fighting on Boar Lane before the game and China spotted a casual in a pair of Tacchini tracksuit bottoms who he thought looked as 'cool as fuck', as he'd never seen them before and couldn't afford them himself at the time. Terry and his brother both had on a pair of Trimm Trabb that day and believe they were the first to wear them in Leeds.

In May 1985, there was major trouble between Leeds and Wigan's lads in London. Leeds were playing Wimbledon in the third last game of the season while Wigan RFC faced Hull in the Challenge Cup final at Wembley. Leeds were chucking bricks pilfered from a skip as between 300 and 400 lads fought on Euston Road.

Again when Hunslet beat Wigan in the last game of the rugby season, a large gang went over for a knock. Eddie was with fifty or sixty out drinking when, after the game, Wigan appeared and fighting began before the police broke it up. Impressed with Eddie's performance, Ronnie, one of the main older lads, told him, 'You stick with me.' At a John Player Cup match between Wigan and Leeds in Bolton, lots of Bolton's football lads turned out, perhaps not expecting to see a large contingent of Leeds lads there. Needless to say, there was fighting and several arrests.

A rugby league cup final involving Wigan and played at Elland Road was the first time the lads first saw Barraclough, patrolling the match on his huge horse. He would go on to be the football intelligence officer with Leeds United. Wigan came through the car park towards the Lowfields after the game and the VYT went into them, with sporadic fights of twenty against twenty breaking out. The police pushed them apart but they kept running back into each other. Barraclough rode past on his horse and pointed out Eddie, who ran and ducked underneath a big truck parked by the Lowfields and stayed there for five minutes. When he thought he was safe to come out, Barraclough spotted him again and shouted, 'Him!' He was nicked. Eddie went to court but was found not guilty. The lads laughed at the police when they came out of court, even more so when one officer called some of them 'little bastards'.

The VYT were brought starkly back down to earth when one of the lads was knocked down and killed after a match in February 1986. York were playing Liverpool at Anfield in the League Cup and the VYT decided to go and organised a coach. On the way home, the driver made several stops to drop off people. Gav lived near Elland Road and the coach stopped on the motorway to let him off, but as he went to cross the carriageway he was hit by a lorry and killed. It was a tragic accident which affected everyone. Several hundred people went to his funeral and the *Yorkshire Evening Post* was flooded with messages of condolence, which prompted the editor to write about how moving the tributes were and say that he had never seen anything like it before. A police presence at his funeral led to running battles with the police in the city centre. He is not forgotten. In 2006, twenty years after he died, the lads organised a get-together in his memory in Leeds.

Days after his death, a flippant remark about Gav by a bouncer on the door of Yates's led to another mass fight. Service Crew and VYT lads were out drinking but got knocked back by the doormen at Yates's. There had been a fight there the night before and the doormen would not let them in despite their protestations. Eventually one bouncer said, 'Fuck off, or you'll end up in a black plastic bag like your mate.' Seconds later, the bouncer was on the floor with his head cut open.

The pub doors shut and, aware of the ensuing scuffle, other lads appeared and joined in the fight until between 100 and 150, young and old, rushed the doors. The doormen from Jaccomellis, a few doors up, also weighed in in the street and were joined by a bouncer from the Griffin bar over the road. Either from previous experience or just common sense, he knew who they were dealing with and said to the other bouncers in a thick Irish accent, 'What are you doing? Do you know who that is? It's the Service Crew. We haven't got two hundred lads to deal with them.' The police soon appeared and helped to break it up and ultimately a few older lads from Beeston went to jail for their part in it. There had always been on-going disagreements with the doormen in the city but everyone was enraged by that comment and felt the doorman in question got what he deserved. Oddly, the lads rejected an opportunity to work the doors themselves in the city centre. 'We just didn't act on it.' said Eddie. 'It should have been the next progression for us, as it was for other firms. We missed a trick there.'

As time went by, the Very Young Team came to dominate the football hooligan scene at Leeds. But when Eddie came out of prison in 1987 after serving twelve months for wounding and affray after a fight in town, the scene had changed and new lads were around who he didn't know. An undercover police operation had taken its toll, the older firm had taken a back seat and numbers dropped off at matches as people moved on and pursued other interests. It was harder to get tickets as well after matches like Birmingham City in 1985 and a highly-publicised incident at Bradford's Odsal Stadium the following year. This prompted some lads to form a supporters' club, based in the Gildersome area, in an attempt to obtain tickets though official channels.

Membership schemes never really worked with Leeds, as the hooligans found ways around any ticket limitations. After the Odsal disorder, the U-card scheme was brought in, which meant fans had to have a red card with their picture and a number on. Forgeries were quickly circulated or cards were loaned out. Some didn't even bother getting one and still went anyway. The Gildersome branch was principally set up by three lads in the 1987/88 season. It was made up of fans from Bradford and Leeds, as the town was halfway between the two. They found a pub that they could use as a base and were put on a routine twelve-month probation. For the first few years it wasn't unusual to have a couple of coaches or double-deckers picking up between eighty and 100 members from the pub.

12

YORKSHIRE MINERS

THE SPRING OF 1984 saw the start of one of the most controversial and divisive industrial actions in modern British history. The miners' strike was a defining – and ultimately disastrous – moment in trade union history. Sparked by the threat of twenty pit closures and 20,000 job losses in the mining areas of northern England and Wales, the strike came as other industries once integral to Yorkshire, like textiles and steel, were also being scaled down. There was a sense of anger at the high levels of unemployment. The early Eighties had already seen the long-running Greenham Common anti-nuclear protest and mass rioting in major towns and cities across England, and the political Left and Right had never been more divided. Prime Minister Margaret Thatcher was either loved or loathed; there was no middle ground. Some miners had toilet paper with her picture on and lads from the mining villages still joke that even teetotallers plan to have a drink when she dies.

Not all miners supported the strike, however. In Nottinghamshire, which shares a boundary with Yorkshire, the majority carried on working. This sparked bitter enmity with their mainly pro-strike Yorkshire colleagues. Those who crossed picket lines were labelled 'scabs' and sometimes suffered threats and even physical assault. Over 11,000 people would be arrested at various confrontations over the year the action lasted.

And so, as fate would have it, Leeds United drew out of the hat for their first game of the 1984/85 season... Notts County away. Eight thousand made the trip to the neighbouring county. On a red hot day, the game was an equally super-heated affair, with non-stop insults traded. County were not known for their hooligan contingent and Benny and his coach from Bradford found a pub before the game with no worries about any opposition. He rang the club on the off chance of getting some tickets for the away end and, to his surprise, was told it was no problem, he just had to come and collect them. They even gave him a discount for buying so many. Some of the VYT chased some locals through a housing estate but when a random bloke standing by his car pulled out a sword they quickly left. Leeds won the match, their first victory on the opening day of a season for nine years, and several thousand ran onto the pitch.

Feelings still run deep. When Leeds played Nottingham Forest in the old First Division towards the end of the Nineties, fifty South Yorkshire fans behind the goal shouted, 'Scab, scab, scab,' for the entire ninety minutes. Former miners say the hatred that existed towards those who 'scabbed' will never subside. Big Tez worked at a Nottinghamshire pit during the strike, which ultimately cost him his place in the firm. He had been at many a battle and was one of those arrested at Piccadilly against Chelsea, but his refusal to strike shocked those from hardy mining areas like Doncaster and the South Yorkshire villages, and that was it as far as their friendship went. Shorty, from South Elmsall in South Yorkshire, who had often 'drunk a few pots' with Big Tez, saw him in the queue for some semi-final tickets at Elland Road years later but they didn't speak to one another.

Not long after the strike, some South Elmsall and other local lads were having a drink in Doncaster after a game and realised a crowd from Nottingham were in the pub. They could hear them using their local expression 'me duck', so they got them all in a corner and grilled them about where they worked. They maintained they were farmers but they were still set upon.

The Notts County match came a few months after David 'Jonesy' Jones had lost his life during a battle at Ollerton pit in north Nottinghamshire. Jonesy was hit with a brick as the miners clashed when the night shift finished, just a couple of weeks after the strike had begun. No one thought he was seriously hurt at the time and their primary concern after things settled down was that someone had been arrested during the skirmish. Shorty asked a copper where the injured had been taken to. He gave Jonesy's name and said he had his name and a Leeds United tattoo on his arm.

'He's dead,' the copper flatly replied.

Stunned, Shorty sat down on the kerb and later had to go to the morgue. Jonesy, who was just twenty-four and a father-of-two, was described by all who knew him as 'a great lad' who had been at many memorable encounters over the years. The National Union of Mineworkers named its memorial lectures after him and another man who died in the dispute. A bar at Liverpool University was also named after him and the lads even heard about a group in communist Cuba that adopted his name.

'After that, it became personal,' said Shorty, who was one of Jonesy's closest friends. 'We go down every year to mark his death. There's a bench where he dropped and we lay a wreath and have some posters done and put them up just to let them know. Every year they used to wreck it. One year we took his mum and when we came out of the pub and she saw what they'd done, it broke her heart. He's not forgotten. He was a great lad and a great friend.'

The strike drew many good lads away from football, at around the same time that the Service Crew was dying. But for those caught up in the dispute 'every day was like a Saturday', fighting with the miners that crossed the picket lines and the police. Some of the younger lads didn't gauge the political significance of the situation but went along for the ride, using it as an opportunity to play up against the authorities. They would be out drinking in Leeds at weekends and then join flying pickets during the week. After one heavy snowfall, some lads built a snowman around a concrete bollard by the front gates to a pit and put a police helmet on it. They taunted some officers and when one particularly unpopular senior officer saw it, he got in his jeep and drove straight at the snowman, trashing the front of the vehicle, much to the hilarity of everyone, including some of his colleagues. One lad was a miner along with his dad, but his uncle was a copper involved in the dispute, and years later at matches he would complain about always being singled out and arrested by his uncle.

Pissed up one night, Shorty and his mates painted some police vans but were so drunk they spelt 'SCABB' with two Bs. The coppers knew who was responsible, especially as they still had paint on their hands the next day. The pickets would also urinate in crisp packets and chuck them at coppers because they knew they would be there all week unable to wash their uniforms, and would tie roman candles together and throw them at the horses. The Standard Fireworks factory was in the area and one worker there supplied them with bangers and air bombs and showed them how best to tie them together. Some collected the county badges off coppers' helmets as trophies. The police, of course, weren't shy themselves when it came to fighting and many miners complained of getting a rough ride. Not all the lads were up for taking them on; some used to joke that while they were getting stuck in at the front they'd get hit by the 'ATBTB' – At The Back Throwing Bricks.

The Frickley Fighters, attached to a mine in South Elmsall, had a spotter on a motorbike who would ride around and tell them what direction the police were coming from when they were defending certain pits. On picket duty, footballing rivalries were put to one side and there would be a mix of different supporters all stood together. After trouble at a game at Barnsley in October 1984, the Leeds United lads were part of a mass picket at Brodsworth, near South Elmsall, on the Monday. When the fighting with the coppers calmed down somewhat and the lads had a sit down, a bloke went up to Shorty and said, 'Remember me?' Shorty had no idea who he was until the bloke said, 'You punched me on Saturday at Barnsley.'

Hutchy, a Man United lad in the village, joined them on picket duty with some of his mates, as well as some Sheffield Wednesday fans. There'd also be the lads from Doncaster, Wakefield and Pontefract, nicknamed Pontecarlo for its obvious similarities with the glamorous resort of Monte Carlo, Castleford aka Cas Vegas, and Featherstone, known as Featherly Hills for the same reason. Little Wayne and Bob Stones, former miners from Featherstone, were highly rated, with Bob's trademark line just before he hit someone: 'I'm Bob from Feath' – bang.

The lads knew if it kicked off everyone would all get stuck in, as they were all game. This was something the unions also recognised and the Frickley Fighters were often asked to travel to other parts of the country to add their lively support to meetings and demos. 'They used to say if the sun shone, Frickley would go on strike,' said Shorty. 'They knew we would barrack people and Scargill asked if the Frickley Fighters and other groups could go to conferences at pits in Wales and Scotland. We were at Orgreave for four or five weeks and we'd move around to others.' Of about 1,600 miners at Frickley, about nine crossed the picket line. Some had their homes burnt down, resulting in one lad being jailed for three years. During the first battle there, which lasted about six hours, more than seventy police officers were injured.

The union paid all fines lads accrued during the dispute and when Shorty broke his arm at a football match, a union official wrote the emergency solicitor's number on his cast. When the dispute was over, the lads lamented the fact that it was 'back to being a football hooligan'. Miners had to survive on very little money during the strike and mates often helped out by buying them beers or subbing them at matches. The weekly £3 supermarket vouchers and £1 a day picket money wasn't enough and was in stark contrast to the £200-plus a week they were used to in wages, way more than most of the other football lads.

Going to away matches became too expensive and Chelsea in April 1984 was one of the few games many of the lads managed in this period. The Frickley lads used to save £10 a week for Christmas through work, but given the special circumstances they were allowed to cash it in halfway through the year, giving them a few hundred quid. They went to their working men's club, the Empire, and got drunk before heading off to Doncaster, then down to London on the Friday night. When it kicked off at a Tube station the next day, all the Leeds lads turned on the police, shouting, 'Yorkshire miners.' The Metropolitan Police had been drafted in to help out during the strike, and miners' songs and chants would be directed at them in London to piss them off. One time on a Tube on a sweltering hot day, the police held hundreds of lads on a train for ages, refusing to let them off, which they thought was a bit of payback. Local police were not immune from the roused passions either. A Sunday League team Sean played for was due to play a team of policemen from Leeds in 1985, but the game was postponed three times until after the strike in May. His team won 2-1 and when Sean scored one of the goals he shouted, 'That one's for the miners.'

The strike eventually folded, the pits gradually closed and, with nothing to replace them, unemployment and drugs flourished. Nowadays in the Empire, where Scargill once made rousing speeches, plaques marking the dispute at different pits that once filled the walls have been moved into the tap room at the back; like the strike, they are gone but not forgotten.

* * *

The 1984/85 season may well have seen the climax of British football violence, before the scene peaked and started to change. It was Leeds United's third season in the Second Division and nationally match attendances were down, with the authorities partially blaming hooliganism. The miners had been on strike since March and matches were a good way for them to vent their anger at police who were perceived to be getting their digs in on the picket line. Leeds would face Boro, Wolves, Pompey, Man City and had another visit from Everton in the Cup. These were all hooligan big-hitters, but the lads found that many other firms didn't want to know, unable to cope with their numbers and put off by their reputation.

In the city the lads were having a whale of a time in the pubs, bars and clubs, relentlessly taking the piss out of each other. The Black Lion, Scarborough Taps and Prince of Wales were the main pubs, especially on match days, mainly because of being in close proximity to the train station. There was no CCTV in the early Eighties but after a while the police would mount a camera on a bridge above the three pubs on match days. The lads also started getting into different pub runs for each night at weekends. Saturday was always in the Templar if Leeds were at home, but Fridays took several different routes. Lads would meet in the Smiths Arms on East Street in East End Park, near the city centre, at 5.30pm for a night of gambling, three-card brag, darts and pool for money before heading off on the East Street run. This involved drinking in the Waterloo, Black Dog, Fisherman's Hut, Spring Close and the Hampton before ending up in The Richmond, a pub-nightclub. The Eastgate run started from the Smiths up to Hoagies, the Vine, the Three Legs, Nag's Head, the Duchess of York, the Madhouse and finally the usual finishing place was Jaccomellis. A third route, the 'shithole run', went from the Smiths, over the road to the Palace, then down the Calls to the New Penny, up to the Mucky Duck – where the Friday teddy boy night was the scene of a few fights – the Duncan, Barbarellas, the Peel and finally Jac's. The New Penny was a rampant gay pub full of 'big geezers', not the camp types, and where some of the older lot had come a cropper in punch-ups in the past. The runs pretty much came to an end in the Nineties when the Richmond, something of a cattle market, was burnt down.

The square mile around the Corn Exchange was known to have some of the roughest pubs in the country in the early Eighties. Those and other favoured watering holes such as the Star and Garter, the Scotsman, the Regent, Robin Hood, the Duncan, the Nag's Head, and the ever-so-charming Snake Pit – the only place to get a drink when the pubs shut at 3pm – were all dotted around the outdoor market and frequented by the traders.

Regular Bank Holiday trips to Blackpool also became a fixture and rows with Man City, Wigan and the locals broke out practically every time they went. There were also run-ins with Liverpool, Stoke and some Scottish firms on the seaside trips, which started in about 1982 and ran into the 1990s. Every Bank Holiday weekend, hundreds of Yorkshire casuals would descend on the Lancashire resort in vans, cars or by train, often with nowhere to stay. They would go on the piss from Friday through to Monday – although the VYT were too young to get in the pubs at first – with the police often unable to maintain control. These boozy trips would provide a fund of anecdotes over the years.

The long-running trouble with Wigan, which spilled over onto the rugby terraces, actually started in Scarborough. Teenagers Zoz, Jono and Watty were with a load of Service Crew lads in the seaside resort when they saw some Wigan lads getting brayed in the town centre. Cammy, one of the Wigan boys, who knew Jono, was attacked by a load of Geordies, and Jono and Watty stepped in to help bail them out. But later that year, in Blackpool, some Wigan lads turned on Leeds. Wigan were out in force that weekend, as were Leeds, with a lot of Seacroft in the mob. They were in the Funhouse on Blackpool Pleasure Beach – which shows their age – when Wigan tried to take Crabby's sovereign rings. Fighting spilled out of the amusement park and onto the seafront, with bottles being thrown. Four Scousers joined up with Leeds, only for one of them to lose his front teeth. Wigan Athletic played York City about six months later, and Leeds made the trip to attack them. After that, there were constant battles between the two firms. A Donny lad was slashed by some Wigan lads one year, which did nothing for relations.

Everyone went over to the resort one weekend ahead of a match against Man City in April 1985. It was to be a memorable occasion for Flare Gun Foxy from Bradford. 'We had a reputation of being wreckers and whatever you could do to get your firm on to the next level you would do at that time. Firms were always trying to outdo one another and because of that I decided to take a flare gun to the Man City match. I wanted to get Leeds up there.' Everton had used one earlier in the season at the cup match and fired it into the South Stand, which probably planted the seed. Foxy got an army issue type which was classed as a firearm and took it with him for the Bank Holiday weekend. Again scores went over, complete with Head bags for thievery. One lad offered to buy the gun off him for as much as £50 but Foxy said he had it for a particular purpose and he wouldn't be using it until then.

One group travelled to Manchester in a van and stopped for a drink in a pub by Strangeways prison.

'You here for the game?' the barman asked one lad in a flat cap.

'No, I'm hoping to stab someone,' came the reply.

The barman retreated, signalling to his colleagues that it was going to be one of those days.

On arrival at Maine Road, Foxy's bag was searched and the gun was found tucked away in with his clothes. The stewards thought it was a pen at first but then a copper realised what it was and arrested him. He was later found guilty of possession of a firearm and sentenced to nine months in Strangeways. Looking back he admits it did him a favour because who knows what could have happened if he had used it. 'I was thinking of the headlines,' he says now.

Leeds took thousands that day. Some went in the Kippax for a punch-up and after the match, which Leeds won 2-1, the buses back from Maine Road were smashed. Sean, Griff and Angie – one of the girls who knocked around with the football lads and wasn't afraid to get stuck in – caught a local bus from the ground and ended up by the Arndale Centre, more or less surrounded. The rest of the lads were bussed back to Victoria and a load managed to slip out the back entrance and walk around to the front, complete with Head bags, now a bit fuller than when they'd arrived. Just as they got there, they saw Sean and others fighting a rearguard action with loads of Mancs. They ran over and it went off big time. One fashion note taken on that trip was that City were wearing tweed jackets and Hush Puppies.

A few years later, Derek from Calverley went over to Blackpool on a train with some young VYT lads, carrying their Head bags and on a shoplifting spree. They nicked a camera from one shop and started mucking about taking photos, including one with Derek and the younger lads all stood behind him. Eventually they ditched their stuff at some digs and went out for the night. The next morning, as Derek was eating his breakfast, a bloke walked in, sat down in front of him and asked him what he was doing, who he was with and where he had been. He then introduced himself as a police officer and told Derek he was being arrested for affray and assault. He was carted out of the B&B, put in a Mini Metro and taken to a police station, where he was given a white jumpsuit to wear. They started quizzing him and asking if he knew certain lads, which he denied. They then put a photo on the table in front of him, the one taken the day before with him and the younger lads. What Derek had not realised was that they had all pulled out Stanley knives when they were posing behind him.

The coppers told him he was the leader of the 'Leeds United Headhunters'. He was amazed, and amused, and asked why they thought this. They said it was because they all had Head bags and he was at the front. What he also didn't know was that the night before there had been a huge fight with some bouncers at a seafront pub called the Foxhall and the bouncers had apparently come off worse. The police must have tracked down where some of the lads were staying, gone through their stuff, found the camera and developed the pictures. Legally, however, they had nothing on him and let him go, but several other lads were later jailed.

The year Leeds were promoted, they played Sheffield United on Easter Monday, which again came after a weekend by the sea. Their favourite nightclub in Blackpool was called Shades. It was a massive place and there were about forty Cockneys in there this weekend. It was thought they were Millwall and one of the Leeds lads was giving some of them a bit of hassle. Paul from Gildersome, a bit worse for wear and unaware of the tension, went over to them and they gave him some grief, so he hit one of them. The whole place erupted. It was a hectic scene of fighting and drinks going everywhere. Another time at Shades, Paul had been chucked out and was eating some chips outside as some Cardiff City hovered about. They knew Leeds were inside and, as Paul leant against a wall, he could see the Cardiff gathering but not in sufficient numbers. He was amused to hear them say they were waiting for Leeds and reckoning they could take them, but told them he doubted it, as there were loads in the club. Eventually they drifted away.

At the start of the 1984/85 season, Leeds' chairman appealed for calm throughout the coming season in the match-day programme. For Wolves at home, a couple of games in, he wrote in the programme: 'Are you a part-time hooligan?' and pleaded with fans not to join in with the hardcore element. It made little difference and Grimsby away in September was similar to the 1982 visit. Three vans travelling together were packed to the roofs with lads and were pulled over by the police near Doncaster. The officers suspected they were flying pickets, only to end up with eighty-odd football lads on the hard shoulder of the motorway. They had to push people back into their vans with the doors to make sure they were all inside and told them just to carry on. Once in Grimsby, there were several arrests after fighting in the streets when the pubs shut, refusing to serve the lads any more. Gangs were reportedly wandering along the High Street and surrounding roads armed with bricks and two lads were hit by a police car. Eddie ran some locals only for them to return and do him and Mason.

At Charlton in November, a game where nobody expected any grief, they were caught out by a memorable ambush by Millwall at New Cross. A coach was organised, with some top boys on, while others went down on the train. Crombie Boy, who had been going since the Seventies, was woken up when they arrived in north London. He heard some of the more right-wing members on board banging on the coach windows and making nazi salutes to passing Jews as they made their way to synagogue. The coach dropped them off at Kings Cross, and they were free to do their own thing. They'd heard that the police would be at every station from Charing Cross to Charlton, so some hopped on a number 53 bus and eventually got off at Woolwich, where Charlton met before matches. However, they found no opposition there, so they hopped on the train and were soon at the ground.

Leeds won 3-2, meaning everyone was pretty happy on their way back to Charing Cross. Chelsea were at home to Coventry, so they expected to bump in to them at some stage but what they didn't expect was a visit by Millwall, who were away to Bradford. However, some of the VYT suspected they might encounter the South London terrors at some point, because Sully and Stix, two lads they used to meet up with who were from the Millwall area, said they would be about. There were between fifty and eighty lads – most in different shades of Lyle and Scott – on the service train when it pulled into a quiet New Cross station. Moz got off briefly to stretch his legs while others carried on playing cards and drinking beer.

'Isn't this Millwall's area?' asked Leonard innocently.

Almost as he spoke, the carriage windows went through and Millwall appeared out of nowhere armed with makeshift weapons. Railway sleepers came through the glass, knocking out one lad, while Millwall grabbed tools from an open holdall on the platform: crowbars, hammers, spanners and axes. Dutton chinned one axe-wielder but most of the Leeds were taken aback. There must have been 150-200 Bushwhackers and it was chaos, with women screaming and innocent passengers who had been leaving the train running back on again. Another window was put through as the train started to pull out. Moz had been chased down the platform by someone with a machete and Skiz said it reminded him of Frank Sinatra in the film *Von Ryan's Express*, only Moz made it. It was a classic hit-and-run.

At the next stop, some lads were seething and wanted to go back, but there was no point, since Millwall would almost certainly have gone. Everyone was now psyched up and wanted to find Chelsea for some payback – and at Charing Cross, the Headhunters were waiting for them. They piled out onto the station concourse, some of Leeds' finest, with the nutcases from Seacroft, Harehills, East End Park, Armley and Bramley, all on the warpath and right in front of them was a similar number of Chelsea. As Crombie Boy points out, if Chelsea ever had a reason to hate Millwall it was now, because they had fired Leeds up good and proper and they went straight through the West Londoners. Leeds chased them all the way up to the Strand, in amongst the theatre-goers, with others being dealt with by St Martin's Church.

There was later a bit of a battle with Luton outside Kings Cross Station before people went off for beers. After chucking out time, those on coaches went for a takeaway and encountered more trouble, as Crombie Boy recalls:

I was never much into the drugs thing, but I'd got some 'rainbow speed' from Manchester Dave, which was probably just speed mixed up with coloured hundreds and thousands, knowing that skanking cunt. Anyway, I took it. The pubs chucked us out and we were mooching around the streets of Kings Cross waiting for the coach. I guess it would have been around midnight and some of the boys had gone to a takeaway for some supper. All of a sudden, loads of shouting and bawling, and it's kicked off again outside the takeaway, this time with a big group of local blacks, so once again, we all pile in. By now, the speed has well and truly kicked in, and I remember grabbing a small supermarket trolley from one of those all-night stores and using it as a battering ram on this feller.

I don't think they were used to the white man taking them on on their own manor, and Leeds more than held their own. The locals were on the back foot, then that familiar sound, nerr nerr nerr nerr, and the coppers turned up. The black lads were off like a flash. Those boys weren't stupid. We may have been football thugs, but to the coppers the blacks were even lower down the food chain than we were. They knew they would have been nicked, and probably got a good kicking for their troubles. The police were right racist bastards in those days.

Anyway, they just wanted to see the back of us, so they loaded us on our coach and escorted us as far as St Albans, told us to fuck off and never come back. We finally arrived back in Leeds at 5.30am, thoroughly knackered. This game made me start to think that it was about time I gave it a rest – for a while!

Nobody expected much at Oxford United later that month, but Leeds were beaten 5-2 and Eddie and fifteen others were found wanting when they went in their end and were relieved to be pulled out by the police. Others managed to dismantle the television gantry and chuck bits on the pitch and the Oxford goalie was hit by a missile. Eddie Gray was on the verge of pulling off his players and conceding the game.

When Birmingham came to Leeds they got right down to Jaccomellis to pay the lads a visit. Derby had got quite far into town one year but Blues managed to go further. Eddie was among twenty VYT by Jac's, waiting for them to arrive, with the rest of the lads inside or dotted about other pubs. When the Zulus marched into view battle commenced but Leeds couldn't hold them. Eddie darted into Jac's to get the others but they were slow on the uptake, many not believing that the Zulus could have got that far into the city. The lads outside got quite a battering and several of the Blues mob were arrested.

In the city centre ahead of Everton in the third round of the FA Cup, about 200 Scousers came round by the Scarborough Taps and Leeds got at them from two sides in a pincer movement. Everton have since wrongly claimed that the two mobs of Leeds were battling with each other. The visitors won the game 2-0, ending

Leeds' cup run, and one of their lads fired a flare gun in the stands. Leeds had been told to expect a surprise at some point during the day, and they weren't disappointed.

One result Everton can claim was on a Sunday in Leeds around 1990, when they appeared out of the blue about an hour after the game. No-one had seen their mob all day and after the match twenty or thirty lads, including Eddie, China and Daz H, were milling about by Jac's when Eddie happened to look up Albion Street and saw fifty lads walking down. The game had long finished and they must have been tucked away somewhere, waiting. Caught out by this move, and impressed, the Leeds lads went to face them at the bottom of a hill. The next twenty minutes saw constant tit-for-tat by Buckles Newsagents, with the shop's news stands used as ammunition. Everton had a young mob and did well, especially one lad of Chinese appearance. They had a good battle as the cops didn't turn up for ages and when they did no-one was arrested; they merely escorted Everton to the train station.

13

THE BIRMINGHAM RIOT

WHEN THE FIXTURE list came out at the start of the season, there was much delight at seeing the last match was away to Birmingham City. Their Zulu Warriors were one of the most dangerous firms in football, and an end-of-the-season clash promised fireworks, as well as the prospect of being a promotion decider for both clubs. By the time the game came around, Leeds did have a chance of promotion but needed four other clubs to lose. Blues, on the other hand, had already secured their place in Division One but needed to win and for Oxford United to lose to become champions. With a feeling of invincibility within both mobs, it was a fixture for the hooligans to relish but no one could have predicted how explosive – and tragic – the day would turn out to be.

The anticipated clash between the Service Crew and the Zulu Warriors was given added spice by the issue of race. The Zulus were, famously, a multi-racial firm with a very high percentage of black or mixed race hooligans. Leeds, rightly or wrongly, were perceived as one of the most racist mobs in England. Yet, as is often the case, it was more complicated than a mere white versus black scenario.

Stevie Li came from Chapeltown, an area with a large ethnic minority population, and had firsthand experience of trying to bring more black lads into the Leeds firm in the Seventies and Eighties. Now forty-six, he started going to games in the mid-Seventies and became part of the 'townies', the group of lads from all over Leeds who adopted the city centre pubs and bars as their base. Chapeltown itself nestles between Leeds and Bradford. White and black lads growing up together was the norm there. With mixed English and Chinese parentage, Stevie admits the racist behaviour within the firm got to him, although he was never a victim of it himself. As a main face from the area, he was one of the few who tried to bring Chapeltown lads into the Service Crew but, as he explains, the handful of 'staunch' racists within the firm meant the sizeable black contingent knew it was not possible to join up. He also explains how the racist reputation Leeds obtained through a few ardent NF types stuck, causing them to be labelled one of the most prejudiced of all of the firms:

Some of the Leeds lads around in the Seventies were into racist things and a lot of the younger lads took that on their shoulders and made it look ten times worse than it actually was. Ten years later there were hardly any racists, apart from the staunch ones, but it always looked like the main Leeds firm was racist. It was a fashionable thing to be racist then – the lads did that sieg heiling and all that – and it stuck over the years, even though it wasn't really the case.

Quite a few didn't get involved in it at all from the start but the late Seventies and early Eighties were the 'Years of the Race Wars', as we called it. The Precinct was a main pub we'd go to back then and next door to it was a bar/club called Gladrags. We'd go there in the late Seventies for the ska and soul nights on a Thursday. There'd be the scooter lads on one side and skinheads or NF lads on the other and it was a great night until the last record when it all kicked off, week in, week out. During the 'Race Wars' we'd come out of the Precinct and there'd be 150 Chapeltown outside and it would start going off but I'd see my neighbours and friends there. Whenever we bumped into each other – black lads and white lads – it kicked off every time. At first it was more white attacking black in town but then the black lads realised what was happening and then they did more and retaliated. But all they really wanted to do was come in and support their team. They are born and bred Leeds fans, so why not? They didn't want to follow Liverpool and Arsenal and the like but they just knew they couldn't go to Elland Road, it was an unwritten rule.

On a personal level, any of my mates from Chapeltown could go anywhere with me and I would never take them anywhere where they could get hurt. I suppose people knew me and I've taken loads of Leeds lads to blues [clubs] and it was always fine. The majority of lads weren't really racist but because I am half Chinese it did get to me. A few Asian lads came with us and black lads. That was acceptable, just not on a big scale. Those black kids that had grown up with white kids, they were okay to get in, but it just didn't happen for the larger numbers.

They wanted to join the Service Crew and in the beginning, in reality, it only lasted a few years and all of a sudden it grew out of all proportion – from 50-100, to 200-300 and then everyone was Service Crew, so that's when we stopped going. Before that, there were all the individual areas and on Saturday night it didn't matter what you were or where you were from. I would say I was the main person to come from Chapeltown and from day one I've always seen and mixed with black kids. They would ask, 'Why do you knock about with the BNP and NF?' and I'm telling them it's something I have to do because I follow Leeds United passionately and I can't choose what other people follow or do. I never got any grief and in reality I should have; if you're seen to be knocking around with those people then I understand what they mean. I also never got any grief off football lads for defending the black lads. I was always in a difficult position. It was very hard trying to be neutral. I think I was in a unique situation although I never feared for myself.

My mates from Chapeltown would say, 'We can't go,' yet they loved Leeds and the atmosphere. It was a shame. When I was with them and I'd taken them to matches or pubs, there was never any trouble apart from the odd young kid or idiot who shouted racist shit. I think it could have worked if they had joined us but some of them old racists just wouldn't let it happen. Like the Zulus in Birmingham, they have turned the racist thing around and everyone has blended and I'd love that to happen here. Some of the black lads here are so proud of the team and their city that they've got Leeds tattoos on their backs but they've never had the *opportunity to show their feelings. It made me feel angry. If I knew then what I know now I might have tried to do something more about it: brought more in, then a few more and maybe I wouldn't be talking about this now.*

Birmingham City too had had racial problems in the Seventies, but by the time of the Leeds-Birmingham confrontation in 1985 these were largely behind them. The Zulus have always said Leeds that day were the biggest firm to ever land at New Street, at least until they dispersed into the pubs or were taken off to the ground. Leeds dispute the claim that they were then forced out of those pubs by marauding City fans. They maintain they were happy to face Blues at any time and gave as good as they got when they met. They also claim a victory in the park behind Blues' end, before scattering others queuing at the turnstiles. Debate would also continue over the years about who went looking for who inside the ground. TV footage taken inside the ground clearly shows it was the police versus Leeds at one end of the pitch and Blues at the other, as a long, thin blue line tried to keep them apart. However, the Zulus feel that if more Leeds had got together on the pitch maybe they could have overrun the police and fought each other. Whatever their differences, neither mob can deny just how wild the day was, tragically ending in the death of a young Leeds fan attending his first match. As Flare Gun Foxy said, 'It was the nearest thing to anarchy I have ever seen. Absolutely unparalleled.'

A week before the two firms met, Blues had been away at Middlesbrough, and after quite a bit of trouble there, fifteen of the Junior Business Boys – their equivalent of the VYT – found themselves in Leeds trying to get home. They were instantly spotted by Eddie and the VYT but instead of fighting they started talking, with some even going off to a café together to discuss the impending battle at St Andrews. Back at the station, David George, one of the main Juniors, saw a van pull up and about forty Service Crew jumped out and proceeded to attack them, forcing them either to stand and fight or run outside. After a bit of a kicking they made it home and were now looking forward to the match even more.

When the match day arrived, some of the Leeds mob went on coaches and others directly by train, but someone also came up with the idea to go via Manchester. This was done whenever possible, either on the way to or back from matches, just to see if any Scum were about. In Jac's the night before, all the talk was about getting the 9.10am to Manchester Victoria. Hasty late-night phone calls were made to those who had been planning to take the 10am straight to Birmingham, not good when people's parents might answer.

As many as 600 lads bowled through central Manchester the following morning en route to Piccadilly Station. It was a sight to savour. Some lads were tempted to go downstairs to St John's Market, where decent leather jackets were to be had, but were persuaded to stick with the mob. At Piccadilly the police kept them all outside for a while until the train to New Street was nearly ready to leave. They packed the carriages to the ceiling and it was the first and only time some saw the luggage racks full of lads lying face down because there was no room anywhere else.

New Street Station, once a favourite hunting ground for Birmingham City's hooligans, was too 'on top' with police by 1985 and the Zulus had a limited presence when Leeds arrived. Those who did see the emerging Yorkshire mob were impressed by the sight. Then the 'Zulu, Zulu' chant was heard and some Leeds retorted with 'War!' The rest of the Zulus, including the Junior Business Boys, were around the corner in their headquarters, the Crown pub, or scattered about the city centre waiting to meet the visitors. It wasn't long before fighting kicked off around the nearby Chinese quarter, which saw several pubs being trashed and one CS gassed. As sirens filled the air around the city, the police set about moving the majority of Leeds on to the ground.

Many of the older Leeds lads had chosen to go on coaches. One went from the Lion and Lamb, carrying the so-called Seacroft and Whinmoor 'Mentals', with them and the Wortley Yids taking the piss out of each other all the way down, while the Harehills Evil Bastards went from the Fforde Green pub. They arrived about 11am and were dropped off by Aston University without any police escort. They found a beer festival taking place and were invited in for just £5, with numerous free pints. According to Shoot:

I'd just started the second pint when there was a right row going on in the entrance. Somebody had run off with the takings, so we had to do one. Others hadn't bothered with the festival and gone to the pub down the road and something had gone off there. Eventually the Old Bill arrived and boxed everybody in but let us have a few bevvies before marching us up from there to St Andrews, about 80-100 strong, via a right trek. We got to the ground about 2.30pm.

Upon arriving near the away end, we saw groups of Brum for the first time and everything went off. The group got away from the police and ran past the away end and down the side streets behind the main stand. Eventually we came to the park behind the end opposite us, the one that had that shitty clock timer in the corner, and Brum made a stand at the side of the park but got run. Leeds were right at the back of the main Blues end and scattered the people queuing up to get in the ground. There was a bit of verbals over the walls with the lads already in the ground telling them to get back outside, before the police arrived en masse to round everybody up back to the away end. As for the match, everyone knows what happened there.

Those who walked to the ground from New Street could see Zulus loitering around. Yet at the ground the police seemed to drift away, perhaps assuming the Leeds contingent would go straight into the stadium. Instead most mooched off to find the Zulus. One officer said to a colleague that he was surprised how many Leeds there were.

'What did you expect?' said someone from the crowd.

Fighting broke out outside and one of the VYT tried unsuccessfully to fire a flare into the Blues ranks. As the trouble spread to those queuing, the police arrived in force. They tried to get the VYT inside but the lads were having none of it and remained at large until the police opened a gate and ushered them in. Eddie spotted one of the Zulus that he knew, a lad called Elvis, and broke off from the mob to talk to him. He went walking round the Blues' end with him before rejoining Leeds.

Most of the Leeds fans were in the tightly packed Tilton Road End. Dribs and drabs went across to the adjoining section of home fans, with some taking photos and others hurling abuse. Eddie was among those trying to get into the seats towards the Zulus and when the police intervened he faked a leg injury and was instead taken into the treatment room with a handful of other Leeds lads. Inside they encountered six Zulus and scuffling broke out within minutes. The match seemed almost secondary, more so when confirmation came that Man City – one of the teams that had to lose for Leeds to have any hope of promotion – were ahead in their game. Not long afterwards, a refreshment stand was taken apart by Leeds and pieces passed through the crowds.

Johnna and Dave M say the trouble with the police started when an officer hit a lad hanging on a fence who was dressed as Rupert the Bear, in yellow trousers and a mask. Leeds surged forward and more officers lashed out at them. It culminated in one of the worst riots ever seen at a football ground. When Blues scored, the home supporters could see Leeds clambering onto the pitch as their more law-abiding brethren chanted, 'You're the scum of Elland Road.' Some retreated while others went into the sections to the right of the Tilton where they saw people in the executive boxes above them watching television. They could see huge plumes of smoke and flames on the screens and they motioned to those inside asking what was happening. One man wrote 'Fire at Bradford's ground' on a piece of paper and held it to the glass. It was shocking news and word spread amongst Leeds, although no-one knew how serious it was at that stage.

The match was stopped and the police formed a line across the entire width of the pitch to persuade Leeds to return to the Tilton. Chaotic scenes followed. Amid a hail of missiles, several mounted officers appeared as others hobbled off for treatment. Even a kettle was hurled; it later became infamous and one Leeds lad, Lee, claims to know its origins: 'In the *Sunday People* report on the violence, when commenting on what was thrown on the pitch they said even a kettle was thrown on. Well, the kettle was at the feet of two blokes in front of us and Darren from Meanwood went two steps forward, picked it up and threw it. At the time it was funny as fuck.' Attempts by Eddie Gray, accompanied by Blues officials, to calm things down at the Leeds end failed and they beat a hasty retreat as more missiles fell. Riot police then emerged and massed ready to quash the trouble, as loudspeakers confirmed the match would go on no matter what.

The second half got under way after some of the debris was removed from the pitch. Leeds couldn't claw back City's 1-0 lead and the Brummies were victorious at the final whistle. At that point, the Zulus poured onto the pitch from the Railway End, while Leeds started ripping out plastic seats and hurling them forwards. The police now had to keep the two firms apart and battled against repeated surges by both sets of fans as the Zulus pulled up and threw advertising hoardings. Police footage of events shows Blues getting further up the pitch than Leeds but they scattered whenever the cops charged, halting their attempts to get to the other end. Both sets of lads met in the seats but the police succeeded in keeping them apart on the pitch. Who knows what would have happened if they hadn't?

The bedlam continued beyond the end of the match, with some Leeds having an impromptu kickabout in the goal before eventually, after 6pm, the away fans made their way to the left of Tilton to go outside. Police remained pitchside watching them go but the tightly packed fans filtering out were then hit by bricks chucked by Blues from outside. In the resulting crush a wall collapsed onto cars and people outside. Diddie and Wayne from the Service Crew were among those helping to remove the bricks but were beaten back by truncheon-wielding officers. It wasn't until later that people learned that a fifteen-year-old boy had lost his life.

Trouble continued outside the ground. Diddie hit someone he saw brandishing a knife, only to realise afterwards it was a woman; like Leeds, the Blues had a few women that ran with them. Shoot recalled:

We had at least two that were close by when the wall came down and they were in a right state, one had to be helped all the way back to the Bullring. There was a strange, subdued atmosphere on the walk back to the station. It seemed like after a fierce battle, when everybody needed to take stock of what had happened and the news that Bradford had a massive loss of life and possibly one at St Andrews. It was a total non-event all the way back to the Bullring.

We waited with the train lot until the coaches were found underneath the bridges. We all started to get on when Brum appeared at the back of the second coach and that's when it got on top. Loads of Zulus came around the corner and the lad who got hurt from the wall got another clout – it wasn't his day. It took a while before the police restored some order and the coaches could leave.

Another traveller on the coaches said quite a few were missing on the way home: 'Only half the bus made it back from Brum, the rest were nicked in the incident before the game. It was funny as fuck with Eddie C in the cells, the coppers did not know what to make of him. Eddie Gray put his head into the police hut to tell us we were the "Scum of Leeds" only to get, "Fuck off you Scotch cunt," from Eddie C.'

Lee was heading back to the station, where talk was of the inferno at Bradford. 'If the Bradford fire hadn't happened, Leeds would have been kicked out the Football League forever that day,' he said. 'But as it was, it drew media attention away from what had happened at Birmingham. We were put on the train home, the oldest train I have ever been on and I've been on a lot of trains. There were no toilets and no coppers. I had a thought that what had gone on was so bad they were going to run the train into a dead end and kill us all. Apparently all the pub doormen had been told not to let in any lads they thought had been at the match, so we had to go back to the Becketts Arms.'

More than 100 police officers were injured and the same number of fans later appeared before the courts. The Government was compelled to order an inquiry into both the Bradford disaster, which claimed fifty-six lives, and the Birmingham riot. Mr Justice Popplewell was assigned to lead the inquest. Days later, thirty-nine Juventus fans died during rioting at the European Cup final against Liverpool in Brussels, to complete a shocking week for football. Justice Popplewell's eventual recommendations included the roll-out of an identity card scheme for fans and Leeds became the first club to implement it. Leeds United and Birmingham City were each fined £5,000 by the FA, which was criticised as a 'weak' penalty by the media.

As a footnote, when Leeds played at Birmingham City in 2006, I suggested the lads from both sides met for a drink before the game. I had previously written a book with the Zulus and knew some of them would be keen to meet up and swap memories. Eddie, Paul, Alan and Benny met Zulu leader Cud in a bar in the city centre and exchanged stories of that infamous day as well as other clashes. Cud praised them for sparking things off in 1985 and agreed that, as Bradford made the headlines that day, Leeds and Blues were saved from much harsher penalties. Both complimented each other for their escapades over the years as well as discussing the obvious difference in the ethnic make up of the two firms. It was interesting to hear them talk in more detail about certain days whilst trying to match names to faces and characters they'd encountered. Overall, it showed how different things are now, more than two decades later.

14

'THEY ARE BASTARDS'

A RUN OF disappointing results at the start of the new season led to the sacking of Eddie Gray in September 1985, ending more than two decades of his association with the club. Angry fans made their feelings known at a match against Middlesbrough at home in October, but by then it was too late. He was replaced by another Leeds legend, Billy Bremner, while Peter Lorimer also ended his time with the club, departing soon after.

All eyes were now on the club and its fans, especially when they faced Millwall in November, the first time for many years they had met the infamous South London hardmen. It was a clash awaited by both hooligan gangs. When Leeds had played at Fulham on the opening day, Millwall were at Huddersfield, and about forty lads went there instead. They saw some Millwall wearing T-shirts with 'Leeds United RIP 9/11/85' across their chests. Strict controls on ticket sales didn't stop several hundred of the main firm heading to the capital. The night before the game, some VYT lads were out on a bender around Chapeltown with Eddie C and went back to his house with a curry before getting a few hours kip and then setting off. Their coach contained 'an excellent mob' according to Tobin, who was probably the youngest on board. 'We parked up behind Kings Cross, started walking and saw about three hundred lads at the top of a road,' he said. 'We assumed they were Millwall or maybe Arsenal. There were only fifty of us but we ran into them and their mob moved back in shock. Seconds later, we realised they were Leeds.'

Eddie Kelly was with a few who ended up sleeping in Euston after going down on the Friday. The plan was to meet up later on the Old Kent Road but people inevitably got split up. At New Cross Gate station, the lads passed one pub that was already smashed up. The walk to the ground was volatile, with Millwall

191

pouring out of the pubs and missiles being lobbed from both sides. Mounted police blocked pub doorways to keep the home fans inside. On the Old Kent Road, Eddie C made his legendary 'This is the A team' remark to a copper who asked who they were, after he had just taken another mob of Leeds to the ground.

There was trouble during the game with a few police getting injured but after the whistle nobody moved. There was a sense of both firms wondering what would happen next, perhaps out of mutual respect. Everyone assumed it would kick off but for once it wasn't clear how. In the event it was little more than a stand-off, though twenty VYT who didn't have tickets were chased by police with dogs through a fruit market, and back at Kings Cross some lads fought with Luton.

When Millwall played at Elland Road in April, Leeds expected a hefty turnout and many of them were out early in the pubs and around the train station. They saw that about 400-500 had made the journey. A huge police presence prevented large-scale trouble but there was fighting when some of Millwall's coaches arrived late. Nine Leeds went in Millwall's end, led by Eddie C, and when Leeds scored, they surged forward. They were hemmed in at the front of the end and turned to face the Millwall masses. Fortunately for them, they were quickly arrested. When the cops got Eddie C, he told them all he needed was 'another nine soldiers' and they would have taken their end. He had been heard earlier on praising the mob that had come out: 'Look at these soldiers. This is an army.' They were later jailed.

The trouble at Millwall in November meant Leeds fans were banned from attending away matches but the ruling was impossible to enforce and was reversed after two games, Carlisle United and Wimbledon. Lads still got tickets for those two all-ticket games. Dave Bassett, Wimbledon's manager, said in the match programme that the club had received ticket applications from across the UK, including Cardiff, from people 'who I'm sure are not Wombles'. The club was forced to open up the area behind the goal because so many had turned up, and the same thing happened at Carlisle.

Johnna was living in London and went down to Wimbledon on the Monday before the match and bought forty tickets. The queue was right down the street and it was full of Leeds fans. The ticket office staff knew what was happening but just charged the fans a couple of quid extra on top of the ticket price and no-one queried their actions. On the day of the game, about 2,000 Leeds occupied the main stand and another 1,000 were behind the goal. The stewards afterwards let some lads into the players' lounge beneath the stand. They were having a drink when the players came in. They seemed okay with the lads being in there and chatted to some of them, saying they were amazed at the number of fans at the game. The FA Cup draw was about to be made, so they all watched the television. Johnna was talking to Alan Cork from Wimbledon about football in general when his team drew Millwall.

'I can still remember his face when they got Millwall,' said Johnna. 'He just said, "Oh shit," and I started laughing. I said jokingly, "We'll come with you if you want." Then Peter Lorimer came in. He was a hero to us lot, part of the Revie machine. We stopped there until the Leeds players left, then went into London for a laugh.'

Leeds didn't think much of Middlesbrough away from home but knew a visit to Teesside wouldn't be short on trouble. When they had gone over the previous season, the police had apprehended them at Darlington and held them under some arches at the station, making them miss the game. So when Leeds played at Boro in March, they knew what might happen. When the train pulled into Middlesbrough they jumped over a wall down a big drop and ended up in a pub, with some heading off into the city centre. About 100 got into a precinct in the main shopping area. As a few bought burgers from a street vendor, two lads came out of Boots and smacked a lad called Bud, giving him a shiner. There was a small scuffle but the police arrived at more or less the same time and rounded them up. Just as they set off in an escort, the two lads appeared in the middle of them and started moaning at Jono, a Service Crew main face, complaining that Leeds had arrived too early. Jono laughed and asked them if they should have booked an appointment.

It wasn't long before the police found the Leeds group in the pub and walked them back towards the station, with Diddie and Little Bez bringing up the rear. They saw some Boro, scuffled with them briefly and ended up walking towards the ground, having managed to lose the police. When they reached one street, twenty Leeds were at one end with up to 100 Boro at the other. They spotted a builder's skip in the middle and it was a race to see who could get to it first. Leeds won, pulled out everything they could and went into them but Boro didn't run. It ended with CID pulling up in cars and officers jumping out as Diddie, Sean and Angie were getting stuck into them. Diddie was arrested, gave a false address and was later released with a clip round the ear and the words, 'I don't want to see you in bother again, lad.'

Inside the ground, with the adrenaline pumping, everyone was saying they should go on the pitch so Diddie went charging on – but no one followed him. The next thing he knew the police were chasing him. He jumped back over the fencing into the Leeds fans, who threw him backwards and up into the stand so the police couldn't reach him. Boro fans in the Clive Road terracing climbed over a wall separating them from the seats and forced both home and away fans towards one end. Around 100 of them were standing on seats and 'rampaging about', according to one newspaper. After Billy Curry scored for Boro, their fans charged across the pitch from three sides towards Leeds, who also got on the pitch, taunting and goading them, as a handful of police struggled to keep them apart.

At the end of the game, Leeds were kept back. Boro threw bricks and bottles over the wall from outside and, as Leeds surged towards the gates, a toilet block collapsed. The eventual opening of the gates led to battles on the park beside the ground, before the police organised an escort. A tight twenty-five slipped away, including Silver, Dave L, Eddie L, Russ from Boro and Dean from Oldham, and began to make their own way to the station. 'As we walked we spotted a local kid sat smoking on a bench chuckling at us, but not for long, as Silver went over and knocked him clean off his perch,' recalled one of the group. 'We carried on walking and encountered a firm of Boro who had a go at us, with little groups of five and six constantly tackling us. At one point we were defending ourselves in a doorway and we would regroup and launch ourselves, pushing Boro back a bit. But once again the police were soon on the scene and put us back in the escort.'

As they approached the station, the two Boro lads from earlier on appeared again, right in the middle of them. Nobody did anything as the police were all around them and they were ushered into the station by a side gate but this pair wouldn't give up and got onto the platform with them. Just as the train was filling up, Gaz hit one of them with a shovel he found standing against a wall on the platform. The train pulled off to the sound of laughter at the balls of those two lads. After more than twenty arrests and damage to more than 200 seats at Ayresome Park, Leeds were slapped with yet another FA inquiry.

The last game of the season was Norwich City away and the opportunity for a piss-up in Great Yarmouth afterwards for the rest of the Bank Holiday weekend. League champions Norwich won 4-0 and their players refused to do a lap of honour until the Leeds fans left the ground, but the lads stayed put for as long as they could and carried on singing, as they had all through the game. In reality there was little to sing about, with the team finishing fourteenth in the table, having also been knocked out of the FA Cup that season by lowly Peterborough. About 1,000 fans later gathered in Great Yarmouth, both hooligans and ordinary 'scarfers'. Drink was the order of the weekend and some lads invaded a mud-wrestling competition. Most departed on the Sunday and the town that Leeds had colonised began to fill up with Cockneys. The rumour went round that most of them were Millwall fans but no-one knew for sure.

Pat, one of the lads who would be arrested in Operation Wild Boar later in the Eighties (see Chapter 15), was with twenty others at a pub with about 200 Londoners inside. With alcohol distorting their thoughts, they decided to attack them. 'We were drunk and it was silly but that's what we thought,' said Pat. Bouncers on the door managed to prevent major trouble – and a probable major kicking for the Leeds lads – but they still scuffled with some. 'Eventually the Cockneys came outside and were going to fish and chip shops but we continued to antagonise them by knocking the food out of their hands,' said Pat. 'There was no way we could win – we knew we would get murdered – and eventually they turned on us, so then we set off and ran across the street then shouted, "Stand!" The large mob behind would catch up with us and then we'd run again, which carried on through several streets back to our digs.

'The Cockneys followed us and were coming from both ends of the street. We grabbed a crate of milk bottles and threw a fire extinguisher but we were getting mullered as it spread inside the B&B. The next thing we heard was police sirens. We ran into our room and jumped into bed with our clothes on and started snoring, even though the place was thick with gas and debris. The police came into our room and said, "What the fuck are you lot doing," as we snored under the duvets. By this time the owner had come downstairs from the top floor asking what the hell was going on and looking at the state of his B&B. He kicked us out and the police took us onto the street, where there was still a big mob waiting for us, throwing things.'

The cops told them to drive home but they said they were all too pissed. The police said they didn't care how drunk they were and told them to get in their car and they would escort them out of the area. So eventually, with a patrol car in front and another behind, they were led to Great Yarmouth dog-racing track. The police took them to the middle of the track, told them to stay there until 9am and said they would come back then and get them. The lads had a tape of The Pogues' *Rum, Sodomy and the Lash* and two bottles of whiskey, which they set about polishing off while dancing in the middle of the dog track until the early hours.

* * *

After a tightly packed schedule of derby matches – Sheffield United, Barnsley and Huddersfield – it was Bradford City away in September 1986, just as the FA's all-ticket ruling was lifted. Bradford had been using the Odsal stadium after the fire at Valley Parade in 1985 but had also played some games at Elland Road, which had provided a good opportunity to fight their hooligans.

Several hours before the match, hundreds of rival fans started to arrive in the city centre. Rioting broke out in Ivegate, Forster Square and on the Manchester Road. Bricks were thrown at cars and buses and dozens of shops windows were smashed in Ivegate, along with every window in the Crown and the Unicorn, which were Bradford's pubs. At about 2pm, thousands started arriving at the ground, where fans were searched for weapons and alcohol. One group refused to pay and forced their way in. About 100 Leeds paid in Bradford's end and, after fighting broke out on the terraces, many escaped onto the pitch. The referee carried on with the game as the police tried to break it up. Seats were ripped up and thrown towards the pitch as the scuffling continued.

Some lads, bored with the game, set fire to a small patch of the grass embankment. A copper told them to put it out but before long, pebbles and stones were being thrown at the police by the fast-food vans. Some took refuge by one van and then fans started shaking it, forcing the workers to jump out.

One told a newspaper afterwards that as the van was overturned, along with the generator, they saw a man throw a match onto the petrol and it burst into flames.

'They were animals, they didn't care about our lives,' said the worker. 'We were inside the van when people began stoning the crowd. Some hid behind the van, that's what caused it. They began shaking the van to try and turn it over and we opened the door and jumped out. As we did that, someone grabbed the takings. I saw someone overturn the generator and he then threw a match onto the petrol and up it went. When they were shaking the van it caused the fat to boil over. We scrambled out just in time. They are not football fans, they are bastards.'

With smoke billowing into the air above the players' dressing rooms and shouts of 'Fire!' the frightened crowds started to move away towards a hamburger stall. Then a shout of 'Gas!' went up, as apparently the pipes from two cylinders at the hamburger stall had been cut and escaping gas could be heard and smelt. As people scrambled to safety from the risk of explosion, stewards opened the pitch's perimeter fencing and hundreds went onto the grass. Women and children were in tears and many men looked shocked

197

and scared. Firefighters and ambulances soon arrived and the match was abandoned. Leeds tried to get to the grandstand where Bradford were as police did their best to keep them apart, while other officers tried to guard a camera installed to film any trouble. Eventually people started to leave the ground in large numbers and buses and coaches were organised to ferry the fans away. More fighting broke out outside the ground but some fans returned to the terraces as the players came back on the pitch to try to finish the game, which Bradford finally won 2-0.

The clashes continued after the game. A gang of white, black and Asian youths reportedly rampaged along Manchester Road and two officers were attacked when they tried to calm the situation. One suffered a broken leg and the other had to be given oxygen by paramedics. Coach windows were smashed by fans on board in Cleckheaton Road, while other roads near the ground were littered with broken glass and debris. As the FA announced yet another investigation, the *Yorkshire Evening Post* surmised that there was ill-feeling between the fans after a seventeen-year-old Bradford fan had been fatally stabbed during a punch-up in the city earlier in the summer. Club chairman Leslie Silver said the events were a 'disgrace' and they had asked for the all-ticket rule to remain in place, as he felt there had been no trouble while it was enforced. Shop workers later told reporters that gangs had been roaming around causing trouble from midday, with one saying, 'I felt as if war had been declared and no one told me.'

Nine people were taken to hospital, including one Leeds lad who was stabbed in the stomach in a fight near the bus station. More than sixty people were arrested and most were from the Bradford area, with twelve from Leeds and others from Blackburn, Scarborough and Ipswich. Charges included grievous bodily harm, assault and criminal damage. Others were later arrested in dawn raids. The media made much of the arrest of a Swedish Leeds fan, who later served twenty-eight days in Armley Prison after admitting using insulting words. Magistrates in Bradford heard that Paul Sodermark threw a lump of concrete at people fleeing the blazing chip van. The twenty-one-year-old had spent £8,000 in two years travelling from his home in Hagersten to support Leeds and newspapers said the millionaire's son had 'spent a fortune ferrying a private army of thugs to take lessons in football hooliganism'. He was apparently the leader of AIK's Black Army of soccer thugs in Sweden and was also involved in fighting during a friendly between England and Sweden around that time. 'Some people have fishing for a hobby, we have fighting and we learn many tricks in England,' he was quoted as saying. He is still in touch with the lads today, meeting them on European trips.

The media were unforgiving about events at the match and the *Daily Star* called for the club to be shut down:

> The louts of Leeds have got away with it for far too long.
>
> They have terrorised the terraces, tormented town centres and driven away many decent, honest followers of football.
>
> Too often they have been let off the hook. We are sick to the back teeth of the prattling succession of managers, directors and administrators who have told us: 'It's only a minority.'
>
> That 'minority' has been involved in thirteen savage incidents over the last forty months.
>
> Today, we regret to say, the authorities have only one course open to them. Leeds United MUST be closed down.

Yet even more bad publicity would follow, with Leeds away to Millwall and West Brom. The Millwall game was one of the first to be moved to an 11am kick-off. Griff, Sean, Derek, and Eddie C went down in a van the night before and toured the West End pubs. When they reached New Cross the next day, Eddie C was at the top of the stairs with leather gloves on, saying, 'They're the Martians and we're going to zap them all.' Millwall's bizarre range of thugs of all ages was apparent as they walked to the ground in an escort. Some of them tried to get in amongst Leeds and when Derek saw one old guy with a bald head he thought he might be a bit scared by it all, but instead he produced a huge knife.

At West Brom in December, Leeds lost 3-0. Petrol from a club mower was used to burn down a shed, nineteen fans were chucked out of the ground and seventeen arrested. It was a bad-tempered match with Ian Snodin involved in a kicking and punching incident with Albion's Barry Cowdrill. Carlton Palmer joined in and the brawl escalated to involve a dozen players, with Palmer and Snodin eventually sent off. In the second half, John Stiles, son of Nobby, was also sent off for a lunging tackle and had to be dragged from the field by manager Billy Bremner.

In the FA Cup, Leeds were due to play non-league Telford in January. West Mercia Police refused to let the game go ahead but West Bromwich Albion stepped in and offered the use of the Hawthorns. Leeds went on to win 2-1. After victories against Swindon and QPR – an entertaining match culminating in Brendan Ormsby scoring a header at the Kop end – Leeds faced Wigan Athletic away in the sixth round. Only about 2,500 tickets were made available for Leeds fans, so they were hard to come by. Sending someone to wherever Leeds were playing to get more tickets was a common practice in those days and Johnna and a couple of mates decided to try it.

'We asked for ten tickets but the office said they needed to have some sort of proof that we were from Wigan,' said Johnna. 'We didn't know what to do at first, then started knocking on every door in the street asking residents if they would buy us some tickets, but no joy. We asked a few others who were buying tickets but the ticket office had seen us approach the first one so they wouldn't let any of them buy more than a couple each. After several hours, and feeling pretty depressed, we went to a local for a pint to discuss what to do next. We had seen a guy repairing a telegraph pole at the end of the street and someone suggested trying him. He agreed and had some ID on him. We asked him to get as many as possible and waited anxiously in the pub. He came back with three tickets about ten minutes later, saying that was all he could get. We offered to buy him a drink but he refused and although he hadn't got as many as we wanted, at least we had ours.'

During the build-up to the game, fans were warned that the police would be stopping everyone coming off the motorway from the direction of Leeds and if they didn't have tickets, they would be turned back. As not everyone had a ticket, there was much debate about what to do. The lads decided to go to Blackpool on the Saturday night and then travel from there to avoid detection. Thirty or forty met up in the Queens pub outside the train station before setting off in separate groups and arranging to meet in Blackpool. Johnna, S and J and some lads from Bedford were going over in a car and discussed the best route to take. As they did, a lad that had turned up with the Bedford lot started having a go at an old bloke in a Liverpool scarf and had to be dragged off him. They set off after getting some beers for the journey.

The lad who had started on the Liverpool fan was driving and when they got to the motorway he dramatically accelerated. When Johnna asked him what he was doing, as they were trying not to attract the attention of the police, he said he was testing the car's capabilities as it was new and he thought it should be able to 'take some stick'. They drove a little further when he suddenly pulled the handbrake at 70mph. They spun round for what seemed like an age before coming to a halt in the middle of the central reservation, with everyone disorientated. They jumped out of the car and Johnna was about to launch himself at the guy but S and J grabbed hold of him and dragged him away. They said he came from some local hard family where they lived and there might be repercussions if anything happened to him. Johnna angrily said he could have killed them but the lad airily said it was all right and he'd done it before. Unimpressed, they got back in the car and set off, with Johnna wanting to get there as soon as possible to get away from the mad driver.

On arrival, they parked up and set off to find the masses, with Johnna asking his Bedford mates why the hell they'd brought the nutter with them. They said they couldn't get anyone to drive and told him about another time he had driven them. They had hired a car to watch Leeds at Plymouth and by the time they had got to Heathrow, he had written off the car and they had to be towed back to Bedford. They said he was okay, he just had a thing about cars, especially other people's.

They found the rest of the lads in a pub by the seafront and settled in the bar, which was packed. Some of the younger lads from East End Park were at one end of the pub playing pool. As the drinks flowed, things got a bit boisterous and a crowd congregated by the pool table, as the East End Park lads were playing for quite a bit of money. One player had a shot on the black to win. As he bent over, taking his time, the driver from Bedford appeared, put his head in between the pool player's legs, lifted him up over his head and burst into, 'We are Leeds, we are Leeds...' The player's cue unsurprisingly slipped and he missed the black. Everyone stopped what they were doing and the place went deathly quiet, except for the driver singing his head off.

The lad he had picked up shouted to be put down but the nutter took no notice, so others helped him down. The East End Park lad went mad, railing at the 'wanker' who just lost him loads of cash. Another East End Park lad pulled out a knife and the rest were getting ready to join in. The driver was dragged out of the way down to the other end of the bar and after a while things calmed down. When his car passengers asked him what he thought he was doing, he said he was just having a laugh.

'You might get away with that at home,' he was warned, 'but not here.'

The East End Park lads moved on to another pub and gradually everyone else started to go. In just a few hours, the nutty driver had threatened an old man, nearly killed his passengers, wound up everyone he had come into contact with and almost started a major fight between the lads. Even those he had driven now wanted rid of him. They still needed him to drive the next day but they knew that if they stayed with him, he would somehow jeopardise their chances of going to the match, as he was such a liability. So when he went to the toilet, they all looked at each other and legged it. They walked for a couple of minutes, instead of going to the nearest pub, to make sure he wouldn't find them, and managed to avoid him until closing time, when they got some food and dossed down in a B & B with the other lads.

When they went to the car the following morning, the back window had been smashed and the nightmare driver was asleep inside. They banged on the door and asked him what had happened. He said he had nowhere to sleep and it was freezing so he put a brick through the back window to get inside. When someone sarcastically said, 'And it was warm then?' he replied that it was bloody freezing because the back window was smashed. They left it and said they should just go to Wigan.

Not long after setting off, the car slowed to 30mph and refused to go any faster, sounding like it was going to conk out. They stopped at a garage because the driver said he was hungry but he promptly threw up inside the car after eating, which stunk the car out. They set off again and it took them ages to get to Wigan, plus it was freezing with the window broken. Just as they got to the slip road to come off for Wigan, the car stopped. The driver had a tinker with the engine, declared it was 'fucked' and they all got out and started to push the car up the slip road. The Bedford lads were fuming, as one of them had put down the hire deposit in his own name and would probably have to pay for repairs. They were hungover, tired and stuck with the most frustratingly dangerous and stupid person.

When they finally made the top of the slip road, a police car stopped in front off them. They told the lad not to say they were Leeds fans, as they might be turned back or stopped from going to the game. The copper walked over and asked if they were all right. They said they were trying to fix the car. He told them there was a garage about a mile away and asked what they were doing there.

'We're Leeds fans and we're going to see Leeds beat your crappy little team,' chirped up the driver.

They looked at each other with steam coming out of their ears and gave the kid a look that could not be mistaken for anything else but anger. He just said, 'Whoops,' and turned away. Luckily the officer just laughed and said, 'We'll see,' before driving off.

Everyone was thoroughly pissed off with him by now. One of the Bedford lads got back in the car, said he couldn't face it any more and wasn't bothered about the game – he would just stay in the car. Johnna, J and S had also had enough and walked off to catch a bus to the ground. When they got there, there were clearly more than the supposed maximum 2,500 Leeds fans. They went to the Wigan end, handed over their tickets and went inside. They immediately bumped into some fellow Leeds fans. They told them about their experiences of the past twenty-four hours and everyone burst out laughing.

Leeds won 2-0 despite the assurances of Wigan centre forward Bobby Campbell, who had promised the Bradford City fans he would knock Leeds out, as he had previously played for City, was a cult figure there and lived in the city. There wasn't much going on outside the ground, as Leeds were everywhere, so J and S had no choice but to go back to the car while Johnna jumped in with some lads from Bradford. He hoped he would never encounter the loony driver again. So far as he knows he has not been back to watch Leeds and the East End Park lads haven't caught up with him either.

A week later, Leeds were at Crystal Palace, where Andy Gray scored a penalty against them to dent their promotion hopes and afterwards branded their fans 'racist thugs'. Abusing black players wasn't uncommon at Leeds and, try as they might, officials couldn't shake the racist reputation. The local Trades Council launched an anti-racist fanzine around the same time which was on sale outside the club on match days. But with its good intentions the magazine was never going to change the mindset of some fans. Some had refused even to count goals scored by black players in the past. Gray said Elland Road was the worst ground to play at and he hoped Coventry beat them in the semi-final the following month. His wish was granted as Coventry scored in extra time in front of a crowd of more than 50,000 at Hillsborough. Ten days before the match, 18,000 people had queued up at Elland Road to get their hands on the 6,000 tickets. Three were injured in the crush. Two main roads had to be closed at one point due to the amount of traffic and tailbacks grew on the M621 as fans from all over the north descended on the club, with some braving the cold and arriving the night before. The queues stretched around the ground but the club limited tickets to one per person.

The last game of the season at Brighton and Hove Albion saw the Sussex club relegated to the Third Division after Leeds beat them 1-0. Groups travelled down to Brighton the night before the match and it wasn't long before fights broke out with late-night drinkers in the town. Two hours before kick-off, shops and an amusement arcade were targeted as well as tourists on the seafront, who quickly dispersed as deckchairs, stones and bottles were thrown. Six Leeds fans were arrested, with five charged with public order offences. Leeds vastly outnumbered the home fans and police with dogs tried to keep them in check in the East Terrace but failed to stop some climbing over the fence and onto the pitch to carry Brendan Ormsby aloft. A football was produced and the lads proceeded to have a kickabout by one goal as others tried swinging on the crossbar. The police drew their truncheons and mounted officers eventually cleared the pitch.

It was a typically rowdy end to a season for Leeds. Meanwhile, behind the scenes, West Yorkshire Police were preparing to bring down the supposed 'ringleaders' of the Service Crew.

15

OPERATION WILD BOAR

WILD BOAR WAS a police operation in which four officers infiltrated the Leeds United football firm. One of the first and most successful of a series of undercover investigations of English hooligan gangs, it began around October 1986 and culminated in raids at more than a dozen addresses the following March. Those arrested, aged between seventeen and thirty, were charged with conspiracy to commit affray and later faced a six-week trial.

It seemed the authorities had had enough of the trouble associated with Leeds United and the newspaper headlines that followed – though many would say they were a few years too late. Major incidents of violence such as the Millwall rampage at Luton, the Birmingham City riot, the Heysel Disaster and on-going violence at English international matches had also made hooliganism a political issue, and the Home Office decided something needed to change. Covert operations were seen as the way forward.

Wild Boar was run from a former county council building close to the West Yorkshire Police training school in Wakefield. Officers remained in constant contact with senior staff and the Crown Prosecution Service during the six-month operation. At around the same time, other football firms were being targeted, although operations against West Ham and Chelsea would ultimately founder in court. Sgt Mick Fickling posed as David 'Simmo' Simpson, a window cleaner. His friend Paul 'Gibbo' Gibson was in fact DC Paul Crehan, who said he was a poacher and even supplied some lads with the odd pigeon or rabbit to help maintain his cover.

His credibility was enhanced when he was actually arrested at Bradford Interchange Station after a match. Simmo and Gibbo ingratiated themselves with Leeds fans and gathered intelligence, as well as being on-the-spot eye-witnesses.

In court, Fickling said he believed the Leeds ringleader was David Brown, nicknamed 'Para Dave' after his time as a bandsman in the Parachute Regiment and later in the medical wing. Brown apparently led a group called Para's Little Army.

Another main face was said to be Pat Slaughter, who was training to become a lawyer and had just passed his second-year exams at Huddersfield Polytechnic. Fickling told the court about a fight in a pub ahead of a match with Crystal Palace, when someone announced, 'There's a team of niggers outside', to which Slaughter allegedly rushed the doors of the pub encouraging others to get at them. A group of five or so black men ran towards them with knives and bats and Fickling said the twenty-one-year-old Slaughter shouted, 'Stand Leeds, stand.' Several ran back into the pub and grabbed stools and glasses before going back out onto the street.

Twenty-three-year-old warehouseman John Milner was alleged to be the firm's banker and the organiser of a coach known as the One Punch Battalion Battle Bus. He collected money for the trips and kept a log of battles fought by those on the coach. Racism was a constant refrain of the prosecution and the jury was told that defendant Martin Pickard had assaulted a black man on a trip to Ipswich and boasted to friends, 'I battered that nigger over there.' Another defendant had chipped in, 'Come on nigger. My mate smacked you in the mouth. Come on cunt. Have you got any bananas? I'll cut your liver out....You're dead, boy. You are one dead coon.'

Although defence barristers suggested Fickling provoked others and showed a photo of him with his fists raised alongside other fans, the sergeant denied he ever initiated or encouraged any trouble. Another possible threat to the case came towards the end of the trial, with rumours that the jury was feeling intimidated. This prompted the judge to remind them of their duty. 'A society's only safeguard is a police service prepared to do its duty and juries prepared to do theirs,' he said.

The following day, five of the defendants were found guilty. David Brown, despite mitigation that he was suffering from post-traumatic stress disorder due to the Falklands War, where he had treated the injured under fire at Goose Green, and the murder of an uncle serving in the Royal Ulster Constabulary, was sentenced to four years in prison, as were John Milner and Patrick Slaughter. Martin Pickard received a two-year sentence and a seventeen-year-old was ordered to spend fifteen months in youth custody. The rest were acquitted.

Judge Crabtree, baffled by football violence, said of his years watching games as a lad, 'When things did not go as planned on the pitch, the men used to throw their cloth caps in the air. That seemed to do the trick.'

* * *

Pat Slaughter is from the Chapel Allerton area of Leeds but no longer lives in the city. He agreed to talk about what happened to dispel some of the myths that have dogged him since the trial. Pat grew up spending time in the Boys' Pen at Elland Road during the time of skinheads and scarves, before most adopted the casual look and became 'flicks' or dressers, as they were called in Leeds. He is well aware of the racist reputation Leeds has but he had a left-wing upbringing and went to Anti-Nazi League rallies and 2Tone gigs, The Specials at Potternewton Park being one memorable concert. At the time of his arrest, he was studying law. He finished his degree in prison and after his release went for various legal jobs. He was over-qualified for many of them but his criminal record counted against him. He ended up travelling for a few years and taught abroad before returning to the UK and earning a Masters in Criminology. He continues to teach.

As far as his co-accused were concerned, he rarely associated with Para Dave. Brown had been around for quite a few years and was known as a game lad, but after the court case some couldn't help but think he had been foolish. They had had their suspicions about the 'new faces' when Simmo and Gibbo appeared, took them to be old bill and left them to it. Dave, however, clearly never sussed them.

Pat Slaughter remains bitter about his experiences, as he recounted:

The police were given a remit to hunt these lads down and finish the firm. They were sent on an impossible mission to a certain extent, to smash this firm which they thought was highly organised and that members swore an oath of allegiance to. Over the years police intelligence, although clumsy, did give them some idea about where lads were drinking and going out, so they sent the officers in and Para Dave handed it to them on a plate.

They were looking for someone sophisticated. They found someone who talked a lot and who must have been such an easy touch for them. As soon as Dave saw two blokes who were prepared to listen to his stories, he latched onto them. The people caught up in this were the ones who basically loved the football and still wanted to go to games. There was really very little going on at the time. However, Dave was organising a coach with another lad called Porky and sometimes the VYT, and occasionally I would go in it with my mates.

Leeds were supposed to be playing Swindon in the Cup, about February 1987, but it got snowed off and Millwall were playing at Bradford. I had a thing about Millwall, I knew a couple of Millwall guys, so I said to a few mates why don't we go there. Obviously there is a bit of rivalry between Leeds and Millwall as well. We bumped into Para Dave that day and he said he was going too and why didn't we come with him. To be honest, we didn't really want to go with his mob because we thought they were knobs. He was going over on the bus from Leeds and about seven or eight of us decided to catch a train to New Pudsey and then get a bus to Bradford.

As luck would have it, we caught the same bus as Dave. We saw him on the back of the bus with about twenty others and we all sort of said hello and apparently he said to one of the coppers, 'That's Pat Slaughter, he's game as you like.' So they must have thought, right, remember him, and made a mental note about me. We got to Bradford and we sort of got tailed up with their lot and decided not to go to the game and have a few drinks. I'd never seen these blokes before and I remember thinking they didn't look quite right, their age, their clothes were a bit off, but at the same time there was no reason to think anything, plus Leeds has always had a big support so often there were new faces about.

We got to the station. There were about twenty-five Leeds, including these four coppers, and there was some anticipation that Millwall might turn up but in the end about a hundred Ointment came through on the concourse. They ran at us and we ran at them and for my misfortune I was at the front and I hit the first kid. It was all over very quickly, the police came and the only one arrested was one of the undercover coppers. That was all very amusing in the trial when they were going through the transcripts and he was saying, 'I'm a copper,' and the officer arresting him was saying, 'Yeah, right.'

Through the rest of the operation I sort of bumped into them very occasionally but nothing much happened. Then at Palace away, in March 1987, I was in a group of about twenty to twenty-five and we were at Kings Cross waiting for more to come in. Para was there and he said to go with him – there must have been about forty or fifty of them – as they were going into central London to fight Chelsea and West Ham. We were laughing and thought, no you're not, so we peeled off and avoided the whole of central London and went for a drink. But two of the coppers also peeled off from them and came with us. We went to Balham and we got to a pub there called the Bedford Arms. We're having a drink, there were about twenty-five or thirty of us and I remember holding court about how bad the police were in the miners' strike, so that wouldn't have gone down too well with them.

We'd been there about half an hour and two lads that had gone to get some fish and chips came in saying they were getting battered – no pun intended. So we all ran out the pub and there were four or five lads outside. It goes off a bit and we start chasing them down the street. They duck into this house and come back with bats and knives. They came at us and seven or eight stood and the rest ran. We're trying to have it with them but basically we're getting beaten and I got to the door and got hit with a bat. Then a couple of cars pulled up with more lads and they got out as well with weapons. When I got to the door the undercover copper who pretended he was a poacher picked me up. My head is smashed and bleeding and he helped wash the blood off.

I said, 'We can't have that. We've got to go back out, one lad is still out there and they'll stab him.'

By this stage, the bar staff are trying to shut the doors and then everyone goes through them and it's gone off in the street. Basically we are the ones taking the hiding and they are all tooled up. We had to get that lad away and eventually the sirens come. We stood and talked to the police about it and said we'd just been done and the bar staff confirmed it, saying we were just having a drink.

And, basically I got done on those two incidents out of the six-month operation. These were the two most violent incidents they saw because Para Dave took them on this boring tour of six months of nothing. Then they concocted this total and utter nonsense that I was the organiser or whatever, but if you talk to any of the top lads most of them were pissing themselves about it and thinking, who are these people? A couple of them came to court for the trial and they had to leave because they were crying with laughter.

So when the raids came about a month later, I think about twenty-six of us got nicked, including Skiz and Griff, in the first week. They put us in the cells and then we were up in court and remanded and that was it, my world was turned upside down. Before this, we had come to think that they probably were coppers and we had discussed it, but we said we haven't got anything to worry about because we're so low down the pecking order, they won't want us. Then our solicitor is coming into the room saying, 'Well, actually, they think you are the top man.' It was mad.

Then I was in this big trial charged with conspiracy. Bonkers. Because there were twenty-six of us, they said there were too many to try in one go, so they split it up into two trials and because I was supposed to be this main face I was in the first one. I was sat in the dock with Para Dave, who I thought was Para Div, and basically ten people I didn't know or talk to. When the trial started there was big media coverage. Then there were Sun editorials and we're reading the papers thinking, oh my god. There was not one victim and the only person who had been arrested during it all was one of the coppers. There was not one person who said that these boys had done something wrong.

The trial was bizarre. There was this huge sort of media presence. I wanted to get Michael Mansfield as my barrister but the Guildford Four had an appeal on so he was with them – I am glad they got him though. So I got a London barrister from quite a radical chamber. She went to a couple of barristers' parties while the trial was going on and she was told that the judge, Judge Crabtree, was getting calls from London every day asking how it was going, which gave the impression that there was a lot of political interest in it. It was a six-week trial and our barristers came to the conclusion that the police and prosecution didn't really have that much on us and said we shouldn't give evidence, which in retrospect was a bad decision.

One thing that did upset me in the trial was the stereotyping. At the incident in Balham, they made out that it was racially motivated and I was supposed to have said, 'Come on, there's a firm of niggers outside,' and that absolutely crushed me. All my mates who were witnesses said, 'One thing we do know about Pat is that he isn't racist.' I thought they weren't really piecing the evidence together and one by one they were finding them not guilty.

The seaside town of Blackpool became a regular Bank Holiday destination, and battleground, for Leeds during the 1980s. Here some of the Very Young Team come under attack from the Wigan Goon Squad on the promenade.

Tobin of the VYT with Shaun Ryder and Bez before a Happy Mondays gig in Sheffield. The dance/rave scene lured many away from the terraces.

Drinking and singing in the sun: a win at Bournemouth in May 1990 would see Leeds return to the top division, and up to 10,000 away fans made the trip, most without tickets.

A contingent of Leeds fans in Ku Klux Klan garb at Bournemouth. Charges of racism have often been levelled at a minority of their supporters, with good reason, but the firm did have some non-white faces.

Serious rioting breaks out outside Bournemouth's ground as police in helmets and shields move in. 'DISGRACE' was the banner headline in one national paper.

The other side to Bournemouth: some of the 900 riot cops drafted in to deal with the trouble pose happily with fans. 'They told us they enjoyed it as much as we did,' said one lad.

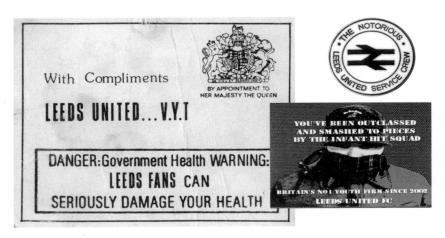

Calling cards and lapel badges: an essential part of any firm's PR campaign!

An intelligence document listing peole who West Yorkshire Police considered main targets at Leeds in the 1990s.

Tottenham Hotspur away in 1991 and a mob walk along Seven Sisters Road. Leeds-Spurs fixtures have regularly produced fireworks over the years.

Cardiff City at home in January 2005. Mounted police led eight charges in an attempt to disperse Leeds thugs who fought them for nearly an hour after the game.

More than 7,000 Leeds fans in Milan in November 2000 when United drew 1-1 and qualified for the knockout stages of the Champions League. Bottles of urine and other missiles rained down from the Italian ultras in the tier above.

Madrid away in 2001. Benny, China, Eddie, Musky and friends. The travel company used Eddie and others as stewards on these trips, which ensured no trouble at hotels or on transport and meant the lads went for free.

The Infant Hit Squad arose in recent years, one of a new breed of 'youth' firms that seemed to spring up almost simultaneously around the country, although improved policing greatly hampered their activities.

The older lads today recognise that CCTV, banning orders and other security measures, not to mention age and responsibility, have effectively ended the hooligan 'heyday' for good.

The slogan on a fan's shirt at Derby County in the fateful 2006/07 season sums up the sentiments of many supporters, both hooligans and ordinary fans alike.

Eddie Kelly (centre) and friends gather in 2006 outside the Adelphi pub in Leeds on the twentieth anniversary of the death of Gav, one of the lads, who was tragically killed in a road accident after a match.

When one lad was cleared, the public gallery cheered and clapped and when the jury were walking out apparently someone did a throat-slitting gesture to the jury bailey. Then the jury bailey that night heard one of the jury saying to the jury chairperson, 'Well, are you going to find anyone guilty after that?' The jury bailey reported the throat gesture and that the jury were feeling intimidated. We had been remanded and when we got in the next day something was different. We found out at the same time the case against West Ham had collapsed, the day before I think, and we thought, well, that's good for us. So, we're all thinking this will be okay and our mates gave us the thumbs up and then the judge came in but no jury.

Then out of a side door the riot squad came in and the judge ordered them to clear the public gallery, the inference being they had been interfering with the case or something. They let two members of each family stay in for each defendant. The jury came in, then the judge makes this rousing speech about in the interests of justice, justice must be done and you must not be intimidated it is your duty, etc., so the stakes have just risen. In the end, seven of us are convicted and the judge adjourns the case for a month for reports.

The next day the Sun and Daily Mail editorials were all, 'Now the jury have the strength of their convictions to find these people guilty let's hope the judge has the strength to imprison them.' I remember being on the young prisoners' wing in Armley when Eddie was in there and I used to have the Independent delivered every day and when I was reading it in the exercise yard he'd walk past and just tut.

We went back and I got sentenced to four years for conspiracy to cause affray, the same sentence as Para Dave. The second trial didn't happen, as they knew they had come so close to a cropper that they abandoned it. But as some of the lads in the second trial had already pleaded guilty, they were sentenced, but they only got small sentences. This was when they changed police tactics from covert to overt. I was just bemused by it all. I remember reading about the same judge a month or so later. He jailed an eighteen-year-old lad for just three years for burgling a house in Barnsley and raping an eighty-year-old woman.

The main reason the other football trials collapsed, Chelsea and West Ham, was that it was found that the police notes weren't contemporaneous, they had gone back over them and filled things in. We raised that in our case, as in the police notes they referred to someone by name and then later on as someone they only knew by a nickname, and that day when the jury was not in and the judge came in, that was what we thought was going to happen. We later appealed and it came before the Court of Appeal ten days before I was due to be released and they knocked it back. We appealed on severity of sentence and on the judge's summing up, but it failed.

I served about two years: four months in Armley and the rest in Lindholme in Doncaster, which is an old RAF base which has the barracks and the parade ground in the middle. There was a riot in Lindholme. There were loads of Leeds lads in there and we heard there was going to be this riot. Once you have been in Armley, which is the most horrible place in the world and people were hanging themselves left, right and centre, and then you're in somewhere like Lindholme, which has a library and access to fields, why you would want to riot there I don't know. But, we heard a rumour there was going to be one and then all these lads came out with pillow cases over their heads like the KKK. Some were setting fire to the library and then they got into where the tobacco was and others who were junkies, Scousers and Mancs mainly, got into the hospital where the drugs were, but nothing is labelled and they're all injecting themselves with all sorts. I saw people fighting, people setting fire to things and others with needles hanging out of their arms.

Para Dave was in Armley and stayed on reception there when I left. One thing I will say about him is, although he was a bit of a big mouth and still to this day I think he is an idiot, he was game and did loads of stuff, and others will say that too. But one thing that really did make me feel a bit ashamed about the way I felt, because I wanted to knock him out – don't know if I could or not – but on the day we were sentenced, his commanding officer from the Falklands came to court and gave this account which moved me to tears if I'm honest. He said that when they were there and he was in the medical wing, they were stuck in this valley and the first lot had gone running down and a few had got shot and some had retreated. But there were still some there and, according to his officer, and I have no reason to disbelieve him, he ran down and got to them, tried to pull them back and tried to treat them and actually got pinned down for twenty-four hours underneath two dead bodies.

I didn't see him again until we appealed and we shared a cell for the night in Brixton prison. It was just flat, the whole thing had become flat by then. I know Eddie put it to him that he had grassed but it wasn't the evidence of a complete grass. But it was very, very unsophisticated and stupid evidence and he had put me right in the frame. I do harbour a bit of resentment to him but mainly it's for a system that allows the police to lie, backed up by the legal system, which is then reintroduced in newspapers.

It has been hanging over me all my life, especially in the academic jobs I've had. A member of staff at one place I worked at, after she read what I was supposed to have said, started telling people that I was racist. It never goes away and it basically culminated in me leaving that job. I really resent those coppers and I'm sure they did really well out of it. Hooliganism is completely blown out of proportion. There are some lads who are doing some fairly naughty stuff but on the whole not much really happens and the amount of attention it is given in the media in proportion to what *happens is ridiculous. In crime surveys, if you ask people, 'Have you been a victim of crime,' how many people say they are victims of hooliganism? Most people I know who have been 'victims' are quite happy about it. There are very few innocent players in it all. But overall, I look back on it all with a sense of nostalgia.*

16

RAVING MAD

ROUNDHAY PARK BECAME known in the 1980s for momentous outdoor concerts. A natural amphitheatre, it featured some of the biggest names in pop and rock and hosted tens of thousands of music fans from all over the world. Roundhay itself is a tough area to the north of Harehills, with Seacroft to the east. Lads from that area have a reputation for their thieving and earning abilities. For the Leeds lads, the Park also became a mecca for trouble with Mancunians and Scousers, who touted tickets at the major music events.

Before the M62 was completed in the mid-Seventies, linking Liverpool and Hull across the Pennines, football coaches would pass through Roundhay on their way to places like Newcastle, Manchester or Blackburn. Often they took a battering from the locals – a foretaste of things to come. In July 1982, when the Rolling Stones played to more than 80,000 people there, 100-150 football lads, young and old, charged their way in past the Hell's Angel security team – with one Angel getting slashed and the rest chinned.

Three years later, Bruce Springsteen performed at the arena, on what again proved to be a wild day of fighting and drinking in the summer sun. Everyone was on a high. The riot against Birmingham City had just happened, some had also been involved in well-publicised trouble at a Scotland-England game at Hampden Park, while the miners' dispute that affected many lads had come to an end earlier in the year. Hundreds were out on the hot Sunday morning and congregated at Jaccomellis and the Prince of Wales. Sean and three other lads were selling T-shirts and posters and headed off to Roundhay to check if the Scouse and Manchester touts had arrived. Putting football differences aside for business purposes, as is often the way, Everton and Liverpool had hooked up together, as had City and United, to sell the usual gig paraphernalia. The area was teeming with people and the touts were doing a roaring trade.

The pubs were filled with Leeds lads all along Roundhay Road, supping their beers in bare chests. The Manchester touts, mainly positioned on the right-hand side of the road, got a bit cocky with some Harehills lads, resulting in them getting chinned and relieved of their goods. The Harehills lads then sold the T-shirts and posters to Sean at £2 each, which he flogged on to punters for £4. Other lads were stealing gear out of the back of vans by the Oakwood Clock, where the disgruntled Mancs started to gather. Then a huge firm of Leeds, about 500-strong, bowled up the road. It went off straight away and the forty or so Mancs made a brave stand before getting battered, concert-goers scattering as the brawling spread.

By mid-afternoon everyone was the worse for wear from booze but had made it into the park either by pushing the barriers down or sneaking in down the steep bank at the back. Some scuffles broke out between some black lads and Harehills and Chapeltown, and more fighting kicked off by the stage, though it wasn't clear who was involved. Police on horseback broke it up just before the concert started. Sensing that the police presence wasn't helping the atmosphere and that people were getting crushed by the stage, Springsteen came on and asked, 'Can West Yorkshire's finest leave the auditorium?'

Ambulances arrived to ferry away the crush victims but some were attacked as they drove out. Pockets of fighting erupted in several areas of the arena and when some older Salford lads were spotted near a refreshment stand, off it went again. There were around a dozen of them and only eight or ten Leeds involved at first, but that soon changed. As Leeds were in Division Two and hadn't met Man U or City for several years, it was a joy to be tussling with them again. One of them hit Terry M, prompting Leeds to dive straight in, but truncheon-wielding cops appeared to break it up. Towards the end of the gig, most drifted away to the Fforde Green pub to continue drinking, satisfied with the mayhem. A van load of Chelsea fans then drove past shouting at those outside the pub. Unfortunately for them, the traffic was gridlocked. They became stuck in it and their van was hammered by 50 lads.

By 7pm, many had returned to the city centre and were in Jac's and Yates's, a couple of doors down, when someone shouted, 'It's going off outside.' Everyone poured out onto Boar Lane to see fifteen Scousers fighting with some Leeds at some traffic lights by the train station. One Leeds lads was slashed but the slasher was hit with a dustbin. Twenty Leeds ran them into the station, where the British Transport Police laid into them all with batons and chased Leeds back out on to Boar Lane, while the Scousers stayed safely ensconced inside. All in all, it went down as a memorable day.

The following year, Genesis played in the rain and this time the police were better prepared. Most of the touts selling shirts and tickets were from Leeds, and though one or two of the few Manc touts did get chinned, most were left alone. A mob of Sheffield United arrived but were sent packing after encountering some Leeds on Roundhay Road before the concert. Several hundred lads were again out for the day and ended up in the city centre later on.

When Michael Jackson performed there in 1987, the gig wasn't nearly as raucous as in previous years. Most had got bored with the scene and with football, although there was some fighting with gangs of black lads at the concert. The late 1980s generally saw fewer of the hooligans going to matches. Those that had joined up for the fashion and reputation faded while others became distracted by the rave scene. Soon there was only a hardcore left – the likes of Eddie, China, Mason, Sean, Jono and Derek – along with the lads from outside Leeds. It was the same within other firms and fighting tended to be less prevalent.

In October 1987, a match with Plymouth Argyle was the same weekend as the Great Storm, the worst to hit southern England for nearly 300 years. The high winds and their devastating effects inevitably caused delays for those on trains, but about fifty travelled down safely on a bus. They headed for a night out in Torquay after the game to drown their sorrows after a 6-3 thumping. An alcohol-fuelled evening ended up in a nightclub called Claire's, with a hardcore of twenty going the distance. The bouncers had already had a chat with the lads asking them to behave but near the end of the night the lads became aware of a gathering of about sixty blokes looking in their direction. It seemed like the club's security had put out the word for reinforcements and had been quite successful.

A solitary glass hurled in Leeds's direction kicked things off and tables were overturned and drinks sent spilling as the fight spread. Leeds were on one side of the dance floor with their attackers on the other. The lads hammered the locals with glasses from a table until they ran out and they were set upon and got a battering. As one, Paul, tried to escape, he ran over all the tables surrounding the dance floor but got cornered and floored, rolling around in the broken glass on the floor, before escaping through a fire exit. He was hit with a pint jug a few times, breaking his cheekbone, but he was one of the lucky ones. Another lad, Yogi, got opened up from one side of his stomach to the other and was also stamped on, causing his eye to swell up to the size of an orange – the reason why he hasn't gone to a match since. Another lad, from Barnsley, was slashed by his ear. It was a bloody night.

Outside the lads were rounded up and put in the back of police cars as others did their best to mingle in and get away. Paul headed back to the hotel despite looking like something out of a horror movie with his face and top covered in blood. Cops circled the area looking to pick up those involved, although the incident was instigated by the bouncers.

Later that month, on Halloween, Leeds were away to Sheffield United. One of the lads, a teacher at a school in Sheffield, sorted a pub to visit before the match but the landlord bandied the news about, so when their double-decker arrived, carrying eighty lads, the locals were waiting. The Leeds group initially got off but in the end decided to find another pub and drove a few miles down the road into Catcliffe. Avoiding any trouble that early was deemed the best thing to do, as they were on probation as part of the supporters' club.

They noticed they had been followed by some Sheffield, who settled at a pub a bit further up the road. Some started playing pool, and others were chatting about whether they should have stayed at the previous pub regardless of Sheffield, when the landlord shouted out, 'Who's running the bus?' as some Blades were in the street trying to get Leeds out for a fight. 'Most of us agreed that if they wanted to have a go, we would deal with them when we set off for the match, although the younger lads were keen to start something,' said Johnna. 'Everyone just carried on drinking but Muffy got the phone number of the pub the Blades were in and started hurling abuse at them. Some coppers came in and asked if there was any trouble. We said we'd been followed to a few pubs by Sheffield, who were trying to have a go, and they listened and then left. We thought they would go over to them and have a word or at least get them to clear off but they did neither and just left a patrol car outside the pub. When I went out for a minute, I could see the Blades outside their pub, looking like they might be going to attack any minute. Then the police car drove off, which I assumed was to get back-up.'

It was nearly time to leave for the match but a few lads went out towards the Sheffield lads drinking outside their pub. Muffy from Bradford was the first one into them. He got put straight on his arse and more Sheffield started coming outside, armed with pool cues, pieces of wood and bottles. One guy had an axe. Punches were exchanged and Leeds were backed off down the road as they dodged the weapons being hurled in their direction. Some Leeds were still in the pub and not involved but others who'd seen what happened came over and picked up the weapons. Then fifty lads surged towards Sheffield, who panicked and fled, jostling one another to get back into their pub. A few stranded outside were beaten as the rest barricaded themselves inside. One lad smashed the window of the pub and a few had a go at him for it. Eventually the lads got back on their double-decker and drove off as the back window was put through as a parting gesture from the Blades.

They were nearing the motorway when they were surrounded by police and told to pull over. The whole bus was rounded up and taken to Rotherham police station, where they ended up on an identity parade. They managed to catch the last eight minutes of the game, which Leeds were losing 2-0 until two quick goals saw them nick a draw. Six lads were later jailed and given two-year bans, including some who weren't even involved in the brawl, while no Sheffield were arrested.

* * *

After dominating so many terrace foes throughout the Eighties, some perhaps began to take for granted the Service Crew's reputation and began to believe their own hype.

But every firm can underrate the opposition and get caught out, as Leeds did when some of them were turned over at Aston Villa. Derek from the VYT bought tickets for the Villa end off Brummie Chris ahead of the match in March 1988. He and a few others, including some Service Crew, went in but a copper turfed them out, saying, 'You've come to cause trouble, so get out and walk round and cause trouble.'

They did walk around – and Villa came at them and got the better of them. They were outnumbered but some still felt they could have done much better and were caught out by believing they were untouchable.

At the season's end, the lads were enjoying another Bank Holiday trip to Blackpool when they met some girls from Wigan who introduced them to a completely new scene: ecstasy. Acid and speed had been around for a long time and loads of the crew smoked dope but that was about as far as it went. So when the Wigan girls told them they could get some pills, it was a new one on the lads, but they told them to bring some over to Leeds the following weekend. They met up in the George pub and the girls had some tablets on them for £25 each. Gooey and Gouldy bought some, went to the toilets to take them, and waited. Twenty minutes later they were looking at each other saying, 'What the fuck is this? It's unbelievable!'

They left the George waving their hands in the air and made for the Warehouse, the main club in the city. They bumped into some older lads on the way who laughed at their behaviour but they told them – in between the rushes – that it was like nothing they'd ever had before. Inside the club, they took the dance floor by storm, loving every moment. They immediately knew they were onto a good thing so set about getting some more of these pills over the next three weeks. They soon tired of paying £25 per pill but the girls said their supplier wouldn't drop his price. Instead they suggested they try a club in Manchester called the Hacienda. The lads both thought, fuck that, as they feared getting their heads kicked in, but desire overcame caution and a short time later they went over one Saturday to try their luck.

They soon found out they had discovered something pretty special. They came back full of stories but didn't have a very receptive audience. Their dope-smoking mates weren't convinced about the music, the drug or the choice of city, but Gooey and Gouldy kept going on about what they were missing. They knew the rest were dying to try it really and would eventually cave in. On one trip, they got chatting to some Man U lads on the train to Victoria Station. One of them, Scotty, who was quite well known on the footie scene, said he had a few Es for sale for £15 each. They hooked up with his crowd after the Hacienda and went back to a shady all-night drinking den called the Kitchen, in the forbidding Crescent flats in Hulme. They got back early in the morning, with Gouldy going off to do his community service.

After a few weeks, all the lads back in Leeds wanted a piece of the action. Gouldy got to know another lad, Pete from Warrington, in the Warehouse one night, a football lad who sold smiley acid house T-shirts and posters. He told them he could get some pills. So when Gouldy finished work on a Friday, he would get the train to Victoria, buy them at £15 a tablet, bring about twenty back and dish them out to the lads. Andy le Sauter, Eddie's brother Paul and Raffs were among the first to sample them and when everyone saw what state they were in, dancing on the stage in the Warehouse, word spread. A dozen including China, Dooner, Mally and Spiff, started going across to the Hacienda for Nude on a Friday night, and by early 1989 there were up to thirty of them. Word had spread in other cities too and lads from Stoke, Boro, Huddersfield, Blackpool and Oldham were now rocking out at the legendary night spot.

Eddie remained unconvinced and didn't try E until about 1989. But when he did, he went over to Gouldy, fists clenched and totally wrecked, and said, 'What the fuck have I been missing?' However, he got knocked back on the door at the Hacienda a few times and didn't bother going back. The rest were there practically every weekend throughout 1989 and became totally caught up in it all and got heavily into the drugs.

The drugs cancelled out any rivalries between Leeds and Manchester, plus the two teams hadn't played each other for several years so the mutual animosity had waned slightly. The Manchester lads took them under their wing and it was all about having a good time. C.C.Rogers' 'Someday' became a particular anthem, played at 1.45am.

Eventually they stopped getting their pills off Scotty and started buying them from a lad called Tony who knew Paul M, a notorious gangster from Salford. One night they'd had some gear laid on and went back to a house with Tony. Next morning there was a knock on the door and it was Mr M, looking for payment. None of them had a penny on them so they all hid behind the curtains. He eventually left and they paid up later, which was probably wise. Gouldy didn't realise just how infamous Mr M was until some time after.

Blackburn also became a bit of a hotspot. They would go to the Red Parrot and acid house parties after meeting at the Warehouse. Thousands of people would join convoys driving around Blackburn looking for the illegal rave after ringing a number to find out where it was. Then, towards the end of 1989, others started putting on raves in Leeds. Eddie E and Tony A organised one in a marquee called Space, off the M62 in Rothwell, and Gouldy, China and a few others sold tickets in the Hacienda. They got a DJ from Manchester, Steve Williams, and Eddie had an eight-foot polystyrene E cut out and put in the tent. By the time most lads got there it had been busted by the police and Eddie, Tony and a few others were arrested. Eddie told the police the E was for 'Eddie'. It was reported on TV and in the newspapers that ecstasy and cocaine had been found at an acid house party in Leeds.

Eddie and Tony fell out over it and went their separate ways. Tony put on Ricky's on a Saturday night at the Gallery and Eddie opened Studio One on Fridays at the bottom of North Street, about a mile out of the city. Gouldy DJ'd there, as by now he was buying records and also putting parties on. A Harehills lad called Gaddaffi would break into a warehouse and sort out the electricity, then ring Gouldy to come and set up his decks. They got away with it a couple of times but were eventually rumbled and the police confiscated Gouldy's DJ equipment and more than 500 records. He wasn't charged with any crime and after six months his solicitor wrote to the police to get them back. He then started DJ-ing at the Warehouse on Fridays and opened a record shop called Trax in Lower Briggate. He had it for a couple of years but it became a hangout for all the hoolies, shoplifters and the unemployed, who ultimately scared away his customers, and he was forced to close it in 1991 without making any money.

Predictably, by then everyone was getting trashed far too often and a few were getting nicked for possession or dealing. Though many were just sorting out their mates, that was not how the police saw it. One lad, Toddy, had been laying Es on to some of the lads but had been writing names in a book and keeping track of who owed him money. He was arrested after the lads had been to an acid house party in West Ham, after a rave in London called Karma Sutra was cancelled. The police were waiting for him when he got home and found his notepad and the eighteen pills he had in his pocket. During questioning he told them the full names of all the people in his book.

Three days later, the police went to Gouldy's house and found a bag with faint traces of speed in. They interviewed him for six hours and he denied it was his name in the book, maintaining it was a different Gouldy. The officers told him the names of friends who had admitted getting drugs off Toddy and said he was the only one who hadn't confessed and it had to be him. He stuck it out and in the end was given an £80 fine for the bag they had found, while everyone else seemed to have talked their way into three or four years in prison.

Friends began to fall out over who was going to sell pills in the Warehouse, and the good times did not last long – too many drugs followed by anti-depressants to combat the comedowns, nickings and fallings out left a sour taste. Everyone became sick of it and by 1990/91 the heyday was over. Many went back to brawling, just as the dance scene mushroomed and went from underground to overground. When they had discovered the Hacienda in 1988, there would often be only a couple of people in the queue outside, but by the end of the following year people struggled to get in as the crowds stretched around the corner and back to the nearby bridge.

Even before the rave scene, some of the VYT got to know a few of the up and coming indie bands. Scottie was one lad who loved his music and had pretty much every track produced by Manchester-based Factory Records. He showed the lads a magazine article about a band called the Happy Mondays and the way they looked struck a chord. The lads decided to follow them despite never having heard their music. When they found out they were due to play at Scrumpy's in Leeds, about forty went, which was pretty much the sum total of the audience, apart from some Salford lads. They got talking to Shaun Ryder and Bez from the band, and saw them again at the Warehouse, where Sean from East End Park had a fight with Bez on stage. Bez later wrote about it in his autobiography, saying he thought he'd better get the first one in so he cracked Sean. Jimmo and Dave Granger helped patch things up and in the end Shaun Ryder stayed at Jimmo's house. The scuffle broke the ice and led to several drug-addled nights back at various houses in Sheffield, Leeds and Manchester after gigs.

Scottie went on to form the Bridewell Taxis, who supported the Mondays at a few concerts as well as the Stone Roses and Inspiral Carpets. The Taxis were six lads from East End Park who made a name for themselves in the early Nineties during the Madchester scene. They built up quite a support, produced several records and still perform now. The lads also got to know The Farm, James and some of the Stone Roses, in particular Mani, who they found to be a really good lad. When The Farm played in Leeds, a lot of hooligans went along and the band feared trouble, but once they realised they were basically a good bunch of lads they all got on and later kept in touch. Tobin and Wayne featured in their video for the re-release of 'Altogether Now' as the anthem for the Euro 2004 tournament.

Wayne first saw the Stone Roses at the Hacienda and told Tobin about them, and they both went to see them at the Warehouse, where they got chatting to singer Ian Brown. He tried to buy Tobin's yellow leather jacket for £50 and a bottle of Remy Martin but as it was a present from his wife Tobin didn't want to part with it. He polished off the Remy anyway. While Tobin felt The Farm and the Mondays were 'lads', he thought the Stone Roses took themselves too seriously at the time, with the exception of Mani, and had tried to jump on the bandwagon of the scally subculture. He had first seen them in the *NME* dressed as Goths and twelve months later they were kitted out like football casuals.

In 1988, when Gouldy and few others came stumbling out of the Hacienda, a local lad they had got to know said there was an acid house party at the CIS building, the tallest building in the city at the time. He told them 808 State were playing, so not knowing anyone else in the city they stuck with him. Gouldy was introduced to Mani and said he and a few of the East End Park lads had heard of him and the Stone Roses. Around 1986, James played at Cinderella Rockerfeller at the back of the Merrion Centre, a memorable gig with their anthemic song 'Sit Down' forming a big part of the night.

Those who did go to matches during the rave era had notable battles with Leicester City, West Ham and Plymouth. At Filbert Street, Johnna, Muffy, Darzies and other Bradford Whites paid in the home seats above the away end goal after walking around all the bars near the ground and not finding any Baby Squad. They sat right in the middle and noticed that Griff and some of his lads were in there as well. As they watched the game, a lad came and sat behind them and said, 'How are you Leeds lads doing?' He didn't sound aggressive but Muffy turned around and said, 'Fuck off, we don't need any babysitters,' in reference to the Baby Squad. The local lad returned to the group he was with and they kept a watchful eye on them.

At half-time, the small Leeds group went to the bar and got some drinks, making sure they had a good defensive position in case of attack, but nothing happened. They went back up for the second half and clocked Griff, nodding in acknowledgment but not speaking so as not to give away their numbers. They were pretty sure Leicester hadn't seen Griff's little team. As the game went on they became more boisterous but still nothing happened, although they were sure it would kick off during the eight long minutes of injury time because they were all on their seats shouting at the ref. There was a flurry of activity around them, as it must have been obvious who they were, but still nothing happened.

Finally the ref blew his whistle and then they saw the Baby Squad standing by the exit tunnel. They made their way across to Griff and his mob and joined up with them, which clearly surprised their rivals, who backed off down a tunnel. A couple of them were shouting at their mates to have a go but they kept walking towards the exit. A couple did try coming at Leeds but when their mates didn't follow, they retreated. In the end they just walked out of the ground and Leicester were gone.

October 1989 brought West Ham United away and despite the recent decrease in numbers, this was an exception with an incredible mob of maybe 600 out. There were so many they filled the Duke of York in Kings Cross, the road outside and some nearby. The two firms hadn't met since their momentous 1982 battle and Leeds were keen to find them. They sat in the pub for a few hours debating the plan of action. Eddie C was out with his lads, who generally did what they wanted, so they went for a scout about. They were half expecting the ICF to come to the pub, or for Chelsea to turn up, but after a while it became apparent no-one was going to show, so they set off.

There were too many to get on one Tube train so some had to get another, but the others waited for them to catch up, just in case. They needn't have worried, as there was no welcome committee, the streets being full only of shoppers. 'Lads were going up to the market stalls asking where the ICF were,' said Johnna. 'We were amazed they weren't about but stayed alert, fearing an ambush at some point. As we made our way down Green Street, lads were looking in the pubs but found no-one except normal football fans. We couldn't believe it. Everyone started to lighten up a bit, while still expecting them to appear at any minute. Nearer the ground, we saw a black guy from the 1985 ICF documentary called *Hooligan* who said in his interview that he used to go to Arsenal but he'd get attacked by five Leeds fans and no one would help. He seemed to be enjoying the fact that quite a few lads recognised him but when we asked where all his boys were, he shrugged his shoulders.'

They hung around outside till near kick-off but when no West Ham showed, the consensus was that, in those drug-addled times, they must be 'E'd up' somewhere. Leeds filled the whole South Bank with some 7,000 fans. There were also little pockets of lads all around the ground, who could be seen jumping up and down when Vinnie Jones scored the only goal of the game.

Afterwards they started walking up towards the station, filling the road.

One West Ham bloke was going mental, shouting, 'What's happened? This isn't real, where are we? They're taking the piss and just walking around where they like!' Some of the lads had a look in the pubs but again found nothing, so they all got the Tube back to Kings Cross for a few beers. The anticipated battle royal never materialised.

As the season drew to a close, Leeds were sitting pretty for promotion under the new management of Howard Wilkinson, after eight long years in Division Two.

A win away to Bournemouth would secure their place in the top flight, so thousands headed down to the holiday resort on a baking Bank Holiday weekend.

17

BOURNEMOUTH AND BEYOND

ON A MAY weekend in 1990, the *Independent* newspaper reported a major improvement in crowd behaviour in England. 'Hooliganism,' it declared, 'is not fashionable any more.' Hours after the paper went on sale, thousands of Leeds fans ran riot in the holiday resort of Bournemouth, and football-related disorder was reported in no less than twelve other towns. The *Independent*'s optimism had been spectacularly misplaced.

Up to 10,000 Leeds supporters made the journey to Bournemouth, approximately 8,000 of them without tickets. Anticipating trouble, the police twice asked for the game to be rescheduled but the Football League refused. Crowds started arriving from Friday lunchtime, some in T-shirts with the slogan 'Bournemouth Invasion 1990'. When the mayhem did start, it was a reversal of the usual roles: it was many 'normal' supporters, rather than hardcore hooligans, who seemed intent on having a tear-up. Indeed some of the lads were walking around looking at the scarfers smashing things up and practically tutting. They personally were not up for wrecking, certainly not on the scale that took place. 'Anyone with brains just sat back and watched the young pissheads wreak havoc,' said one of the Donny lads. 'Petrol tanks on motorbikes were set on fire and a ciggy machine was thrown out of a first floor window. It was mad.'

Everyone seemed to congregate in one main pub, where a few Chelsea and Man City fans were also having a drink and some lads got chatting to them. Muffy from Bradford came in at one point looking shocked, saying he thought he had just killed someone. Some local lads came at him and he had his knife out and one came really close up to him and then fell on the floor. He said he needed money and to swap clothes so he could get away. People started giving him cash until he smiled and said, 'Cheers lads, you'll believe anything,' and went off to the bar.

Eventually the police closed it and, with little else to do, fighting kicked off between bored fans and police, which went on into the night. Hundreds tried to kip on the beach but the police moved people on during the night, which soured relations for the following day. About ten lads, including Ronnie, Charlie and Pat, found themselves locked out of their digs and ended up in the fun park on the front. They got talking to some junkie grafters from Liverpool and everyone was fairly out of it on pills, acid and speed. One of the rides was a space shuttle simulator and Charlie said for a laugh maybe they should sleep there. He tried the open-top door and it opened, so in they climbed and eventually passed out, only to be woken at 7am by a fairground worker testing the rides. Who knows what the guy thought when he opened the capsule and they stumbled out, dishevelled, hungover and disorientated after their recent trip to the moon.

A couple of hours later they bumped into Ricky B in a car with a couple of the older main faces. They were in a similar state. Their mate had been arrested and they were going to the nick to find him. As they drove into the police yard, Ricky flashed his bus pass to a constable on the gate and told him they were CID. They were let in and walked through to the cells but were sussed as they were trying to pass their mate some tobacco.

China and some of the VYT had been out of their heads in Leeds on the Friday, and headed down during the night, arriving the worse for wear at about 8am. They headed for the beach and joined the masses, where some were dressed in Ku Klux Klan costumes. The flags were out, fans were playing football on the sand and everyone was drinking in the sun. It was clear when they arrived at the ground, however, that the police had sent for reinforcements. With so many ticketless, they were unable to get in, the police started to order them about, and pockets of trouble broke out.

Not everyone was involved at first, with some splayed out comatose on the bonnets of cars and others just hanging about. A few forged tickets were knocking about and one lad had both genuine and forged tickets and a ticket for Bournemouth's end. He used a forged one to get in the Leeds end but found it was way too full. Outside the ground, thousands gathered in the gravel car park. As the mood deteriorated, mounted officers started charging at the crowds, who would move apart and then retaliate. This went on for some time, with the odd burst of 'Yorkshire miners' from the lads. Trouble escalated with the rumours – both false – that police had run over and killed a fan and that two lads had jumped out from behind a tree, taken an officer off his horse with a branch and stabbed him to death.

And so to the game. Leeds went 1-0 up in the forty-ninth minute and promotion became a real prospect, causing some lads to try and calm things down in fear of reprisals by the footballing authorities. When the referee blew his whistle for full-time, riot police and officers with dogs struggled to contain the fans pouring onto the pitch as the Bournemouth players fled.

Gradually the crowds moved back to the beach to celebrate and the party went on into the night. Vast numbers of police were now everywhere, resulting in lads taking back routes to get back to their hotels, with some even creeping through bushes. Again fans were critical of the police. One group sat drinking around a small fire on the beach claimed officers simply waded into them. Another group on the beach had dropped some acid and watched the mayhem unfold around them in a kaleidoscope of psychedelic colours before one of them decided to jump on some random beer monster walking past and started rolling around the beach with him. All the beer monster seemed to say was 'Grrrrrr' and the pair ended up in the sea, with the beer monster forcing his spaced-out attacker's head under the water for longer than was safe, so his mates stopped laughing and asked for him back. But he wouldn't release their pal, so they waded into the sea and ended up knocking him out. Both men were then dragged back onto the beach. Once their pal realised he was okay, he grabbed the beer monster and started dragging him back into the water but they stopped him.

The next day the papers were full of condemnation of the behaviour of the Leeds fans. There were calls for the club to have points deducted and therefore be stripped of the Division Two title. They were also criticised for hampering the chances of English clubs being allowed to once again play in Europe. Photographs showed various incidents of trouble, including fans pouring onto the pitch and one lad kicking a police officer or St John Ambulance worker who lay motionless on the ground outside the stadium.

Other papers criticised the Football League for not re-arranging the fixture, saying the riot was 'predictable, predicted and avoidable'. The *Daily Mirror* thundered, 'Only the League turned a blind, and now blackened, eye to the warnings.' It also quoted League president Bill Fox as saying, 'With hindsight we have to regret that we did not give the police request any consideration.' The *Yorkshire Evening Post* chimed in, 'The greatest day in the history of Leeds for the last eight years and it had to end like this. This time seaside thugs fighting police weren't Mods, Rockers or Skinheads but the modern menace of soccer hooligans.' The next day the paper listed ways to make 'Leeds yobs pay'. Its suggestions included fans each paying a £1 levy for every home game, with the money going to Bournemouth, and armbands being worn by players as a mark of respect to football.

All of the national newspapers reported the devastation: deckchairs burned, beach huts smashed, every car outside the Dean Court ground damaged and the Criterion shopping arcade wrecked and looted. Trouble apparently spread to Poole and Weymouth as fans got taxis out of Bournemouth. More than twenty people were injured and 120 arrested and three courts heard the ensuing cases. Meanwhile 250 miles away in Leeds, the fans were celebrating in City Square in anticipation of the Championship trophy being presented to the club on the Tuesday at a friendly against Italian side Genoa. More than 800 in a Leeds fan club in Norway were also celebrating. 'As far as I am concerned, this is a new beginning for Leeds United,' said LUFC's managing director, Bill Fotherby.

In fact it was a weekend of trouble around the country, with over 400 arrests at more than a dozen matches, involving Birmingham City, Chelsea, Sheffield United, Grimsby, Barnsley, Portsmouth, Swansea, Leicester, West Ham, Preston North End and Aldershot. The Labour Party called for a full inquiry into the 'ineffectiveness' of national police intelligence and the Government hinted at 'special measures' being applied to Leeds. In response, club chairman Leslie Silver struck a wrong note when he pleaded, 'After Hillsborough, when there was a terrible loss of life, nobody was drummed out of any competition. Fortunately, here, there was no loss of life. Some sympathy should be extended to Leeds. We've tried to ensure there were no problems.' A total ban on Leeds fans travelling to away matches was deemed a punishment for the well-behaved fans and the police said it was impractical as fans would get tickets somehow anyway. In the end the club was neither punished nor fined; it merely received a reprimand from the authorities.

'As far as we were concerned, that day was down to the pissheads and normal fans that follow Leeds,' says Eddie Kelly. 'Most of the lads were spaced out on pills, speed, booze, whatever, and we just sat back in the sun and watched it all unfold. There were so many ordinary fans at it, it had very little to do with lads, but it wasn't made out like that in the press. Leeds has a wrecking reputation and the media lapped up what happened that day. We don't like the fact that the "lads" are seen as the ones behind it all, it certainly wasn't true on that occasion. There was no-one to fight in Bournemouth, except pensioners. If the police had embraced the fact that everyone was just having a drink it would have been fine.'

* * *

THE 1990/91 SEASON kicked off at Everton, normally a nasty place to visit – but true to the spirit of the times, it was relatively trouble-free. It seemed the Scousers weren't really interested in the Leeds fans in their end. Outside a nearby pub, the street was full of Leeds wondering where Everton were, joking that it was going to be an easy season. With the drugs and the rave scene at its height, lads seemed less interested in fighting.

Some took magic mushrooms on their way to QPR in November in the Rumbelows Cup. Their giggling soon turned to paranoia, with lots of looking at the floor when they first got to the ground. Afterwards, Griff, Musky, Derek and a few others sauntered down to some QPR lads, thinking they wouldn't amount to much, but ended up getting scattered and chased by lads brandishing pieces of wood – not the first group to come a cropper at Loftus Road.

It was a bit of a shock to be caught out by lowly opponents but they were back on familiar territory when they played at Chelsea a few months later. The police began searching them as they came out of Fulham Broadway station, and the predictable sounds of weapons dropping to the floor could be heard. A mob of Chelsea were being held over the road but a few Leeds, including Gaz from Donny, darted across and went straight into them. They were rounded up moments later and chucked in the cells where Gary 'Gaz' Edwards, the author of a book about following Leeds called *Paint It White*, was also being held. Gaz was up in court a week before Leeds were again due to play Chelsea at Stamford Bridge in September 1991. A copper at the court said to him, 'No doubt you'll be there again on Saturday?' to which he assuredly replied, 'Yep, I'll be there.' The case against him was thrown out but one Leeds fan from Brighton was fined £250 and offered to pay a paltry 50p a week, which was surprisingly accepted by the courts.

Now Leeds were back in the top division, one fixture everyone looked out for was Spurs. The rivalry between the two firms hadn't faded as far as Leeds were concerned and they were keen to pick up where they had left off several years earlier. At White Hart Lane in 1991, a tight firm of lads from Seacroft and Beeston, including Jono, Mick and Zoz, fought a hard battle with them. The lads arrived late and were looking where to go in by the Spurs end when they encountered them. They came at Leeds and although none of them moved, Spurs equally didn't hesitate one bit, which was impressive. During the skirmish, Zoz was fighting one, with Skiz next to him. When the lad kicked Zoz, he grabbed his leg and kicked the other one from underneath him and as he went down Skiz caught him with a volley in the head. 'A right James Bond move,' recalls Zoz.

Sean, who was also there, picks up the tale. He and six others would end up in court for the fight.

By the time we played Spurs, we had played Man U at home and away, Liverpool away, Everton away, Man City away, all good days out but this was the one we'd been waiting for, probably since the day we went down. We'd many scrapes with the Yids over the years and missed some of their action in the Eighties due to being in Division Two, and likewise for them, so it was all hands on deck. They turned up at Leeds early on in the season and we gave them it on the South Stand steps. As the game went on they had a big mob of black lads turn up in minibuses and our law made them sit on concrete outside Elland Road for the duration of the game. Then it went off in town with them, but we had all our lads there.

We were raring for this match and this was it, it had arrived. We went down on coaches from the Granville and we had a great firm, all our main lads there, not big but who cares, we had what counted. We got to Kings Cross and had a few beers there and met up with the train lot and the Cockney Whites, then someone said, 'Let's go,' so we all went to the Tube. I thought, there's a good two hundred here, maybe more, and it's quality – but when we got off at Seven Sisters we had about five hundred lads. I was more than made up with this firm. Tottenham didn't have a prayer, I thought to myself.

Going down the road, about thirty of us got out of the escort. We walked halfway down and some Spurs confronted us. They lasted all of ten seconds and were off on their toes. Nearer the ground another little firm came at us on the opposite side of the road. Eddie K belted one of them and Angie got stuck in. They didn't last that long either and we were having a laugh by now, it was going to be our day, I could feel it in my blood. I looked over the road at the escort and thought, I wouldn't want to tangle with that lot. It was a top firm.

There seemed to be a scuffle at a pub between the escort and Tottenham, as they had come out and tried it on with our lot, thinking they'd budge. Not a chance. Marshall, Lumby, Watty, Chalkie, Dave B, Kiddy and all their firm just got straight into them. By now the law were shitting themselves and must have known not to fuck about with this lot. As we approached the ground it was getting busier and livelier but I still felt it was our day. We had a little run at them at a bus stop and they backed off, then they came at us with about eighty and nobody moved. I think John from south Leeds cracked one of them and it stopped dead. The law then put us over the road in the escort and just as they did Tottenham attacked us. Our lot just went straight in and scattered them. The law got it under control, a few batons here and there, and right in front of a copper one of theirs butted Gaz L and jumped back behind the copper. We were fuming trying to get at him but we couldn't due to the law. They even came into us with a horse to separate us.

They shoved us outside our end. All our coach lot were coming up to the ground so everyone said, 'Let's get in.' About fourteen of us decided to have a walk so we went quickly away from our end to the other side of the ground. I was having a piss against a wall with Terry the boxer when all hell let loose. All we could see was arms and legs flying in. Jeans buttoned up and in we go. It was mad. Spurs had waited and then attacked us round the back of their end, the Paxton Road, but we had a good little firm. They had a big, tall, skinny black lad in a leather. He must've been about six foot six. One of our lot – I know who – shouted, 'Get the nigger,' and everyone of our lot went for him. God he was off, honest, he could shift. Then I picked up a cone and cracked one of them over the head as they came into us again.

It seemed to be stalemate. Then a tall kid ran into me on my right side and I put him down with my left and as he was on the deck I booted him. I knew he was staying down, I'd hit a match-winning penalty at Wembley. It was him or me. Then Jono dropped another one of them, Zoz booted one and we backed them off.

We had some good lads in that fourteen, a mixture of Beeston and Seacroft. A police car came and Jono got nicked, the law backed us off about forty yards from the main road and sent us back the way we'd come. There was another little skirmish with Spurs and Terry and Zoz battered a couple. A copper ran up and grabbed Zoz and I told the copper he was wrong and the kid had just attacked him, so he let him go. You can imagine how grateful he was not to be nicked there and then.

We got into the ground late and as soon as I saw Griff he said, 'You've been at it, haven't you?' I replied, 'Unbelievable. We've just done 'em round the back of their end.' He said he could tell by the expression on my face. We watched the match until it was time to go and we walked up Seven Sisters Road in the pitch black and just took the piss all the way back up. Even Big Trevor walked out of the escort with us up the road. Nobody was gonna do that firm. It was the best since Millwall in 1985. It went off outside of a Safeway supermarket – nothing safe about that for them, I can tell you, though one of them lobbed a tin of soup at us from ten yards that would have done some damage if it had connected.

As we got back to the Tube station, there was a gang of them outside a bus stop. Eddie charged into them and we chased them up the road. As we went down into the Tube, I saw their main man, the one with the ponytail and stubble. We'd nicknamed him 'Walshy' after Paul Walsh, their centre forward. This was it, he was going down. I was just about to drop him when Griff said, 'Leave him till we get to Kings Cross.' I was fuming but he was right, it was camera'd up.

When we got back to the station, Jono was there, as the law had let him out. He'd been charged with violent disorder but at least he was coming home with us. We found a little off licence round the back of either St Pancras or Euston and as we were coming out with our cans of beer for the coach trip home a roar went up and all these lads came running towards us. I cracked one of them over the head with my pack of four and they flew all over. The lads, about thirty of them, ran off with our lot chasing them. One of the cheeky bastards picked up a couple of my cans on the way.

I sat with Jono on the way back and he was sick as a Blackpool donkey to be nicked. We still had a great day out and a laugh though and he eventually got not guilty with his case. I was on cloud nine with the way the day went and I'm sure that all our firm were too. Tottenham have always given us problems, so this was sweet. We'd showed them up on their manor, just like all the rest of them in London but this was 'the one' to our lot. We had done it at West Ham, Chelsea and Millwall in the Second Division and they are better firms but Tottenham was the one we wanted to have a result at. We'd not been there for years and that day we really became number one.

My joy was to be cut short just six months later as the police made a number of arrests in Leeds and I was one of them. They came for me at work. It was to do with the Paxton Road End incident. They interviewed us all and made up their minds we were fucked. I was taken to Holbeck nick and interviewed by DS Mark Hanson and his sidekick Joe Lennon. I got the hot-and-cold, good cop-bad cop treatment. They showed me the video tape and fucking hell it was clear but I still told them I thought they'd made a mistake, me being arrogant to the last.

My ex-wife Carol was a star, as she had not let them in the house and sent them to my work and as they were on their way she rang me to inform me they were coming. She got a load of photos out of the house and other things that could be a hindrance to me. We did about four court appearances in London and things didn't look too good but the coppers tried to be too clever and edited the video evidence. It worked in our favour and the case against us – the Tottenham Seven – got thrown out of court. I even got about £2,800 back in expenses and court costs as I was working for the DSS then. So I took Carol on holiday to Rhodes.

And the guy who Griff stopped getting a hiding, you have a charmed life, as we met a year later on Seven Sisters Road and I should have just chinned you then. You owe

Griff a pint, mate. I understand him to be Trevor Tanner and he has written a book on his exploits. He nearly didn't get the chance but as all of us footy fans are good sports, good luck mate, I hope that you make a comfortable life for your family, but be honest and admit you got done that day. We always have a good day out against you at home or away, all the way back to the late Seventies. That day I was proud to be Leeds looking at the lads we had with us – simply the best.

In February 1993, Leeds were again at White Hart Lane. Around 100 drank in the Duke of York in Kings Cross, where one of the lads from Leicester was sat with his brother against one side of a stained glass window with his feet resting on a table. He was near the entrance, nodding and saying hello to the people coming in and out of the pub, when the door opened and a lad walked in that he thought he recognised. He stared at him, trying to place the face. He finally realised it was 'Terry', who he had met through a Spurs mate he had been to a few games with. Terry, however, was not there to renew acquaintances. He pulled out a can of CS Gas and sprayed it into his brother's face.

Unbeknown to Leeds, about thirty or forty Spurs had gathered outside. Suddenly the window was put through with a brick that narrowly missed them. In the shock of the first few seconds, Leeds didn't react, but equally Spurs didn't take the initiative and run in. Instead they lobbed a gas canister or distress flare in through the door. The pub filled with smoke. No one knew what was going on, with some thinking it was a terrorist attack. Then all the windows were put through and Spurs shouted, 'Come on Leeds.' Griff bolted into the street with a few behind him as chairs and stools started to be lobbed outside. He was joined by the Leicester lad, who was nearly hit by the brick and who was now thoroughly vexed. Spurs were dispersing and turned onto Euston Road towards Kings Cross. Leeds gave chase, outnumbering them two to one. They caught up and a few punches were thrown in the middle of the street as a couple of the Londoners stood.

The police were by Kings Cross in vans and ran across the road with dogs to calm things down. The Leicester lad was by the central reservation with a handful of others and Spurs were on the opposite side, a bit further down. He had seen red and had his sights firmly set on Spurs. He saw one lad in a pink jumper by a row of taxis but, because of his tunnel vision, he didn't see the line of five police officers leaning on a nearby barrier watching him. He went for the lad in pink and chased him around a taxi several times, shouting, 'I'm gonna get you.' Needless to say the coppers moved in and put him in handcuffs. The officer who arrested him was from the British Transport Police and a Celtic fan and they chatted en route to Wood Green station. The officer asked him what he thought he was doing in full view of all the coppers. They nicked him at about 2pm, he was fingerprinted, photographed and charged within forty minutes, and he still got to the match. A month later he was fined £150, bound over for a year and given a twelve-month ban.

The following year, Spurs were at Elland Road and it ended up with about forty of them, tooled up, against ten Leeds by the bridge near the ground. People had been saying that Spurs were coming but Derek for one didn't think that much of it as he parked his car – until he saw Sean covered in blood. He went to the bridge and saw that Spurs had all sorts of weapons. Leeds backed them off a bit but then they came running back and managed to get China. Derek went back in and dragged him out. Barraclough, the Leeds copper, was there and told Derek that Spurs were 'cheeky bastards' for coming over the bridge and said he hoped they had run them.

A lot of the lads liked Barraclough. They thought he was firm but fair and part of the old-school way of thinking. Derek and Steve W, a lad who came through in the Nineties, would even chat to him from time to time, which went against the grain as most didn't like to associate with or acknowledge the coppers. He told the lads to watch their backs on the odd occasion at matches and was far more popular than the other football intelligence officers that were linked to Leeds – Calvert, 'Black' Stan and another nicknamed the Silver Fox. Derek was shopping with his wife in town once when he bumped into Barraclough, who was also with his wife, and he introduced Derek as 'one of the lads'. And when

Derek was off work with a broken elbow after he was hit by officers from West Midlands Police, he sued for compensation and Barraclough made a statement for him.

In Amsterdam once, he came in the pubs with the Dutch police, pointing out the lads and saying they would be well behaved. When they went back in later, everyone was naked and totally pissed and someone got Barraclough in a playful headlock as the Dutch coppers watched in disbelief. And in Monaco, when Leeds were playing them, about twenty were in a bar out of town when Barraclough appeared in his civvies, obviously not expecting to see any of them. The lads were amused to see him kitted out in designer-label gear, as they had only seen him in uniform before. Some even claim he had a little Leeds badge on his shirt, but they can't be sure.

In 1999, Spurs were at Elland Road in the FA Cup and brought a good mob. It was a highly charged game in front of a capacity crowd, marking the first occasion George Graham had returned to Elland Road since quitting as Leeds manager in 1998 to take the job at Spurs. Clearly well organised, about 150 Spurs thugs gathered in a working men's club in Beeston and then got up as far as the Wagon and Horse pub. Fighting kicked off as soon as they came out of the ground and it was a good little battle with Spurs doing well.

Back at White Hart Lane in the replay, Eddie and one of the lads who had petrol-bombed a train carrying Chelsea fans to Leeds were walking from Seven Sisters Tube when they got into an altercation with a Spurs lad. The lad, in a yellow ski jacket, who was with a few mates, looked the pair of them up and down and then punched Eddie, saying, 'Come on then.' Eddie didn't budge and verbals were exchanged. 'What the fuck you gonna do now,' said Eddie, 'because that had no effect?' The lad hesitated, seemingly taken aback, at which point Eddie added, 'You soft cunt.' When police appeared the Spurs lad tried to get Eddie nicked by saying he had racially abused him – which was actually true – and he was stopped and searched for a few minutes, allowing the Spurs group to move on. After the game, as Eddie and several others got back by the coaches, a Spurs mob emerged near a school car park, including the guy in the yellow ski jacket. This time they picked on the wrong mob and got battered.

The police nicked five Leeds, including John from south Leeds, Gaz P and Arnold. Their solicitor came recommended from other lads and sat in court as various witnesses gave evidence. The lads said they were attacked by Spurs as they were walking to the coaches and had to defend themselves. One witness said that although he didn't know the lads, he had seen them at matches and wanted to give evidence after seeing them being assaulted. The lads were laughing when he described how big and menacing the Spurs were. One of the magistrates then told him she had been in court for many years and knew Tottenham fans were 'right hooligans' and said she believed him. The lads were all cleared. Outside the court, however, their own solicitor told them, 'You don't fool me for a minute!'

The next day, Leeds played Celtic in Glasgow in a friendly in front of a crowd of 50,000. About 300-400 lads went for a big piss-up, including Gaz P fresh from his court appearance, dressed in a smart jumper, slacks and slip-on leather shoes. When asked why he was dressed in such a 'straight' manner, he said, 'I'm dressing differently now, I'm not getting dragged into this any more.' As they walked down the road, three big Celtic fans came round a corner and went straight up to Gaz and said, 'Alright mate, are you the Leeds Service Crew and one of their famous casuals?' He wasn't happy but everyone else was killing themselves laughing.

Later Eddie, the good Catholic boy that he is, stood in the middle of a packed car park by the ground surrounded by Celtic fans and shouted, 'Freeeedom!' The general response was, 'Fuck off you English bastard.'

18

THE SCUM

DESPITE THEIR SIDES not meeting since the early Eighties, the loathing that existed between supporters of Leeds United and Manchester United had not abated. So when they were matched for the first game of the season at Elland Road after Leeds' promotion, the talk in certain circles was of little else. A Leeds mob gathered to wait for them at the Wheatsheaf pub, to the south of the city – which would be the scene of many more battles through the Nineties as 'the Scum' came in that way on the A62. The Scum appeared in their escort and ran at Leeds, scattering them, prompting one cocky Mancunian to say, 'You're not in the Second Division now Leeds.' In his autobiography *The Men In Black*, Man United leader Tony O'Neill wrote of that day, 'We'd done Leeds good and proper.'

The teams met again in the first of two semi-finals in the Rumbelows Cup in February 1991, which saw Eddie Kelly and Little Billy from the VYT escorted out of Man United's end after Chris Whyte scored for Leeds. Scotty and his mob were in the Scoreboard End and didn't spot Eddie and Little Billy lurking in amongst them. The pair decided to attack the nearest lads to them and counted to three and went for it. United were 'shocked to fuck' and backed off around them. Eddie and Billy had their backs against a wall as they fought United and ended up clambering over a fence into the Leeds end, to rapturous applause, as they jeered Scotty and his boys with the words, 'You fucking wankers…there's only two of us!'

The following season saw the two teams in a heated race for the title – the lead changed hands seven times – and it was Leeds who finally pulled clear to top the division, denying Man United their first championship in twenty-five years. As well as league matches, the teams also met in quick succession in the FA Cup and in the Rumbelows Cup.

The Scum

The first of a trio of games in seventeen days, all at Elland Road, came in December 1991. Again everyone congregated in the Wheatsheaf and it was Diddie who first saw them outside. He went out and told them to wait, then told everyone in the pub. They poured out, only to see Man U set off on their toes. There were more Mancs but it was dark and when the pub doors opened and people came spilling out they must have thought Leeds had superior numbers. They soon realised their mistake and as some Leeds mingled in with them near the police at the ground, they could hear them arguing among themselves, saying they should have taken the Yorkshiremen.

For the Rumbelows Cup in January, no more than thirty lads were drinking in the Wheatsheaf ahead of the midweek match as the Scum parked up by the Ringway, not too far away. They had to walk past the pub en route to the ground and seventy or eighty came marching down the road as Paul and Diddie were by the pub. They suggested meeting up after the game and Man U seemed to agree and carried on by.

Paul and Ward then told everyone inside and they all came out as the Mancs walked through some traffic lights and around a corner. They went straight after them shouting, 'Come on then,' and waded in. United made a stand but got done and ended up getting hammered each time they stood, which was three or four times between the pub and the ground, a fair distance. It was their main mob and there were a few game lads who retaliated but the rest didn't want to know and after the first stand Leeds knew they had them. They stopped again by the tunnel by the Lowfields, where Leeds went into them again. Eddie was in the middle of them rolling on the floor with Gary P, one of their main lads, and Paul got pushed into the tunnel with them and got ammonia in his eyes. The police did eventually manage to corral Man U and they almost came to blows with one another when they discovered their seventy-odd had been done by a small group of Leeds.

The game was, however, a victory for the Reds. 'Leeds scored first but then we got topped, the usual situation when we play them,' recalled Paul. About an hour after the end, between forty and fifty Leeds were walking up by where United had parked and sussed their cars, as there were too many to belong only to residents. They set about slashing their tyres and smashing their windows before getting some drinks from a shop and then hiding in an alley next door to wait for them to return. The Mancs must have thought they were home and dry, as it was some time after the match, but as they came up the road with the police, Leeds ran out and into them. They weren't ready for it and they stood for a bit but then broke ranks, with Leeds in pursuit. They ran back down a hill and other Leeds coming up behind them saw some hiding in a bus shelter. This little tale, the lads point out, doesn't get a mention in *The Men In Black*.

The following week it was the third round of the FA Cup. Again everybody met in the Wheatsheaf and stayed there until about ten minutes to kick-off. As they walked down Gelderd Road in groups towards the ground, the last ones out of the pub encountered some United at the crossroads the pub sits on. It kicked off for a while with the police running back down the road to get involved. There were sporadic fights after that as both mobs, plus the police, were mixed in together with ordinary spectators.

Leeds were enjoying a renaissance under Howard Wilkinson, who brought in new players while the youth structure also began to bear fruit. One player he bought was a certain Eric Cantona, whose later defection across the Pennines did not go down well, although he had shown only brief moments of greatness with Leeds. When Man U were at Elland Road a few months after he was sold, the police were right to again expect trouble, with fighting before and after the game. No one disagrees that Man U have always brought it to Elland Road over the years and Old Trafford has also been the scene of many memorable battles. 'You never saw any Man U without tickets in Leeds, although Leeds would go ticketless to Old Trafford,' says Gaz from Donny, who was nicked there three seasons on the trot. 'The touts say Man U expect to pay more for tickets but if they're offered for fifty pounds in Leeds you'd get battered for asking such a high price.'

Some question how many Man United managed to get into Leeds unchallenged by the police on more than one occasion in the latter part of the Nineties. Two or three times, more than 200 of them got in taxis from the train station and reached pubs where the Leeds lads were either penned in by the police or battled away outnumbered. Man United have said they think Leeds police are slack, but certainly at Manchester one year it seemed like a set-up for them to get at Leeds, with only intelligence officer Barraclough wading in as the few local coppers there stood by and watched.

On that particular occasion, the Stretford End was being rebuilt, which meant a tiny ticket allocation for Leeds of only several hundred. The lads in the Gildersome supporters' club had gone and when they came out everyone was saying stick together. Barraclough knew there was a mob waiting for them and was straight with the lads about what they would encounter. Battle commenced by the bridge not far from the ground and in the melee Barraclough was seen to get a bit of a hiding and had to retaliate. When he got back onto the coach he was shaking his wrist, apparently as a result of punching a Manchester fan, and when the lads asked how his hand was he said, 'Sshhh.' Some time later, Leeds heard that some young Mancs went into a pub claiming to have done them, but older lads set them straight, saying they should have but they hadn't.

Big Tony, who ran travel for Man United fans and latterly for Leeds when European football was a regular occurrence, got smacked by Griff during a heated fight by the turnstiles at a night match one year. He went down and had to crawl out on his hands and knees, and every time he got up he was knocked down again, a fight he is happy to give credit to Leeds for. Whenever Eddie Kelly got stuck into Scum's lads, refusing to give up like a terrier that won't let go, Big Tony and others would ask, 'Who's that little fucker, we just can't get rid of him.' He eventually got to know Eddie and some of the others stewarded for him on a few European trips, ensuring free travel for them and trouble-free journeys to and from the games – usually.

Not everyone wanted to use Tony and not everyone in Manchester liked the fact he helped Leeds. He pretty much followed on from Scotty, the Manc lad who had got to know the VYT during the crazy days at the Hacienda. His travel stewards – Manchester natives – usually got set upon after the lads had sunk a few beers. He had put an advert in the paper for UF Tours – Unofficial Tours – so some of the Leeds lads booked with him when Leeds faced Stuttgart in 1992.

They all stayed in Frankfurt and got a coach to Stuttgart, which took about an hour. On the way they were all pissed and shouting, 'Fucking kill the driver,' which inevitably he heard. They arrived to be greeted by Eddie Kelly, who had travelled separately, with the words, 'Why have you come with that Manc bastard?' Eddie had history with Scotty from the Wheatsheaf battles; at one fight he had been telling United to wait for the Leeds firm to appear properly when Scotty punched him in the face. He hadn't forgotten. On this occasion, Scotty turned to Gouldy, one of the Leeds lads he'd met at the Hacienda, and asked him to sort it out, so he put his arm around Scotty, walking him away, as Popeye did the same to Eddie.

Stuttgart was a carnival atmosphere and the first time many of the lads had been to Europe. After more heavy drinking, they got to the ground on a coach Scotty had put on and then jumped off into a crowd of locals. Several of them were arrested, and when the coach later went to collect them to go home, they found the driver had told the police they had threatened to kill him. Police were at their arranged meeting point, along with the thirty or forty lads. They drew their truncheons and a beating seemed to be imminent, so most kept their heads down, but in the end one copper said, 'You can do this the hard way or the easy way.' They took the easy option, were marched to the train station and got on a train back to Frankfurt relatively peacefully.

Later that season, Leeds beat Man United 4-1 on aggregate to win the Youth Cup. Some Donny and Leeds lads drove over to Old Trafford for the first leg which was attended by more than 30,000 fans, a larger crowd than at all but one of that weekend's Premiership matches. About fifty got into a home section and afterwards, when they got to their cars and minibuses, they found the windows had been put through and someone had shat on some of the seats.

Leeds United's sojourn in the Second Division in the Eighties may have allowed the Mancs to build up new rivalries with others, but they were reminded of the venom Leeds had for them at a match against Blackburn Rovers in 1994. Some Leeds fans booed all through the two minutes' silence for Sir Matt Busby, which received national media attention. It wasn't until the mid-Nineties, when Man United were defending champions, that Leeds beat them for the first time since 1981, and they also managed to knock them out of the FA Cup in the same season. The following year saw Leeds under new ownership and, after a 4-0 drubbing at home to United, Howard Wilkinson was sacked and George Graham replaced him, with David O'Leary as his assistant. His tenure was brief but he stabilised the team and players from the youth team who would go on to become household names began to feature more: the likes of Harry Kewell, Jonathan Woodgate and Paul Robinson.

The two teams met again at Elland Road in September 1997 and there was plenty of trouble when Man United went into the city centre before the game. The police tried to keep them apart and there were tit-for-tat exchanges amongst the traffic as sections of the two mobs attempted to get to one another. Some United settled in All Bar One in Greek Street, which was quickly attacked – as was their escort to the ground – resulting in the police barricading them in for their safety. As the police began to guide United over the pedestrianised bridge by the ground, Leeds went at them, chucking bottles and glasses before racing around to meet them over the road. Video footage shows a policeman against a railing with a cut to his head.

Near the ground, Leeds started to goad and attack the coaches that pulled into the car park and scuffles broke out around the vehicles, with police capturing it all on film. Loads of both normal fans and 'lads' gathered by the traffic lights at the ground and the police had to clear a path to get Man United inside, well after kick-off, and set about shunting them in the away end as Leeds jeered and abused them. Leeds scored first and managed to hold on, while their supporters booed every United touch of the ball and drowned out any chants they got going. Afterwards, there were sporadic confrontations in the car park, again with the police filming.

It was a 5pm kick-off for the match at Old Trafford on Bank Holiday Monday in 1998 and everyone was worse for wear when they arrived, after spending the day drinking in Oldham. 'A group of fifty or sixty of us got off our coach by the other visiting coaches and walked over the bridge to the forecourt,' said one lad. 'There were thousands of Mancs swarming around. There was another coachload behind us but they were stopped. We stuck together like glue and were surrounded but they couldn't budge us, we did really well. We were half shepherded by police and just worked our way through to the turnstiles and got in. It was a memorable day.'

At one point, Benny and others turned round to see a lad in a wheelchair come racing down the road with a Man U shirt and scarf on, shouting out his hatred for Leeds: 'You Yorkshire bastards!' He was speeding down the pavement so fast that he came out of his chair and fell into the road. His mates came to his aid but he was still cursing and bellowing and the Leeds lad couldn't help but laugh at what had happened. 'The forecourt was full and the Scum were swarming around with bricks and other missiles flying through the air,' said another Leeds lad. 'It was several thousand against several hundred and was so bad that similar matches were changed to midday kick-offs after that.'

At Old Trafford in 2000, after the deaths of two Leeds fans in Turkey, some Manchester supporters made throat-slitting gestures towards the visitors and some had the Turkish team's flag, to which Leeds responded with 'Munich 58' chants. In 2001, rumours circulated that the two firms would meet in Rochdale when Leeds played Man City and Man United were at Bradford, but in reality the rumour was based on passing comments about where Leeds would be drinking afterwards and didn't amount to anything. About sixty Leeds went to Rochdale and as many as 300 Scum turned up at Yates's where they were drinking, but they couldn't get past the Leeds lads at the doors, who fought them off.

A couple of months later, in March, the two sides did meet after the game at Elland Road. Man U had been brought in on buses and the usual coppers were out with their cameras and the helicopter was hovering about above. A copper was hit on the head by Elland Road during one fight. Several hundred of them came into Holbeck and the fighting kicked off straight away and reached riotous proportions. Man U stuck together but because the police blocked off roads it made it harder for Leeds to get together and they were low on numbers. The fighting spilled into numerous streets, with small groups of lads battling away as the coppers did their best to break it up.

In 2002, it was another hectic day of trouble in Leeds, with buses getting attacked and a motorbike policeman getting pulled off his bike. Some of the young lads who formed the Infant Hit Squad were out and got a call from the older lot to alert them that Man U were going to be targeted at some point. Everyone in the various pubs around town got together and two double-decker buses came into view and they darted out to greet them. Police footage of the day, from Operation Cadole, shows the buses, escorted by two outriders slowing down as they reach the junction by the Wheatsheaf pub and then getting stuck in traffic. At that point, bottles are lobbed at the buses as Leeds race towards the vehicles, amid shouts of 'Leeds, Leeds, Leeds.' The buses start turning left as the police sirens get louder and the lads are still going towards them which is when the copper gets kicked off his bike. He gets up and his colleague picks up a piece of wood and starts walking towards the lads, who scatter in among the traffic. Another copper filming can be heard saying, 'What is that police officer doing?'

Aerial footage shows Leeds at the door of one of the buses and others by the windows as the buses stop and start in the traffic before getting away. R, one of the younger lads from the Infant Hit Squad, broke his hand hitting the windows and trying to get them off the bus. At no point during the couple of minutes of mayhem do United get off, they just retaliate with verbals and hand gestures.

After the game, one of United's lads told Eddie they weren't going back their usual way, into Holbeck and then into town. Instead, between sixty and eighty of them set off in the opposite direction. About twenty Leeds went after them and it kicked off when they reached a B&Q store. It was a good fight and a few got sparked but no-one could claim a victory. Man United said later that if Leeds had come with more, they would have been on their way. In the distance in the police footage after the fight can be seen a man laid out on the floor by a traffic island. He was a Service Crew veteran called Slant, who had been hit with a metal bar.

Ahead of a match at Old Trafford around the same time, about seventy Service Crew and IHS decided to meet in Halifax to avoid unwanted police attention. They got into Manchester for about half-time, which they had prearranged with Man U, but when they got off the train they were met by riot police. A mob of United behind the police acknowledged Leeds for what they'd done. The lads were promptly searched and put back on the train. Meanwhile Eddie was with about thirty lads drinking on Deansgate and getting calls from a well-known Salford face asking where they were and what was happening. But Eddie had to tell him there was no point them coming in.

In 2003, more than 200 Leeds walked through Manchester city centre hours before a night match without any hassle and hung about the bars near Piccadilly. 'We were picked up by the police and there was a little bit of scuffling going on with them when they took us to the ground,' said one lad. 'They walked us the long way round and we got there about thirty minutes after kick-off. By McDonald's, Sean ran over and hit one lad and a police dog brought him back. We had the usual hassle to get in because of membership cards. Afterwards we were rounded up and were walked the long way again back to Piccadilly. We got to the platform, knackered, with about a minute to spare for the train. The next game at Old Trafford was a total non-event. Our coaches were taken directly over the road from Old Trafford and we were straight in, straight out.'

With Leeds struggling in the league, that game was, at the time of writing, the last time the two teams played each other.

* * *

Leeds United's return to the top flight football saw them renew acquaintances not just with Man United but with many other old rivals. A few pre-season friendlies against Hibernian, at that time one of the most active of the Scottish casual firms, also ended up being riotous. Prior to one fixture in the early Nineties, some lads met an Aberdeen casual called Willie at an England-Scotland match. He told them that Hibs and Hearts had got together and formed the Scottish National Firm that day. They looked like a bunch of rough bastards and in one battle came flying round a corner straight into a mob of Leeds and wouldn't give an inch.

Hibs seemed to have a similar mentality to Leeds, and some said if they ever got the chance to play them, it was one game they needed to be organised for. So when the opportunity arose, two lads went up on a reconnaissance mission on a Thursday night, with others coming up by train and coaches the day before the match. An all-night pub was sorted so that when the main mob arrived at about 5.30am, about fifty lads got settled into the beer straight away, along with some locals enjoying their Tennent's. A couple of Hibs spotters came up the stairs into the middle of the pub, had a look and left. The next thing the lads knew was that the Capital City Service crew had appeared outside. One lad leant back in his chair and looked out of the window while holding a spliff. 'I don't want to alarm anyone,' he calmly stated, 'but there are about a hundred lads outside.' Then the windows came in.

Automatic shutters came down on the bar and Leeds threw objects out of the windows before pouring outside to face the Scots. Hibs seemed a bit shocked that Leeds had come straight at them after their initial attack, but they fought toe-to-toe for a short while before Leeds chased them down the road past a McDonald's and turned right into a park near the ground. The locals beckoned Leeds down the road, saying: 'A bit more, just a bit further,' as they knew they had hundreds more lads waiting in Easter Road. As many as 300 were there to greet Leeds and the fighting was ferocious. At one point Sean and several others were cut off and under attack in a bus shelter. As a van came up the road, Sean ran over and smacked the driver so the vehicle would veer off into Hibs. It worked and they got away. Undercover coppers appeared among Hibs and grabbed some of them, saving the outnumbered Leeds group from a severe beating. There were casualties on both sides but eventually the police intervened. Although Leeds were outnumbered, they felt they had fought well and had the victory because they had taken the pub. Everyone was on a massive high afterwards. One of Hibs came over, said he was fresh out of Barlinnie Prison and passed on his respects: 'You're the best in England, now meet the best in Scotland.'

After the game, as police did their 'trains to the left, coaches to the right' bit, about thirty-five stood by the McDonald's found themselves with no escort and no coppers about. They set off, only to be attacked by 200-plus Hibs at a crossroads. The lads were hemmed in by a metal barrier and some were backing off, although there wasn't really anywhere to go. Then Eddie Kelly jumped over the barrier with an iron bar shouting, 'Come on, you cunts,' and roused Leeds to fight back.

'Put doon your pole,' said one Hibs lad to Eddie.

'There's only one place this is going mate,' replied Eddie, 'and that's round your head.'

The police then appeared, with one officer filming the trouble, which some think was pre-planned. Leeds were taken away in vans, dropped at the train station and put on the train home.

The police filming incidents had become common, along with CCTV cameras everywhere. In earlier years, lads at football could do pretty much what they wanted but things had shifted and more care was now needed. Another trip over the border was for the 'Battle of Britain' with Rangers in the European Cup in 1992. Officials banned all away supporters, for fear of trouble, but thirty or so drove up, including Griff, Sean, Neil from Goole and Gaz and Rowey from Doncaster. Gaz and a mate were at the ground for 5pm and got their hands on two hardhats. They entered the stadium by pretending to be workmen and whiled away the time fiddling with cables and wires and generally blagging it. They even tried to bring the club's flag to half mast. After several hours they were sussed and chucked out, but they did manage to get some tickets for the game.

The last match of the 1990/91 season was at Nottingham and Ronnie, Derek, Dave B and Mason were in a mob of thirty who went looking for Forest's Executive Crew in their regular pub. They were walking through a housing estate when forty or fifty

Forest appeared round a corner. They went for Leeds and Derek, who was at the front, charged into them, pulling a bottle from his pocket. Leeds chased them down the road but Derek and Mason got separated, and as Forest made a stand they started brawling in gardens using fencing as ammunition, with passers-by watching in shock.

In November 1994, when Forest were at Elland Road, Leeds were in the Spencers by the station when someone came in shouting, 'They're here.' Forest were on Boar Lane and Leeds came around the corner to meet them and it went toe-to-toe for a while before they got split up by Yates's, with Leeds on one side of the road and Forest on the other being moved away by coppers. Moose, one of the young lads to come through in the Nineties, was at the front and spotted a Lucozade bottle in a bin. In a rush of blood, he grabbed it and ran across the road to whack it over a Forest head. The police arrested half a dozen participants and when they went for Moose they ended up struggling on the floor with him as the two mobs carried on running at each other, meeting in the middle of the road before the police again calmed things down. Moose was accused of being a catalyst for the trouble and was carted off. Steve W, who had been near the station, and a few others followed Forest to the ground, enjoying a couple of scuffles en route.

Steve, a strapping lad from the Armley and Beeston areas, was another face to emerge in the Nineties. He knew all the lads, and was the same age as some of the VYT, but didn't go to matches until around the time of the Bournemouth carnage. He knocked about with Moose, among others, after getting to know him after various incidents at or away from Elland Road and found they had a similar attitude. As some were still into the club scene and others generally went to football less in the early Nineties, the next wave of younger lads were coming through and joined the hardcore that remained – Griff, Eddie, Slant, Carrot, Skiz, Craig, Bert, Pudsey Macca, Derek and F.

Early on in the decade, Steve attracted the attention of Calvert, the football intelligence officer for Leeds, prompting a mutual dislike. Steve was arrested along with several others for fighting with Forest one year and after a few other brushes with the law was subsequently jailed. He felt his card was marked after that. Calvert seemed to have his eye on him, always watching to try to catch him out, as he had Steve down as a main face, even though really he was just one of the lads.

One fight Steve was known for, mainly because of the visible injury he sustained, was with a well-known hardcase from south Leeds. Steve heard this guy was badmouthing him and when he challenged the bloke, it escalated into a fight. Apparently he had a reputation for biting and as they were rolling around on the floor he took a large chunk out of Steve's ear. He didn't notice until people shouted, 'Your ear!' while the bloke made a run for it down the road and into a house. After he was eventually persuaded to go to hospital, Steve received a phone call from the bloke asking to meet up. He agreed and they met at a sports centre. The bloke had brought back-up in the form of three others. Steve had one mate with him and told him to wait in the car. They started fighting one-on-one and Steve was getting the better of it when his opponent shouted 'Now!' and two of his mates came at Steve with house bricks. Deciding he needed some ammunition, Steve went to his car, where he had a set of golf clubs. When they saw that he was willing to carry on, they thought better of it. Word soon spread that the 'feud' was over, with Steve's reputation somewhat boosted.

Steve was part of another battle with Forest in the mid-Nineties which became known as the 'Baker's Dozen' amongst the Leeds lads who fought about sixty of them at their pub. Leeds were playing Derby and a few set off in a minibus, stopping at some pubs on the way, but in the end they decided to find Forest instead. They went to a pub near the train station, only to see fifty to sixty lads gather outside. Thinking they were Bury, who were playing at Notts County, the Leeds firm ran out and chased them down the street.

They moved on to another pub and had been in there for an hour when three lads came in and had a look around, obviously observing them. As they left, Steve hit one of them by the pub's swing doors. He then saw about another sixty outside, who tried to get in and attack them. Steve and Binnsy stood them at the door to stop them as tables went through the windows. When the cops arrived the landlord backed Leeds, saying Forest started the fight and tried to attack them. It is a story detailed in the book *Inside The Forest Executive Crew*, by Gary 'Boatsy' Clarke, and Steve has also had a few goes with the author and his mates at Kings Cross over the years.

A few weeks later, the match between Leeds and Leicester City was called off due to the weather. Forest were at home to Villa, so a Leeds minibus went over to seek them out instead. They arrived at the King John pub by the station before kick-off and when they saw some of Forest's firm inside, Eddie said, 'All right lads?'

'You Leeds?' said one startled lad.

Eddie intimidatingly tapped the side of his face and said, 'You fucking know we are.'

The locals left their pool cues and departed. After the game, they came back to the pub in ones and twos until there were about twenty of them, at which point Eddie said it was time to act. The thirteen or fourteen Leeds lads stood by the doors, eyeballing Forest, then Eddie kicked things off by booting one of them. Bottles went into the air just as a large contingent of police arrived and started making arrests. That left plenty thinking the police had been tipped off, or at best inadvertently alerted, by Forest. A copper went to arrest Eddie but he claimed he had been glassed, as he was already bleeding, and said he needed to go to hospital. The copper just told him to 'fuck off', so he did, and they left in the minibus.

* * *

Since being back in the top division under the stewardship of Howard Wilkinson, pundits had spoken of a 'wind of change' sweeping through Elland Road. They also noted Wilkinson's controversial decision to remove pictures in the foyer from the Revie golden years in a bid to let new players make their mark. With players like Gordon Strachan, Gary Speed and Lee Chapman, Leeds were alive and kicking again. They played in the European Cup in the early Nineties and, after drawing at Spurs in the last game of the 1994/95 season, beat Newcastle to a place in the UEFA

Cup. The following season they targeted a place in the final of the Coca-Cola Cup, but first they had to overcome Birmingham City in a two-legged semi-final.

As their coaches queued in the traffic by St Andrews, the lads spotted a group of Zulus in a pub and its car park. Bricks hit the vehicles as they got nearer to the pub and they could see what was coming, so some decided to get off and tackle them. Their coach was heaving with lads but in the end only about twenty got off. They opened the emergency exit to find a copper outside on his bike, who said they couldn't leave the coach. Someone pushed him over and they headed for the pub.

The Zulus' attention was on the coaches in the traffic when Leeds ran towards them in the car park. It kicked off with about thirty Zulus and Leeds felt they had the upper hand as it spilt out on the road near a traffic island. More Zulus were there, easily doubling their numbers, with one distinctly dressed in a long leather trench coat. A Leeds lad got hit in the face with a brick and a copper fell off his horse as he tried to grab another during the trouble. As things calmed down, the twenty started walking the short distance to St Andrews and watched their backs all the way, expecting another onslaught any minute. It never came. However, some other lads were attacked when they were spotted parking their cars. They were surrounded and though they stood and fought they were pummelled by overwhelming numbers.

Outside the ground, Eddie was with Paul and Brian from Leicester and a lad called Grays, a main face in Leicester City's firm. Eddie had a ticket for the Birmingham seats and was trying unsuccessfully to get in. Some Blues lads were staring at him and Grays, so Eddie responded, 'What are you looking at? You know who we are.' The Brummies went off, only to return with a huge black lad as Eddie was talking to ex-Leeds player Noel Whelan. Eddie and the black lad started fighting and were rolling around on the floor but Grays didn't join in and was trying to get Eddie to stop, much to his surprise as he thought he was a reputable lad with Leicester. The stewards waded in and broke it up before police arrived. When he did get into the ground, Eddie went into the seats and sat there on his own but the Zulus left him to it.

The return fixture at Elland Road was the scene of much jubilation after a 3-0 victory and confirmation that Leeds were off to a Wembley final for the first time in twenty-three years. Mick T, Crabby and Johnna encountered a vanload of Blues lads on the way to the ground as they walked over the bypass near the turn off for Elland Road from the motorway. They were about to cut through an industrial estate when the van pulled up and the door opened and the Blues lads motioned for them to come over for a fight. Johnna half-heartedly shouted for the Brummies to come to them instead as they carried on walking. They were more interested in watching the match and hadn't been involved in trouble for ages. There seemed to be about fifteen in the van and they didn't look like typical lads, as they were so badly dressed. They were in proper Seventies get-up, looking like extras from *Life on Mars*. One even resembled the Yorkshire Ripper, with black hair and a beard, flares and platforms, with another possibly wearing a three-star jumper. The most vocal of the group was a smallish guy with a balding head who looked like Roland Rat.

Johnna told them it looked like they hadn't been out since Leeds had beaten them at Hillsborough in 1972, and with that they got out and started to walk towards them. The trio stood where they were and when the lads ran into them they all fell backwards into some bushes before the Brummies went back to their van and drove off. The three untangled themselves from the bushes and were all laughing as no one was actually hit and they didn't know what to make of it.

They carried on to the ground and saw the van again nearer Elland Road. The Blues lads started jeering, like they had just done something, but the lads laughed at them. They saw them pull into the car park outside the ground and someone suggested going to find them after the game for a proper battle, but after a resounding victory by Leeds, they couldn't be bothered. Wembley fever took over. However, others did encounter some Zulus and give them credit for what they did. Seven or eight coaches had made the trip from Birmingham. They were escorted into Leeds by a couple of police motorcyclists but hit heavy traffic. Wally, one of the Zulus' main lads, decided to jump from the back of his coach onto the road. Others followed suit, leaving the coaches to continue into the city bereft of passengers – bar one – with their drivers unaware that everyone had got off. They were spotted coming round the back of the old supporters' club and down the steps from Fullerton Park. The Leeds lads that were queuing to go in B-Block in the West Stand saw them come down the stairs and started shouting, 'They're here!' and it kicked off in the car park and under the stand for several minutes and a good battle was had before the police waded in.

A month later it was Aston Villa in the final. A big mob went down to London on the Friday, met at Kings Cross and went round the West End looking for Villa's hooligans, but didn't find any. Saturday was the same, so some went up to Camden, where they had a bit of a clash with Chelsea. On the Sunday of the game, everyone congregated at Kings Cross again, and filling five pubs. Again Villa were nowhere – even a mooch at Euston yielded nothing – so they left some spotters.

As kick-off neared everyone started to make their way to Wembley, stopping off at various pubs en route. They approached the stadium with half an hour to spare and there were many thousands of Villa there, but no hooligans. People were going in the pubs looking for them and it wasn't until five minutes before kick off, just as the lads were about to go in, that Villa appeared. Leeds ran down towards them but Villa legged it and the few that didn't run praised Leeds for having a do with the Blues in the semis. They didn't want to know and Leeds have never really had much trouble with them, apart from one time when a few Leeds came unstuck in their end in 1987.

The Nineties drew to a close with a major battle with Portsmouth at Fratton Park in 1999. A mutual respect had existed between the two firms since the Eighties, and only a couple of seasons earlier they had fought at Elland Road. Eddie and a few others had been milling about near a fish and chip shop when they met a similar number of Pompey. 'Fancy it?' they asked, and Pompey said they did. That was it, with stop-start fighting for a good ten minutes all the way to the railway bridge. Eddie's mob were doing fine until they got to a car park full of Pompey, who then 'booted the fuck' out of them. 'We came back with bottles and had another go,' he recalled. 'It was a good do, we were outnumbered and they were a decent firm. When we were watching England v. Italy in the World Cup qualifiers for the 1998 tournament, the first bar we walked in we saw the same lads. There were loads of them there so I said, "Remember me?" and they were like, "Yeah, you're Leeds, from that row at yours?" We stayed drinking with them and had a good laugh until some of them got too leery towards the end of the night. It was uncanny to bump into them though.'

For the 1999 game, a mob of about 150 went on the train. One group managed to get thirteen rail tickets for £10 each instead of paying a full total price of £750. Instead of getting off at Fratton Park, they stayed on until the last stop, Portsmouth Harbour, and then hit the pubs. The police soon located them and waited outside until they got back on the train to Fratton. They arrived to find a situation akin to the early Eighties, with hardly any police around. Some suggest this was due to a dispute between the club and the cops over the bill for policing games. Leeds walked up to their end and a copper asked, 'Home or away lads?' After the inevitable answer of 'Home' they went down towards Pompey's end. Fighting broke out with about twenty of their lads and they tried to get more to join in but Leeds 'slaughtered' them, according to some of those who were there. More Leeds appeared but were blocked off by police and when they went to go in the ground it was clear that about seventy lads didn't have tickets, so they were made to get a train back to London.

After the game, in which Leeds whipped them 5-1, word had obviously spread about the battle outside and 2-300 of the 6.57 Crew gathered, kept back by police. When Leeds got together, numbering about forty, some were shocked by how few there were, not realising so many had been turned away without tickets. Pompey fought with the police as they tried to get at Leeds, with several getting truncheoned. Some were on the same side as Leeds, mingling in, and soon things escalated.

With their numbers, Pompey could have murdered Leeds if they had run at them but instead there were pockets of fighting in the road as the police lost control. The brawling was soon non-stop and seemed to centre around three streets, with lads chasing and being chased through the alleyways between the houses. Some Leeds described themselves as being 'pebble-dashed' after Pompey chucked gravel at them and at one point Gaz from Donny, a fair-sized lad, was grabbed by a copper but managed to wriggle free. He swapped jackets with a smaller mate and could hardly move in it. A couple of Pompey lads got wedged in one alleyway or ginnel and Paul and Jono laid into them – hitting them with a For Sale sign as well as punching them.

'It's normally a ten minute walk to the station but it took us a good forty-five minutes because of the trouble and running battles,' said Paul. 'When we got there, Pompey were throwing bricks and had us under pressure for a bit and we were ducking behind parked cars. In the end we knocked a wall over and threw the bricks and debris back at them, then chased after them, but the police came and that was that. When we finally got back to Kings Cross we went looking for Spurs but the cops had it under control. We still decided to go home via Manchester on the off-chance but nothing happened.'

On the train to Leeds, they encountered an odd bloke who said he had just got out of prison and was banned from West Yorkshire. He had paperwork on him stating he couldn't enter the county boundaries. He started offering people out and taking the piss but nobody took him up on it. They got back to Leeds at about 3am and over the coming weeks waited for any CCTV pictures to appear in the papers or knocks on their doors, but it turned out the images were too blurred to see who they were. Subsequent conversations with Pompey saw them admit they got battered, despite their numbers and so few Leeds.

Man City in the Cup in 2000 saw a 'right mob' of 4-500 Leeds walk to Maine Road. Big Tony from Man United was an impressed observer and asked Benny and others why Leeds hadn't brought the same numbers to theirs over the past few years. Hassle with the membership scheme at the club and the fact that the 'straight members' snapped up any tickets for Old Trafford had always had a big impact on the numbers the firm took there. For the City game, however, they were out in force, as Eddie remembered:

The Scum

We had an excellent mob that day. Big Tony was like, fuck me, right mob. We got on a bit of the forecourt and there was a bit of to-ing and fro-ing, not that much happening. Leeds were already losing 2-0 by then but we ended up winning 5-2. As we were coming out, the cops suddenly shut the gates and people got a bit crushed. The gates were getting pushed and about forty managed to get out – me, China, Jono, the usual suspects and the best forty you could wish to escape with. We slipped off into a side street, found about sixty City and ran at them. They shit themselves. We chased them, caught a few and left them on the floor, then chased after the others and it went on like this for ages, catching them up and fighting. The ones we'd left behind on the floor would catch up with us and hit us from behind. One lad got me with a right sidewinder from behind and I was like a dying fly on the wall of this terraced house. China was pissing himself laughing at me.

After that, we were in some park with a fence round it and could see a mob of City. The cops were about but we told them, 'They're our mates, let us go and meet them,' and they believed us and let us cut through the park. We piled into City and just kept running into them, fighting and chasing them all the way into the city centre. In the end the cops had enough and hit us with truncheons. 'What are you doing?' we said. 'We're coming into the city centre and they've been getting us.' They ran all day but we did have an awesome mob and they couldn't have done us.

Over the years we've had some right do's with them, especially with their Young Guvnors. Them and Spurs are the ones we met most when we were in the Second Division. But I don't know where City get their reputation from. A few have definitely stood but you need more than ones, twos and threes to stand to make a decent mob, maybe they have too many hangers-on.

A few months later, Leeds were at Sunderland and the lads headed over on coaches. Eddie was off the coach as soon as they arrived and into the nearest Mackems he encountered, with others following him and getting stuck into the Stone Island-clad locals.

As soon as we arrived they were shouting, 'C'mon,' so I hit the first one I saw. Those that came off the coach after me had a go too and a few Leeds got arrested. Their lads were pointing out loads of ours to the cops. It was the only time I'd been to their ground and I remember everyone singing: 'Thank you very much for Michael Bridges' as we hadn't long bought him from them. Afterwards a few of their lads came over but they'd been pointing people out so I didn't have time for them. One lad in a lot of denim was saying something but I just said, 'Fuck off Shaking Stevens.'

19

LIVING THE DREAM

THE EUROPEAN TRIPS dotted throughout the mid-to-late Nineties were bigger on drinking and laughs than they were on fighting. Following Leeds was a pricey hobby for a couple of seasons as the club 'lived the dream', so lads either picked carefully or went anyway and worried about it later. Visiting places like Russia and Ukraine was an eye-opener, although seeing the historical highlights was rarely top of the agenda. Big Tony from Manchester started organising some of these trips for them after approaching Benny and others. The club had a few issues with the lads choosing his trips over its own, but his touting abilities meant he could get tickets for those otherwise unable to obtain them through official channels – which sometimes meant they would end up in the home end.

When Leeds qualified for the UEFA Cup in 1995, officials said fans could only go to watch the team play Monaco if they were in a membership scheme. Loads went anyway and found they could pay on the gate. Lads that had bought tickets beforehand sold them for double the price and then paid the nominal price of £6 or so to get in. Leeds United were charging something like £25. Eddie knew how cheap it was from a previous holiday in the south of France so he went to the ground early and bought twenty tickets. Before kick-off, a journalist for the BBC's *Look North* regional news programme was reporting on the shortage of tickets when Eddie pulled out his wad of tickets and brandished it in front of the cameras, saying how easy it was to get them. Scuffles later broke out with police as lads and fans tried to get into the ground and Eddie started fighting with one copper. When Eddie was punched on the chin, a more senior officer stepped in and made his junior apologise. More fighting broke out with the police inside and Eddie got 'battered to fuck' on some stairs, resulting in his T- shirt and

265

trainers being ripped off. The coppers said, 'Not you again?' and left truncheon marks across his legs.

Some dodgy currency notes had done the rounds of Doncaster ahead of the match, and after police raids one lad decided to disappear and headed out early to Monaco. Others thought an investment in some amphetamine would provide a nice little earner on the trip, so they wrapped it up in condoms and stashed it in the boot of the thirty-two-seater coach. In France they discovered that some of it had got caught in the boot mechanism and had shifted whenever it had been opened en route. The driver must have been bemused to see them continually hanging around the back of the coach as they desperately tried to retrieve their stash.

Some went prepared for trouble, taking flares and stun guns which they carried with them into the bars of Monaco. One lad wanted to try out his stun gun on Gaz but he was having none of it, instead pointing out a random guy walking in the opposite direction. The lad went over and zapped him, causing him to shoot backwards onto his arse from the shock. He got on his mobile phone and within seconds cars started pulling up out of nowhere and police appeared, rushing to help him. He had stun-gunned the Mayor of Nice. It was in the papers the next day and the lad decided to get the next train home.

One of the Leicester brothers, Paul, started the trip at a service station on the M1, where he met a couple of mates at midnight on the Sunday. There they also met travel organiser Scotty and his party, who told them they would be meeting a lad at Gatwick with information and tickets. They parked at Heathrow, as they were flying back to there, then got a coach to Gatwick, where they spent an anxious few hours waiting to meet this lad whilst panicking because they couldn't see any flights to Genoa, where they assumed they would be heading. They didn't know their flight number or what this lad looked like but he eventually turned up with the news that they were flying to Nice instead.

As soon as they checked in they went straight to the bar, drinking six pints in half an hour – those who know the two brothers well know that this isn't beyond the realms of possibility, as they like a drink – and met up with another mate, Ian from Bicester. They were seated at the back of the plane and one of the lads was asked what he wanted to drink. He got a couple of beers and then realised the drink was free, so he asked for all the lager and vodka they had. The air stewardess started filling his table with cans and miniatures as the rest of the plane looked on. He had three cans left as they came in to land but managed to finish them off as they hit the runway. Needless to say, after no sleep and no food he was carried off the flight and things were sketchy after that.

They checked into the hotel and then hit the bars, catching up with the other lads. Paul was a self-confessed nightmare because of the state he was in. There was fighting with the Turks who lived around the train station, with CS gas being let off, but generally everyone was out enjoying themselves ahead of the match. When Paul sobered up later on he was aware that his eye was sore and his knuckles were bleeding, although he had no idea why or how he managed to lose everyone he was with. He wandered around lost in his shorts for a while, then kipped on a bench until daylight, when he tried all the hotels to see if they recognised him, as he could not remember where he was staying. During his wanderings, a black bloke tried striking up a conversation with him and when he told him to fuck off, the bloke said, 'Ahh, English, do you want to buy a diamond ring?' He showed it and demonstrated its alleged authenticity by dragging it down a shop window, scratching the glass. Paul wasn't interested and walked off as the guy from the shop came out and started shouting at the bloke for damaging his window. Their argument escalated into a fight and Paul stood watching through his one good eye before leaving them to it. Eventually he found his hotel after seeing some Leeds fans outside. Paul and his brother Brian provided great amusement on several trips due to their constant bickering, drinking capacity and subsequent adventures.

Everyone was back out in the bars again later. A coachload of schoolchildren pulled up outside one bar by the train station and some started waving. One girl lifted up her top to reveal a Man U shirt, which didn't go down well, and the mood instantly changed, with chairs and tables being lobbed at the coach. The look on the kids' faces turned to horror and staff set about shutting the bar as the police arrived. The lads realised they had overreacted in the heat of the moment and were out of order. They decamped to the hotels, where they started knocking on each other's doors and letting off fire extinguishers when they opened them. Some unlucky lads had their eyebrows shaved off. When an Oriental chap opened his door and got sprayed, he came out and adopted a karate stance and started brawling with the perpetrator.

Although the police were expecting trouble at the match it passed off peacefully and was a 3-0 victory to Leeds. When the Doncaster contingent went home on the coach, they discovered the police had phoned the coach company asking if the lad who had done a moonlight flit was on board. So he got off at Calais and hooked up with a truck driver. The rest stopped at a hypermarket to stock up on beer, where they warned the driver he had a sizeable stash of amphetamine trapped in his boot. He helped them get it out and get rid of it before sailing home.

For PSV Eindhoven a month later, security was tighter and the lads heard the club had stirred up the Dutch authorities, so tickets were hard to come by. Nevertheless, Benny managed to get some for their end. They could see the police were stopping people near the turnstiles and checking if they were Dutch before they could go in. Benny, Brian, a lad from Watford who was half Dutch, Gilly and Dave Maddox from Bradford – who was dressed in a T-shirt on a freezing night and therefore obviously English – saw plenty of English lads being turned back. Benny and Brian persevered and got in the queue. The ensuing conversation with the police went like this:

Copper: 'Where are you from?'

Benny: 'I am from Schweden on my holidays.'

Copper: 'Passport?'

Benny: 'Why do I need my passport when I am out on my holidays? I do not bring it out, I have come to watch the football...'

With that he was let in. When it came to Brian, he repeated the only bit of Dutch he could remember, which was something his mum said at the dinner table when he was younger. He could have asked the copper to pass the salt but he got in too. The others weren't so lucky or as good at using their ingenuity and were amazed at Benny passing for a Swedish tourist when, as Gilly put it, he 'looks less like a Swede than any of us.'

The match police were strict. They had chartered a plane in Amsterdam in preparation for any deportations and rounded up lads who didn't have ID on them – you are legally obliged to carry it at all times in Holland. Many were taken to an aircraft hangar and kept there in plastic handcuffs, without food or water, for twenty-four hours before being put on the plane and deported to Leeds-Bradford Airport. Most had left their belongings wherever they were staying and had to get mates to bring it home. Even those who had come by car were forced to leave their vehicles in Holland.

CS Maritimo in Madeira in September 1998 marked George Graham's last game in charge before he left for Spurs. Leeds won 4-1 on penalties after extra time and as Graham walked off the pitch two lads, Paul and Holmesy, gave him a load of abuse over his departure. He responded by telling them curtly to 'fuck off'. Back at the hotels some lads found out where one of the West Yorkshire coppers was staying and charged loads of champagne to his room. To this day he doesn't know who was responsible but promises he will find out and seek revenge.

Visas were required for the trip to Lokomotiv Moscow the following season and Benny was the one collecting passports and sorting out visas with Big Tony, their travel agent. Between 150 and 200 lads booked to go, and when they all met at St Pancras, Benny handed out their documents in envelopes before they set off to Heathrow. The lads drank the plane dry and then started on the duty free, with bottles of whisky and vodka for £6 or £7. It helped to take their minds off the decidedly ropey plane they were on, as Aeroflot tended to use museum pieces.

The Leicester brothers got into an argument with each other and when the plane was coming in to land, they were rolling around in the aisle, despite attempts by the cabin crew to get them to sit down. They were still scuffling at passport control and when they came to hand over their documents, it became clear they had each other's visas. Armed guards took them to a room for questioning while the rest of the lads, about three coachloads, were left waiting. One of the brothers tried to drop kick the door, which can't have helped proceedings, but eventually they were released. Their squabbling continued at the huge hotel they were booked into, with people just stepping over them by then, letting them get on with it. One of the lads was in a lift with several American couples in tuxedos and ball gowns when the doors opened to reveal the brothers rolling around on the carpet.

Out in the bars and roaming the streets, some sampled the beer and the cheap hotdogs sold by street vendors. The food on offer was generally rank. Some went to a pizzeria in search of Western nourishment but found it didn't actually serve pizzas and when John from south Leeds asked for tomato soup he was presented with a bowl of water with a tomato in. The Leicester brothers ended up in a hotel bar and had practically drunk themselves sober. They were sat in the foyer watching people coming and going when three or four blokes in suits and leather jackets went into a shop opposite them and started helping themselves to the merchandise and ransacked the till. The shop assistant did nothing, but thinking it was some kind of robbery, the lads went over and asked what was going on. The assistant tried to tell them it was okay and not to get involved and the men laughed at them and then left. After this brush with the local mafia, they carried on drinking with others dotted about the bars.

The hotel they were in was massive and overlooked Red Square. There were always blokes in black polo necks on the door offering taxis or 'other services'. Most knew to steer clear of them but one lad didn't and inevitably got stung. The lad, from Farsley, got into one of their cabs but after a few minutes the driver turned around with a gun and ordered him to hand over all his money and any jewellery, and to take off his clothes. He ended up on the wrong side of a four-lane dual carriageway in his boxer shorts. He could see the lights of the hotel in the distance, and as he went through an underpass on his way back in the freezing cold, three junkies tried to mug him.

As well as the local hoodlums, there were numerous 'fit' Russian hookers at the hotel, mostly teenagers or in their early twenties and many of them students. 'They made a fortune, even the ugly one was paid just to fuck off,' said one lad. Smithy asked Benny if he could have his room keys, as he had plans after hiring two hookers for the price of one. When told that all of the trip money was stashed away there and the girls might steal it, the lad said, 'Nah, don't worry, I'm going to tie them up and things.' Another lad from Worksop was seen being led up the stairs. 'Oi, where you going?' shouted one of his mates. 'I'll not be a minute,' he replied knowingly. Other lads were told they could watch one session and chairs were set out in a room, but when the two hookers were brought up they were unsurprisingly reluctant to perform in front of such an audience, and left.

It was icy cold and of the 2,500-odd fans that went, about 2,450 wore big Russian fur hats. Some went to see Lenin's Tomb, under the watchful eye of the armed guards. Before kick-off, one group went into a bar and got chatting to the locals. They were drinking some potent concoction which was being passed around, while the lads were drinking whisky. One Russki asked what they were on and someone jokingly said it was piss, which didn't go down well. Minutes later the army appeared and turfed them all out. After the game, the Russian police were trying to sell their hats and badges for dollars. It was a memorable trip, especially for those who overslept, missed the flight home and had to pay extra and the others who lost their passports.

* * *

As Leeds continued to progress through the group stages, the next trip most went on was AS Roma in March. About 7,000 fans travelled to the Italian capital, many spending several days there. Steve and Moose were among those who got a bus to the ground but ended up getting off onto a long road at the wrong stop, at Roma's end. There were twelve of them, including Griff, his son and a Bristol City lad.

They walked towards the ground looking for a way in when they saw a large mob, some in flying jackets, coming down the road – armed with flare guns, knives, sticks and nunchaku. Steve and Moose decided to run towards them and the mob accelerated. They knew they had bitten off more than they could chew but ran into them, with the remaining ten behind as back-up. The locals swarmed around them and out of the twelve, Steve and Moose came out of it the least injured. Griff's son was stabbed three times, Griff had a flare fired at him which went in his shirt, the Bristol City fan was also hit with a flare and someone else was stabbed in the head.

One Italian came at Moose with a stick but dropped it and when Moose bent down to pick it up his right foot slipped underneath him. The Italians all tried to put the boot in but Leeds fought them off him. They then saw Griff had his son in his arms, with blood everywhere. It was clear he was in a bad way. Fortunately at that point the police came and started sorting people out and taking the injured to hospital. Steve and Moose were arrested but were walked round to the Leeds end and released. About twenty minutes later, they went looking for Roma again and had 'a bit of ding-dong' with them but the police had it under control. Plenty of people said afterwards that they were lucky not to have come home in black boxes that night.

Prague later the same month was another troublesome fixture with the locals. About a dozen lads were chatting to some Prague fans in scarves, only to draw abuse from a bar full of skinheads who supported another local team and who shouted at their fellow Czechs for talking to Leeds. The Twins from Donny went straight into the bar, which emptied, and it kicked off outside. The skins backed off for ten seconds until they saw how few Leeds there were and then came back into them, with their biggest lads demanding one-on-ones. Police stopped it from escalating. In the ground Prague chased Leeds around their section in the stands but were reluctant to come directly at them.

Back in a bar afterwards, Gaz from Donny was leaning against a post with his pint but it wasn't secure and he toppled over. Somehow he managed to keep his pint intact, something a Leeds copper there at the time still reminds him about. A mob of Prague then appeared, resembling a neo-Nazi rally in cropped hair and flying jackets. Gaz and his mate Paul threw a bin at them as others brawled in the street until a bloke let off a gunshot in the air. Most people dived for the deck until it emerged he was a plain clothes police officer, and the Czech police and Black Stan, a Leeds football intelligence officer, ushered everyone back into the pub. The staff said they were closing the bar, so the police lined everyone up against a wall. Benny was next to Paul and every time he spoke to him he got a slap from the cops. Everyone was put in vans and taken back to the hotel. Benny was one of the last ones to leave and thought he was going to get nicked but Stan told the police he was with him and they drove him back in a police car.

The next match was away to the Turkish side Galatasaray in the UEFA Cup semi-final. Every Leeds fan, indeed every football fan, is well aware of what happened there. Two Leeds fans, Christopher Loftus and Kevin Speight, were stabbed to death in a horrific attack in Istanbul. A Turkish thug was arrested and sentenced to fifteen years' imprisonment for the stabbing, but the sentence was later reduced to five years, a decision which disgusted many observers, while five others were given lesser sentences of under four months. Few of the people interviewed for this book wanted to speak in any depth about those tragic events, as the scars still run too deep. 'The locals had been run three or four times but they were picking people off as they came back and they got innocents,' said Eddie. 'There is no closure for either family, as the sentences were a joke. For that to happen to those two lads is a tragedy. They were not interested in violence, just having a drink and watching their team. All those lies about Leeds lads pissing on a Turkish flag were just an excuse for them to get away with their actions. But events like this bring a lot of fans together.'

The first opponents Leeds faced in their momentous Champions League campaign in the 2000/01 season was 1860 Munich. New legislation after the Euro 2000 tournament meant more restrictions and some lads were either refused permission to leave the UK or were sent back after arriving in Munich if their name appeared on a list of not just convicted hooligans but also suspected ones. Certain people had to surrender their passports and special courts were set up near ports and main railway stations to enforce travel bans.

Those who made it to Munich were soon out in the bars and mooching about. Some congregated in a huge square called the Hofbrauhaus, an area filled with bars where tourists are served by women in traditional Bavarian dress. Hitler had given speeches here and sieg-heiling was not just frowned upon but illegal. It didn't stop many from making the straight-arm salute and attracting the attention of the police. There had already been trouble with some Turks, whose domain was around the train station, so the police were well aware of the Leeds presence. The army even appeared among the unimpressed locals and sixteen visitors were ultimately arrested – eleven from Doncaster and others from Leeds, Wakefield and Harrogate, including three identified halfway though the match. They were told they would be serving a twelve-month sentence and, once in custody, were forced to have an Aids test. Gaz from Donny and another lad were the only ones to refuse and after a while, the police brought in some hefty guards to cajole them. They asked what would happen if they didn't go through with it and were told, 'Ve vill hold you down and jab the needle in your armz.' With that, the lads thought it prudent to roll up their sleeves and slap their arms to get a vein.

They were incarcerated in the only Category A prison in Bavaria and found themselves two to a wing, mixed in with Turkish criminals, general nutters and hardened racists who were keen to give them propaganda leaflets. While solicitors worked to secure their release, they got their heads down and dealt with being locked up for twenty-three hours a day while trying to identify the revolting food. Dipping their fingers in mini tubs of chocolate was about as much sustenance as they got. They also got their hands on some German magazines and got a shock when one contained an article and pictures of the murderous events in Galatasaray.

Most lads shared cells but Ado from Donny and Moose from Leeds were on their own. Moose had a Yugoslavian and a Russian as neighbours. Others were dotted all around the jail overlooking a courtyard and would shout across to one another. The Turkish inmates prayed several times a day and after a while it became too much for the Brits. As the sun set one day and the Muslims began to chant, Ado, with legs dangling out of his window, started a rousing chorus of 'Rule Britannia'. The others were quick to join in to drown out the Turkish inmates. Their nightmare was over a few weeks later when they were released and sent back home.

Milan in November saw another lad get deported after some trouble with Italians in a bar. The Leicester brothers, Paul and Brian, had been drinking all day long and got into another of their infamous arguments, which was overheard by a group of Italian blokes in the corner. When one came over with a Burberry scarf over his face, he was punched. One of the brothers dashed off into the back of the bar and hid in some sheds before a woman stumbled across him and screamed. He was apprehended, pistol whipped, hit with a traffic sign and taken to the cells – it emerged that the man he had hit was a plain clothes police officer who suffered a bruised jaw. He was in court the next day and was given a six-month sentence, suspended for five years, and a six-month ban from Italian football effective immediately, so he couldn't go to the game that night. He was also banned from Milan for five years. A year after that, he was issued with a two-year ban from matches in England and Wales by the Home Office.

Leeds drew 1-1 to go through to the second phase of the competition on aggregate after an earlier victory against the Italian giants. There were jubilant scenes, with Peter Ridsdale greeting the fans in the stadium and conducting a stirring chorus of 'Marching on Together'. The players stayed on the pitch and watched replays on the giant screen, arm in arm.

About 8,000 had gone to Milan but only 1,000 made the trip to Lazio a month later, enjoying a good booze-up in Rome without any hassle from their fans. It was then a couple of months before the next run of games, which started with Anderlecht. The day before that match, Paul, Brian and another lad from Leicester went over on the Eurostar and started drinking as soon as they arrived in Brussels. They were out all night and hooked up with a Leeds fan from Hull called Doc, who turned out to be a headcase. In one bar they were randomly taking photos of people and objects for a giggle, but as the drinks flowed Doc glassed the waiter in the face. They thought it best to leave but some undercover police swooped on them and arrested them. They were put in cells which resembled cages for the night, Paul and Brian in one and the other two in another. The Hull lunatic started trying to bite through the bars and was going berserk at being locked up. When the police came to quieten him down they had a go at him with their batons, while his cellmate sat terrified at the back. The police decided the only way to knock him off the bars was to hit his teeth, so they did – and several fell out onto the floor. Eventually, they dragged him out, his face a bloodied mess.

'We were all told we were to appear in court the next day and because of that the police said we needed to be examined by medics,' said Leicester Paul. 'Three of us were taken to a hospital in a van but we had no idea where Doc was. Plastic tags were put on our wrists. I managed to get free of mine and the others couldn't stop laughing because I was waving at the police and then pretending to put them back on. They eventually caught on and tightened them up. A doctor appeared with a hypodermic needle and wrongly thought our mate was the troublemaker from the cells. They asked him to get up. He was asking why and then some police came in and held him down while we were cracking up with laughter. They gave him a tranquillizer and then took us all back to the same cells.

'We spent a night on wooden beds wondering what was going to happen but the next morning we were in court via a computer link, although we didn't realise what was happening at first. An officer told us we were to be deported, which was really what we wanted to hear. We were then taken to our hotel and packed while still in handcuffs. We were driven under flashing lights to Antwerp and dropped off at the airport. When our flight was ready, the police shook our hands and said, rather bizarrely, "Very well done and good luck." We were put on a plane with leather seats and free beer all the way home.

'When we had been in the hospital, we had decided that we were going to batter Doc the next time we saw him because he had caused us all the hassle. But when we saw him at the airport he looked like he had been hit by a juggernaut. He'd taken a real battering and had lost some teeth, so we left it. When we landed we went out in London and had an excellent night out as the match kicked off back in Brussels.'

Some of the lads at the match paid to go in Anderlecht's end, while others blagged Sky TV bibs and passes and got in for nothing. 'We sat in their stand and it was a bit tasty,' said Benny. 'It reminded me of being in Millwall's end. Alan Smith scored two of the four goals and a kid next to us told us to leave because we were English. I came out with a fake accent, denying I was English, but the others were cracking up around me. This kid wasn't convinced and went to punch me, but Musky caught his hand and he fell backwards. The rest of their crowd in the stand were all watching and we thought it was time to leave and tried to get out onto a gangway.' Two skinheads in flying jackets stood nearby and Russ, a Cockney White who was over from his home in Spain, punched one of them as he ran past. They then ran down some stairs and could hear footsteps behind, so at the bottom they hotfooted it into the hospitality area and watched the second half on TV.

Leeds eventually reached the semi-finals, where they drew the Spanish side Valencia. They beat Deportivo to get there and local news programmes showed clips of one emotional fan, in his sixties, hardly able to speak as the tears streamed down his face. 'I just can't explain. It's so many years since we've been this far…it's a dream,' he stuttered. But after a 0-0 draw at home and a 3-0 loss in Spain, the dream was over.

Losing to Arsenal in the domestic league saw Leeds finish fourth and miss out on another stab at Champions League football. The team did make it to the fourth round of the UEFA Cup in the 2001/02 season but were knocked out by PSV Eindhoven. David O'Leary brought in Robbie Fowler for £11 million and Seth Johnson for £7 million, which took his total spend to £100 million. To fund the extravagance, the club took a securitised, twenty-five-year loan of £60 million, which meant results were now vital. They finished fifth in the Premiership, which gave them another UEFA Cup slot but was a poor return on such an expensive squad.

One of the amusing tales from the following season's cup campaign was a trip to Metalurg Zaporizhia in the Ukraine. It was obviously a poor country where a round of drinks cost less than £2.

When the plane carrying some of the lads touched down, the doors opened at the back of the aircraft and people walked out past rusting cranes with grass growing on them. The lads were shocked to see some move and realised they were still in use. In a taxi to the ground, the driver switched his engine off at traffic lights to save petrol and when they tipped him he thought they were buying his car. It was another good trip and the lads were surprised to discover that the locals had heard of the Service Crew, even a woman they got chatting to on a train.

The last European trip was to be in Malaga in November 2002. The lads were well aware that things were coming apart within the club and it meant a lot went for a last blast. Before the game, 100 Leeds walked up to the ground and surveyed the Spanish fans queuing up. One older lad said, 'Fuck this, last chance...' and everyone charged them.

* * *

It had been a rollercoaster few seasons with O'Leary's vigorous spending – signing Rio Ferdinand for a British record £18 million followed by the likes of Viduka, Matteo and Dacourt. But events away from football attracted headlines for the wrong reasons. Jonathan Woodgate, Lee Bowyer and two friends were accused of attacking a twenty-one-year-old student outside a club in Leeds in January 2000. The trial was drawn out over the club's most successful season for years. After a ten-week hearing costing several million pounds, the case collapsed in April 2001 as the jury were considering their verdicts. The *Sunday Mirror* published an article that the judge decided could prejudice the case, forcing him to call a halt to proceedings. A retrial was ordered and the four were back in court in October. *Sunday Mirror* editor Colin Myler resigned three days later.

The attack victim, Sarfraz Najeib, had been bitten on the face and suffered a broken leg, nose and cheekbone, and the media hung on every detail, especially when teammate Michael Duberry gave evidence for the prosecution. Duberry had been cleared of conspiracy charges at the first trial and said Woodgate told him he had been involved in a fight outside the Majestyk night club, something Woodgate vehemently denied. When the trial drew to a close, the jury spent twenty-two hours deliberating before returning not guilty verdicts of GBH on Woodgate, Bowyer and Neale Caveney. The fourth defendant, Paul Clifford, was convicted of GBH and of a second charge of affray and was jailed for six years. Woodgate and Caveney were, however, convicted of affray and sentenced to community service. Bowyer was cleared. The victim's family said the verdicts were a 'tremendous disappointment'. While the judge said there was no racist motive for the attack, Mr Najeib's family took a different view and spoke of a race-hate campaign against them, with tyres being slashed and threats made.

Club chairman Peter Ridsdale had told the media that 'Leeds United was not on trial' and later confirmed the players would be able to continue playing for the club. However, the incident was further inflamed when extracts of O'Leary's book *Leeds United On Trial* were published in the *News of the World* within days of the court case ending. In it he criticised the two players, saying they 'let Leeds United down and the way they carried on in the streets of Leeds is disgraceful'. O'Leary defended the timing of the serialisation, saying there was only one chapter on the trial and that he could not prevent the serialisation, adding that he would not get any money for it. His book also revealed that the club hired a private detective to investigate Woodgate and Bowyer's stories.

For its part in the debacle, the *Sunday Mirror* was later ordered to pay £175,000 in fines and costs for the story that caused the collapse of the first trial. The paper ran a double-page interview with the victim's father who said the motive for the attack was racist, something the judge made clear to the jury was not part of the prosecution's case. Lord Justice Kennedy ruled that the newspaper's decision had been 'expensive and traumatic for the complainant, his family, witnesses and defendants alike'. After the hearing, Trinity Mirror said, 'We accept that we deserved to be punished.'

20

INFANT HIT SQUAD

AROUND 2000, FIVE or six small groups of lads, most aged in their early twenties, began meeting up in the pubs in the city and then going together to matches. As trouble was now more sporadic, they began to arrange rows separately from the older mobs. After a couple of years of doing their own thing, they came together properly to form the Infant Hit Squad. The IHS drained what they could out of a dying scene, before lengthy bans kicked in – one of them ended up in HMP Strangeways for the relatively minor act of throwing a dustbin in a fight with Manchester United. Numerous bans issued after trouble with Cardiff at home in 2005 meant some could not even enter the city centre, so fewer were out drinking as well as going to matches.

The trouble at Elland Road was a follow-on from when Leeds went to Ninian Park in 2002 for an FA Cup tie. Leeds were top of the Premiership and, despite events away from football causing distraction – David O'Leary's autobiography coming in the wake of the Woodgate and Bowyer trial – they were hopeful of success. It wasn't to be, and even more negative headlines followed. Between 400 and 500 thugs went down, many by train via Hereford with the rest going straight to the ground on coaches. They were met by thousands of Cardiff, who later said they had their best mob out at home since a memorable battle with Man United in 1974. About 150 Leeds arrived at the train station not long before kick-off but the police prevented either firm from getting at the other.

And that was how it stayed both during and after the game. The referee was hit with coins and bottles were thrown at Leeds but really the only upset was Leeds losing 2-1. Cardiff fans poured onto the pitch after the final whistle and did their best to get to Leeds, and images of riot police pushing them back made the events appear far worse than they were. The club was brought to book by the Welsh FA after Sam Hammam celebrated the win by walking around the pitch and standing provocatively in front of the Leeds fans but in truth there was little violence.

Three years later, during Leeds's first season in the Championship, things were a bit more lively, although largely with the police. Hundreds were out waiting to greet Cardiff to Elland Road and after the game the visiting fans were kept back as Leeds waited outside, chanting. Running battles lasted for nearly an hour, with traffic cones, bricks and bottles being thrown at the police as mounted officers made repeated charges. It was captured on CCTV cameras and images later released to the media resulted in fifteen arrests for affray, including a soldier and a twenty-one-year-old who had played football for Leeds and Bradford City. The judge said it was 'an horrific incident and had it not been for the cool courage and discipline of the police officers it could have ended with tragic consequences.'

In November 2002, Leeds again captured the headlines when they played Sheffield United in the Worthington Cup. Seats were lobbed towards the pitch in response to an on-the-pitch celebration by the Blades, in yet another game Leeds lost, their sixth defeat in twelve matches. This match was the first time Benny from Bradford saw the younger element coming through, as a good fifty or sixty of the IHS were out that day. He and others watched them kick open the glass door at Sheffield's train station when they arrived and all pile outside, despite a police presence. Benny could see they 'didn't give a shit' and were up for anything. Afterwards, some Blades appeared down a side street as an escort of about 350 Leeds passed by. Steve, Moose and some younger ones broke out and went after them, backing them off and getting a few blows in. When the first one went down, Sheffield didn't seem to want to know, but they came back and kept having a go at the escort all the way back to the station.

The right time for the police to nail the IHS was in its heyday around 2003/04. They were waiting at the train station for every game, had good numbers and were riding high after getting a few battles under their belts. Keeping watch on the station often meant they'd be fighting with much older blokes as other firms passed through. They followed in the footsteps of the older crowd by going out drinking in the Wagon and Horses and Becketts for home games, but later drank in the Hogs Head and Viaduct when they decided to get 'their own' pubs. Numbers swelled to about eighty lads but eventually dwindled to about thirty when some realised football violence was about more than just wearing Stone Island. In any case, the hardcore preferred a smaller clique.

If not at matches, they would take trips to York or Cleckheaton and would later read about their exploits in the *Yorkshire Evening Post*. The lads came from all over the area, as territorial rivalries were not an issue with them. The majority came from Leeds: J, R, Ian, Nick, DB, K, P Tommo, Johnny Mac, Big H, Big Woody, Muff, Batley Bob, Brownie, Danny S, Paul D, Ste D, Fat Marc and DS, Manners, B, Dean, Smithy with his steel-cap boots, Hunter and Haighy from around Wakefield and Jam, Benny and Liam from Doncaster way. There was also 'Weird' Tim from Warrington, Gaz from Oldham and Tys from Bradford and the odd lad from Barnsley and Huddersfield. Ste D, Paul D, Tys and R were the originators of the firm and decided on the name while sat in a pub one day. They wanted something that highlighted the 'younger' element and so went with the Infant label. Everyone had a say but over time it fell to one lad, R, to take the lead. He says his overall aim was to bring everyone together from all areas to form one youth firm, and feels he succeeded in creating one of the naughtiest and most active youth firms in the country.

They followed the Eighties fashion of getting calling cards made up with different messages. Something that had not been around in the Eighties was the internet and now rumours, claims and counter-claims would whiz round sites as fighting became talked about rather than indulged in. Generally, battles were hard to come by, with just a handful each season, and would invariably be discussed for ages afterwards. It seemed in this new age that hooligans were forever on their phones but always chasing shadows, or running around thinking firms had arrived but finding nothing. The IHS once ran through fields and woods from Beeston to Holbeck because they heard some mob was around, but arrived to find no-one there and were left soaking and muddy. When a few

Leeds went in limos to John Sheridan's testimonial at Oldham, they waited for the locals to show up after repeated assurances that seventy of them would appear. Despite the numerous calls, they didn't, even after several hours.

Equally, there was a lot of grief to be had if you were the person supposedly organising things and everyone was asking 'are they coming' and 'they' promised they were but didn't turn up. When firms did manage to meet in town centres, the increasingly ubiquitous CCTV cameras were another deterrent and could result in fallings out as some refused to get stuck in under the gaze of the lenses, while others who did would get caught and arrested.

Goodison Park in February 2003 was the first away ground the IHS went to as a proper youth mob and fought without older support. They picked a tough fixture to start with. About fifty boarded a coach from the casino car park on the morning of the game, including R, Tommo, K, Woody, Dean, Fat Marc, Manners, Haighy, Hunter, Jam, Benny, Muff, Batley Bob, Smithy, Paul D and Brownie. Five or six older lads with them split off and did their own thing on arrival.

They drove to the outskirts of Liverpool and got taxis in to the Arkles, by Anfield stadium, for about 11am. The Arkles is a well-known Liverpool FC pub and R noticed an older lad at the bar counting everyone in. After ten minutes they heard a commotion and went outside. They saw a Scouser walking past with a girl and a pram and when some verbals were exchanged, the Scouser pulled out a bowie knife, before putting it back in the pram. Not surprisingly, this made an already edgy atmosphere even more tense, as the rest of Leeds' mob were by this time at the match. While the others waited in the pub, R went to get something to eat from a petrol station. He got chatting to one of Everton's older faces, who said Everton's old firm were out but were mostly on bans, and anyway they'd be 'too naughty' for the IHS, but he took a phone number, saying he'd send their younger contingent over after the game.

Near the end of the match, Leeds started to come back into the pub for a pint before getting their coaches home. The IHS lingered, waiting for Everton to show and constantly looking out of the windows. About thirty minutes after the match, when pretty much all of Leeds had gone back, R got a call to say the locals were on their way. The landlord eventually sussed what was about to happen and pushed people back inside and locked the front door, trapping a couple outside. He also said the police were on their way. Between twenty and thirty Everton, a mix of young and old, were then spotted coming down the road. The long awaited shout of 'They're here' went up and everyone set about trying to exit the pub. They broke through a window or two and eventually managed to open the doors to meet Everton in the road. Their opponents were carrying pieces of wood from a dismantled fence and a few bottles, which they threw into the on-coming Leeds.

Everton were game and wasted no time piling in. One lad at the front waving an iron bar was put on his backside and hit with it, and another local was cut in his neck. In the toe-to-toe slugfest, one of Everton's older lads, Stewy, was knocked down five times but kept getting up. At one point he grabbed the ankle of a Leeds lad who was kicking him and bit it like a rabid dog, refusing to let go. Leeds got the better of them and gradually some Everton at the back darted off, leaving the ones at the front. Eventually all the Scousers ran off into Stanley Park, before regrouping and coming back for more. Again Leeds chased them off in twos and threes, as R shouted for people to stay together. Feeling victorious, they finally returned to the pub and were standing outside when the police came. They cops didn't seem to care about the fight but told them to go to the station immediately. The lads feared the worse at hearing that, but managed to get there trouble-free and headed home. 'They were ringing us on the way home, vexed about the kid getting stabbed in the neck, but they've been dishing that out for years,' said R.

The first time the IHS were complimented by some of the older heads for their actions was after a row with Huddersfield in 2003. Huddersfield had got the better of some of the older Leeds lads at a day out at the races towards the end of the Nineties, so it was inevitable revenge would be sought at some point. Leeds played Newcastle United at Elland Road in the first game of that season and the younger lads were told to meet up at the Wagon and

Horses afterwards, as something was going to happen. They assumed it would be with Newcastle and eight of them went to the pub to be told the plan. They met Eddie, Macca, Steve, Alan, Moose and Lee, among others, and were told instead that they were off to Huddersfield.

Once things had died down at Elland Road, the plan was to go to Cottingley Station to get a train to Huddersfield. They walked the mile and a half to the station in groups of four or five, dashing through a council estate and hopping through gardens, and about forty lads caught an old rattler in the early evening. When they arrived, they saw two coppers waiting on the platform and feared the worst, but as they walked towards them, one of the officers said, 'Good day at Barnsley lads?' They clearly thought they were Huddersfield Town fans returning from their match at Barnsley.

The Leeds mob carried on and found the pub where Huddersfield's mob usually drank, but it was shut, so they ended up in another pub called the Vulcan. SD went to the bar and ordered a round, but as the fourth drink was poured, the roar went up and everyone ran out of the pub, taking bar stools, bottles and the odd ashtray. They saw at least fifty Huddersfield coming down the road, shouting. Some of them were also armed with stools and one had a chain.

Leeds walked towards them in silence and they met in the middle of a main street, by a crossroads and a church. Leeds spread out, with the young lads eager to prove themselves at the front with the top older ones. They ran straight into them, no holds barred, and one of the younger lads rammed a Huddersfield fan through a car window. Leeds backed them off and when one of them went down they began to scatter around a corner by the church. The lads regrouped, knowing they would come back, and they did but from round the other side of the church. It went off again with pockets of fighting and people scrambling about for several minutes. Then Leeds got together and charged at them a couple of times, and at that point they ran off and didn't come back. SD carried on running after them and the four lads he was chasing turned round and attacked him. He got hammered, with some even jumping on his head. He was only rescued when one of the older lads came round the corner and stepped in. 'He looked like the Incredible Hulk with his jeans ripped below the knee and a huge golf ball on his head,' said one of the crew.

That night there was a boxing show in Huddersfield, with local fighters on the bill, so the lads now headed there looking for more action. Despite being covered in blood, SD somehow managed to get past the bouncers and into some toilets near the entrance to clean himself up. However, the bouncers wouldn't let the rest in and said the police were coming, so they waited outside, trying to phone Huddersfield's firm. They could see into the boxing arena and spotted some of the rival firm, so they beckoned them outside. One of their main lads mouthed off from behind the bouncers, so as SD came out of the toilets he walked out in front of him, turned and butted him straight in the mouth. After a skirmish in the doorway, the police turned up and baton charged everyone before rounding up Leeds outside and escorting them to the train station, dishing out some Section Sixty orders and sending them on their way.

Twelve months later, the two teams met in the Coca-Cola Cup at Elland Road. The Infant Hit Squad met at the Stick and Twist pub at the top of the city centre, which was convenient as the geographical restrictions in the lads' banning orders stopped nearby. They heard some Huddersfield were down by the Town Hall and when one of them got to a pub opposite he saw about twenty lads, the majority black, which he knew meant they weren't Leeds. Still, he asked if they were, and eventually one piped up at the back, 'No, Huddersfield.' The IHS went straight into them, with their outspoken leader from the boxing fight getting put on his backside. Eventually the visitors legged it towards Leeds General Infirmary, with some running inside the hospital to escape.

'We were in Becketts afterwards and we heard they'd been put in Yates's by the police, so ones and twos went down to see them,' said R. 'They were banging on the windows but nothing was really going to happen with police about. We tried getting to them afterwards, waiting about in pubs and then going off to the Wheatsheaf and even through a few dirt tracks back up near Elland Road, but nothing was happening. They had special buses taking them back to the station and although some lads got on with them for a bit, not much happened, as there wasn't a chance to properly get them.'

A couple of weeks after the sneaky trip to Huddersfield, young and old were battling again, this time at Middlesbrough. Fifty lads, about half of them IHS, went by train via Darlington, but were met by police. In the escort to the ground, Boro were walking alongside, mouthing off. Lee from Leeds recognised one of them from an England game and told him, 'I thought you said Leeds never turn up, well here we are.'

As they approached a pub, on the road to the ground, 130-150 Boro came out and tried to get at them. The police did what they could to keep them apart, using batons and CS gas on both mobs. They managed to get Leeds up against a wall and Boro surrounded them, having a proper go at getting to them, and for a moment or two it was going off all over, full-on toe-to-toe stuff. Both firms were up for it and Leeds needed to stick together as the police regained control and eventually got them to the ground. Towards the end of the game, lads started drifting out in twos and threes and set off for the station but they were collared by police keen to prevent a repeat performance.

Aston Villa in 2004 saw the IHS organise a bus at the last minute, only to discover when they went to pay the night before the match that it was an Asian coach firm and drinking on board was a no-no. About twenty-five turned up on the Saturday morning and everybody had beer with them, but the driver made them drink it there and then or put it in the boot, which wasn't their ideal start. So they were looking forward to a drink in Birmingham, but half a mile from Villa Park the driver pulled off the motorway and stopped for thirty minutes because he had exceeded his driving hours according to his tachograph. They were on a housing estate that seemed to be full of black lads, who kept approaching the coach and making gun gestures. The driver wouldn't let them off but eventually the back door was kicked open and they chased off the locals, despite the threats. It turned out to be a dull day as they ended up just drinking in the pub for away fans about 200 metres from the ground.

As the original IHS gradually stopped, or were stopped from, going to matches, yet another generation has emerged, in the same way they did. They have taken on the same name and are visible around the bars and pubs, but they face an almost impossible task of getting away with the violence of their predecessors. Hefty sentences and bans are the order of the day now and most have too much to lose. 'They've made a real impression on the lads for doing their own thing. We're impressed,' says Eddie. 'They've done a good job and I can't imagine another firm having a youth mob like them. It's just a shame so many got nicked and banned so early on, which had an obvious impact and stopped them from carrying on.'

21

CLUB AND COUNTRY

LEEDS HAVE NEVER had much influence on the England hooligan scene, but with international matches being played in the north of England during the rebuilding of Wembley, and with an active younger element flourishing, it became too tempting to ignore. And when Turkey played England in a Euro 2004 qualifier, the fixture attracted interest from lads of all ages after events in Galatasaray. The police were well aware of it and were on high alert, as more than 5,000 Turkish fans were expected at Sunderland's Stadium of Light. The fear of reprisals was widely reported and Northumbria Police collaborated with their colleagues in West Yorkshire to identify potential troublemakers and prevent any major incidents. More than 1,000 officers were on duty and a police statement was issued to quash rumours that an England fan had been stabbed by a Turkish supporter.

In the event, more than 100 people were arrested, half from Yorkshire including twenty-nine from Leeds, before, during and after the game. Several police officers, an England fan and a photographer were injured. Fans bayed at coaches carrying Turkish supporters and crowds surged forward and clashed with riot police on the approaches to the stadium. At one point bottles, car wheel trims and bar stools were thrown at the officers. Inside, police on horses, backed up by officers with dogs, baton charged England supporters who laid siege to the Turkish end. Both England goals led to pitch invasions and, overall, it was a bad-tempered game with scuffles among players in the tunnel afterwards and a member of the Turkish staff accused of making throat-slitting gestures.

The Leeds lads started out early and went across on coaches before spending the day in the pubs. Lee, who has been attending matches since the mid-Eighties, recalled what happened:

We had two coaches. One picked up from the Miggy Arms in Leeds, where the landlady at the time had promised to open up at 9am for us so we didn't have a lot of well-known faces stood around on show. We knew the Old Bill would be out everywhere to stop us going. Some of the lads had received official letters the previous week telling them not to visit Sunderland that day. Without a banning order that should be against your human rights, I think.

Anyway that bloody landlady didn't get up and open the back door. It wasn't a good start to the day but the lads stayed around the back of the pub out of sight until the bus turned up. We promptly boarded and set off to our first meeting point. The other bus went to the Chain bar and picked up there and then at a few other points along the M62. We rendezvoused at Ferry Bridge, where we were picking up the famous Donny Whites. It was a bit out in the open but if everyone stayed on the buses it would be okay. When people started getting off it was like an invite to the Old Bill to come and get us. We got everyone back on with a few sharp words and set off up the A1.

After about an hour, one of the lads went round collecting another £5 off everyone on the bus, to moans of, 'What's it for?' Why people just can't do as they're asked I don't know. We phoned the other bus and asked the Count of Ponte Cristo – a lad from Pontefract – to do the same. I believe he got the same moans and groans but he told them it was the fee for the ferry, which was the way we would arrive in Sunderland. Everyone knew we couldn't just drive in on two coaches, as we wouldn't have got near the place. But we weren't booked on the ferry. When we got just past Middlesbrough and pulled in to the rear car park of a large pub on the A19, there waiting for us was a fleet of taxis, some of them minibuses. That's what the extra dosh was for.

We told the coaches to meet us after the game outside the Colliery Tavern, which is outside Sunderland's ground. Within minutes we were in the taxis and on our way. Rommel or Montgomery couldn't have planned it better. The only problem was, we thought all the taxi drivers would know the pub we wanted to go to, in a suburb of Sunderland, but none of them knew it. So after a bit of driving around and stopping to ask a few people, everyone turned up at the Pallion pub in Pallion, just outside the city centre. One of the lads had done a job there the previous week and asked the landlady if it would be okay for us to come. She said yes but never thought we would turn up.

We stayed there all afternoon. As more Leeds fans came to meet us, having come by train, car or minibus from all over the country, some were starting to go for a wander outside the pub and getting restless, or reckless. I would say we hadn't seen a copper all day, even though they were looking for us and famous faces were walking around outside the pub, some even on the phone.

We decided to get everyone out and told the bar staff not to serve anyone else, that always works. As we piled on to the street everyone was quiet and we marched with military precision the couple of hundred yards to the Metro station. People always like to estimate how many lads have turned up on days like this and I stayed on the door and counted everyone leave. We had a lot of lads that day. As we boarded the train, the police turned up but they were too late to stop it or get on it. They also seemed to be a bit slow in radioing to say they had found us, because when we got to Sunderland Central and came up to ground level, there were just two coppers looking out of a window. When they turned round, the look on their faces was like they'd seen a mob turn up from Bradford: pure disbelief.

We walked up the road and round the corner. We'd heard a lot of the pubs were shut, so when we saw fifty Sunderland drinking outside one we headed straight over and couldn't have been made more welcome. We were in there for about forty minutes when someone said that there were Turks on the bridge. Some of the lads tried to clear the pub and told everyone to turn right when leaving, to go down to the bridge. When I came out and turned right there were a few scuffles going on and police were everywhere, making arrests, but I also noticed there was a very large group of our lot missing. It transpired that they had turned left. They had bumped into the Leeds Old Bill and had a minor altercation. All were arrested and locked up till after the game.

The rest of the day was spent spotting who was fighting with who. We got picked up at full-time outside the ground with only enough lads left to fill one coach. We filled it and sent it on its way, then took the other coach to the police station, where all ours were being held. Over the next three hours, one by one, they let everyone out. Finally the bus was full and we could set off back. It was funny to see one of Leicester City's lads, who was a friend of a friend, come out of the police station and get on the bus and sit down as though it was a bus of Baby Squad. Well, he only got a lift to Leeds.

For all the organisation of the Leeds crew that day, a massive policing operation meant there would be no full-on confrontation with Turkish fans. Eddie Kelly was also among the mob:

We had a right mob that day and we were prepared to batter anyone. It was our day, hence no Man U, they knew what was going to happen. Everyone knew we had the biggest mob, about three hundred easy, and there were a few scuffles breaking out but generally it was okay until after the game. The police had told the Turks parked in one car park to stay there until the England fans had dispersed, which they did. But five or six of our lads were parked in there and when they went to their cars on the top floor they realised every car was full of Turks. They got battered with bars and sticks, whatever, but because of political issues they got nicked despite CCTV showing they got a battering by the Turks. It was six versus loads.

At their trial, they were told more or less to go guilty or just two would get found guilty and cop for the lot. They were led to believe that if they pleaded guilty to a charge of violence disorder, I think it was, they would get a lenient sentence. Two of them got eighteen months and the rest got six to nine months, which is hardly light, just because the police alleged they were only there for the trouble.

For England against Wales in 2004, about twenty-five IHS went over to Manchester with some older lads and went around the pubs. They could sense there was going to be trouble. R was chatting to a lad from Darlington when someone banged on the pub window to say Man United were outside. A mix of between ten and fifteen young and old went outside and saw some lads backing off round a corner. Leeds gave chase and went straight in. They caught a few, who got a shoeing but kept running. They all ended up in a street by another pub, where United regrouped and came back down to face them. As they clashed again, the lads recognised a few Huddersfield among the United mob.

Leeds got the better of them, with Manners grabbing a bin from a doorway and throwing it, which led to him doing a stint in Strangeways. As R was laying into another kid he could hear him saying something and when he turned him over discovered it was his Darlington acquaintance from the bar. He asked him what the hell he was doing with Man U and he said he saw everyone running off so he thought he'd better go too. R cursed him out for going with them, then returned the Adidas Keglar trainer that he'd lost in the fight. He'd contemplated nicking the pair but when he saw the state of them he threw this one back, telling the lad to get new ones.

After that the lads were 'up for it' and went onto Deansgate, going after any groups of lads they saw, Mancs or not. They ran one group by a pub and chased them into a McDonald's, shouting, 'You Munich?'

'No, we're West Brom,' came the reply, and the lads suddenly became aware of customers looking at them over their Happy Meals so, sweaty and breathless, they left rather sheepishly.

They spent the rest of the afternoon walking around on the prowl. They encountered some Peter Kay-sized Bolton lads and had a bit of a skirmish but they disappeared as quickly as they had appeared. Returning to the station, they saw an older Huddersfield lad and made a joke about his lot and Man United having their running shoes on. He had about ten mates with him and it turned out they were on the same train as the Leeds lads. Scuffles broke out in one of the carriages as the train left the station.

Booking everyone to go to Belfast for the England-Northern Ireland game a year later proved problematic, as the police were liaising with their Irish colleagues and this put the best laid plans in jeopardy. More than forty lads booked on a coach to Stranraer in Scotland, the ferry and rooms in a hotel. The police asked for all names, addresses and passport numbers a month in advance and the lads obliged, as none had banning orders against them and they assumed it would be fine. But two days before the game, the coach company rang to say the booking had been cancelled.

The news didn't go down well and the organiser rang the hotel manager, who told him two police officers from Belfast had visited him to say he should know that he was about to let hardcore hooligans stay. He had panicked and called the booking agent. The organiser phoned the police station in Belfast to complain and a female officer said she would pass the details on to the Chief Constable and would get him to ring the next morning. He doubted it but did indeed get a call the following day from the man himself, who couldn't apologise enough. He said the police in West Yorkshire had rung the station to ask them to pass on the message to the hotel manager, which was an error in his officer's judgement, and added that as long as no-one had banning orders, they were all welcome. He even gave the lad his mobile number and said if they had any problems with the police, to ring him.

So everyone went from being £130 down to getting it back after the cancellation, to then having to stump up more cash to book flights if they still wanted to go. In the end, nineteen flew from Edinburgh. A friend in Belfast met them at the airport with minicabs and took them to a farmhouse they had managed to book in the middle of nowhere. 'Even though we lost to the only team you don't mind losing to – one national anthem and all that – Healy scored the goal and we had a cracking time,' said Lee. 'The next time I saw the Silver Fox [football intelligence officer] he swore it had been fuck all to do with him and it was in fact Special Branch that rang Belfast to try to stop us. Make your own minds up.'

* * *

Another disaster with the police came at a pre-season friendly with Hull City on a Friday night in 2003. Coaches were carefully planned to ferry everyone there and everything was fine, with another 'excellent mob' coming together, until the police waded in, as Lee recalled:

> Friday night pre-season away to Hull, even for us it was a big game, for them it must have been their European Cup Final. We met in Normanton, two coaches at 10am and two more were leaving Leeds at 2pm. Eighty lads had taken the day off work and a further eighty had taken a half day, and that was just our lot. It showed that it was a big game. One of the lads had spoken to the manager of a pub in Brough all week to make sure everything would be cool when we turned up. He had put on loads of food and got a load of extra staff in for the day and we were just about to set off down the M62 when the phone rang. It was the manager of the pub, who said, 'I'm just ringing to let you know the police called last night and I had to let them know you were coming, but they said it would be okay.'
>
> My arse okay. We would have been back in Leeds by noon or locked up till kick off. Faces dropped. 'Fucking hell' was the chosen phrase for the morning. Well, we can't go there now, can we? We asked the driver if he had a map and he was a mate so he wasn't bothered. We looked at the map, decided on Driffield and went the back way to avoid the M62. It took what seemed like forever but we eventually landed and made our way to the Buck Inn.

It was an uneventful afternoon session with everyone splitting up and just having a few pints. The Old Bill found us, saying they had seen a familiar face come out of a chippy so they followed him. Probably a load of bollocks but they didn't hassle us, just lined the high street right down to the station. We phoned the afternoon coaches and broke the bad news to them, so they went halfway along the M62 and pulled off. We decided the coaches wouldn't get into Hull, it was too far for taxis and there would not be enough available, so we all got the train and landed in Hull at the same time. A few Leeds got out and chased a few waiting Hull and a few punches were thrown but nothing major.

All week it had been in the papers that the pubs in Hull would be shut all day on Friday, massive local media hype, so the police presence in the station was as big as it could have been. We were held in the station for a while, then put on double-decker buses and escorted to a car park near North Ferriby. They had kept all the Leeds lads who came on trains together. There were four double-decker busloads of us in this car park and we were kept there for ages, not knowing if they were going to line us up and shoot us or what. Then the orders from on high came through: everyone back on the buses. Still no-one was sure what was going on. They pulled the buses out of the car park, surrounded by police motorbikes, and each bus had two police vans to escort them. They pulled on to the M62 and headed west back to fucking Leeds. Yes, they took us back. Unbelievable.

I understand the manager of the pub got a bollocking off his area manager for paying extra staff and paying for a load of food and having an empty pub. Serves him right. What people driving past us that night on the motorway must have thought I would love to know.

One match that had more success in terms of organisation was the last game Leeds played in the Premiership which, perhaps appropriately, was against Chelsea at Stamford Bridge. The fixture soon became known as 'The Magnificent Ten', as ten of 'Leeds' finest' broke off and challenged their rivals by one of their pubs in Parsons Green, a feat not many can claim. Eddie Kelly was one of them:

Before the Magnificent Ten, we'd had a good fight with them in a hotel in Leeds when they came to us earlier in the season. I was stood on my own by the ground and counted twenty-one of their lads and they saw and said, 'Where's ya boys then?' I just asked them where the fuck theirs were. Then later I saw them go into the Queen Hotel by the station, and ten or fifteen of us had a look and saw twenty of them, the same ones from the ground. I said, 'Here's our boys,' and we battered them at the front and in the doorway of the hotel. They just tried to get away and run inside. We left them, as there are lots of cameras around there.

Our last game in the Premiership before we were relegated was at theirs and we went out with a bang. Everyone was going and we were determined to leave our mark. It was all sorted to meet at their pub about 11am, opposite Fulham Broadway Tube – a nice surprise for them. We got there in taxis, two or three hundred, and the pub was shut so we changed tack and went to another called the White Horse in Parsons Green. More and more arrived bringing numbers up to about four hundred. Someone kept ringing Chelsea, saying, 'Where are you? We're here.' But they never showed. Then the cops turned up and rounded us up, the usual sketch, and Section Sixty'd people. It took ages and a few snuck off over the road.

As kick-off approached, there was an escort up to the ground but us stragglers, ten of us, hung back and walked up the road some way behind the others. By Fulham Broadway Tube there is a pub on the right. The road was blocked off by police and loads of pedestrians were about. Me, Browny, Zoz, May, Dougie and a few others went up the road and outside the Tube we saw about fifteen Chelsea. They had *sussed us and were gesturing and all that, so we went straight over and smashed into them and ran them as far as we could. Then thirty or forty came out of the pub behind us on the right and we turned around and ran at them and they backed off. We knew we'd never run – that ten was proper – and we just laughed.*

By this time you could hear the sirens and the police got us up against a wall and then Chelsea came round us, saying, 'C'mon.' We replied, 'You say that now the cops are around, you soft cunts.' We were searched and they took our names, then we heard 'Is Kelly with them?' over the police radio and the cops said, 'Yes he is.' At that point J Smith from Wakey walked past and shouted that he had my ticket for the game. The coppers asked him where his was and he showed them the two tickets and they turned to me and said, 'It's your lucky day, now fuck off,' and I was away! Later, me and Zoz walked around the outside of the ground and saw the first lads from Fulham Broadway and they said we'd done well and all that, though we thought they'd have a go at battering us to save some face. But they were on a hiding to nothing with that original ten, we would never have moved.

Another friendly, this time with Celtic in the summer of 2005, saw another debacle when a coachload of lads was left stranded in Carlisle. It had been an early start and the lads headed straight for the pubs in Glasgow, with little hassle from the police, although some weren't happy when they found out that about half of the mob – around fifty – were not going to the match, preferring to stay in the pubs. The rest managed to escape police attention by leaving one pub via the emergency exits. People split up and when some heard that a lad had bumped into a few Celtic – no-one expected to encounter a major mob – a 'couple of fat blokes' were sent up to the pub they were in. Celtic took the bait and followed them down the street, where about forty Leeds were waiting. 'It was Alan Wells all over again,' is how one Leeds lad put it, referring to the famous Olympic sprinter.

Once back on the bus and heading home, the drivers, with the promise of a few quid, agreed to stop for an hour at 9pm for another couple of pints and a bag of chips. At 8.45 they rolled into Carlisle and two of those on board, who were very much worse for wear, boasted loudly that when they arrived they were going to rape all the women, kill the men and set fire to the shops. They obviously didn't mean it but the bus drivers took it seriously, and when the lads returned, they and the bus had gone. It was Sunday night, with no train until 5am, then two changes and back into Leeds at 10am. Not good. Four or five stayed in a hotel while the rest got in the taxi queue and hired seven-seaters, which cost £70 – and some of the lads didn't have a quid between them. Most accepted it as one of the hazards of such trips, but one guy who hadn't been with them before and hasn't been since went ballistic with one of the rape-and-pillagers for landing them in such a mess.

Meanwhile, despite all the financial pillaging that had gone on at Leeds to buy players over the past few seasons, the results weren't good enough and in the summer of 2002, David O'Leary was out. He left 'an ambitious club in a state of serious disarray', according to the BBC, and the players he brought in were soon to be linked with moves from the club. A succession of managers followed O'Leary but failed to salvage things and the unthinkable happened at the end of the 2003/04 season: Leeds dropped down to the Championship. It was the start of the meltdown which led to the mighty Leeds finally sliding into League One. By August 2003, Leeds also had the most football banning orders in the country, and a year later British Transport Police said their fans had caused more trouble on trains that any others.

One of their last battles in the Premiership was against old enemies Spurs. The year before, four younger lads had been jumped by Spurs in the Duke of York pub at Kings Cross when Leeds were playing Charlton. About fifty Spurs were in the pub when the Leeds youth element went in and Gaz from Oldham was smashed in the face with a glass in the doorway. A few punches were thrown before Spurs backed them out of the pub.

The next time they went down again, the younger element mooched about the pubs in Camden – most were actually banned from matches – before heading to Kings Cross to meet up with others after the game. A few of them were sat outside a pub near the station when seven or eight lads went into the pub and asked if they were Leeds. Assuming them to be Spurs' youth mob, a few more Leeds followed them in, bringing their numbers to about fifteen. The rest of Leeds were drinking in the Flying Scotsman nearby and DS set off to tell them. He got there only to find 'a bit of a carry-on' outside the pub, as a couple of Leicester lads had been chinned by Macca and they were all discussing what had gone on. No-one listened to DS at first as they argued between themselves, and it took ten minutes before he could tell them. In the end he left and no-one followed him.

The lads were still sat outside when he returned and they could see Spurs inside on their phones. Eventually Sarge and Macca arrived, asking where Spurs were. Sarge then booted the door open but as they steamed inside they were showered with pint glasses and bottles. Sarge's eye was cut open, leaving a wide gash and part of his eye socket visible. Leeds waded into them, with more coming in through a side door. Spurs were eventually forced to hide behind tables but the police were soon there and everyone scattered. DS jumped on the back of a double-decker bus and headed off down the road as the chaos continued. Many were arrested and kept at a police station before being taken back to Kings Cross. Two lads were later jailed. The IHS rate the Spurs youth mob, just as their predecessors rated the older Spurs firms, as they always 'wanted to know' whenever they met up.

Life in the Championship kicked off with a pre-season friendly with Hibs. About 300 of the firm made the trip, including about thirty of the IHS. Almost everyone that turned up was banned from games in England. They met fifty Donny lads after arriving off the train and Hibs kept ringing to see what pubs they were in. They split into two groups, with some repeatedly bumping into the locals on street corners as they walked along Princes Street. Leeds kept running at them, hopping over barriers to get to them, but they would run off every time. They acted like they wanted a fight but it never happened – though Cardiff had been up the week before and had apparently taken a battering.

At the ground, a mob of Hibs were behind a ten-foot fence mouthing off at Leeds, which prompted some to charge over to them. One had a go at clambering up the fence but bounced off it and ended up on his arse. One of the IHS was too pissed to get into the ground, so his crew stayed with him and headed back towards the station, where again they encountered little pockets of Hibs. Other lads left the game at half-time and a few more scuffles took place. Near the station as they prepared to leave, the lads had to shout to each other to stay together as some Hibs were seen with knives rolled up in newspapers.

The August Bank Holiday weekend saw Leeds playing at Sheffield United. China, from the Very Young Team, was celebrating his birthday and after the match forty of them went drinking around Leeds. They were in the Hogs Head when they saw about the same number of Sheffield level with the Viaduct pub. They had obviously come into Leeds on the off-chance of finding trouble. China was on the phone to Eddie, who was a few miles away, when he saw Sheffield and by the time he finished the call and walked down with everyone to meet them, Eddie had appeared.

Just two policemen, with batons drawn, stood between the two groups as things kicked off. One hit China over his head but he retorted, 'What are you hitting me for? They came over here.' The lads surged into Sheffield, who stood their ground, and battle commenced. They fought for five minutes, with some pausing to get their breath back before shouting, 'Come on Leeds,' and diving in again. Eventually Sheffield crumbled, scattering under a nearby bridge as more police arrived.

Eddie saw them again at the station, some covered in claret, and went over to give them a 'leaving present'.

'You Sheffield?'

'Yeah.'

Bang.

The next day, the lads feared they had been caught on camera. A friend of a friend knew someone who worked within the city's CCTV unit and rang to ask if anything had been seen. They were relieved to be told they were okay. 'They stood for a bit but, like every other time, eventually ran like fuck,' says Eddie. 'Fair play for coming in but don't bite off more than you can chew, boys.'

Brighton away a couple of months later was, however, a day that some Leeds lads can't be too proud of. It was cold and wet and only 600-odd tickets had been made available but a few headed south to watch Leeds play in front of the smallest crowd of the season. Lee was among the visitors:

Brighton, a place for a weekend of sun and sea and, of course, homosexuals – so never any trouble in the Eighties! We used to take 5,000 and dominate the town, so when someone said they had a spare ticket and do I fancy it for the weekend, I said yes. I knew there wouldn't be many of our lot going but a weekend away is a weekend away.

The match was crap but we stayed to the end for some reason. Around 10pm, about thirty of us found ourselves in the area known as the Lanes when someone said Brighton were on the phone. I looked around the pub and thought, no worries. Through the windows I then saw twenty lads coming towards the pub. I told a couple of lads and went outside to be faced by two ugly twats, one a skinny wanker, who said, 'I'm Hibs, who are you?'

I hate Hibs. While he spoke he put one hand in his inside jacket pocket – shitbag – and with the other he launched his full pint at me. As I turned away, his fat, Boris Johnson lookalike mate came at me and stuck his fist in my face, with the weight of his twenty-two-stone body.

More lads started to come out the pub, ten of us in total. Brighton backed off and decided instead to bombard us and the pub with anything they could get their hands on – bottles, glasses and about fifty pub chairs. There was not much ten of us could do but at least it was more than the twenty inside who didn't come out. They backed the ten of us into the pub and went on to destroy the outside of it until the Old Bill turned up. The night didn't do much for my good looks.

December saw the return of Millwall to Elland Road and plans were in place to meet and greet them after all those years. Many of the banned brigade, old and young, were drinking in the White Hart in Beeston. Fifteen minutes before the end of the game, about thirty set off through the back streets by the ground and ended up in a street opposite the away end, where they waited. A few peeked out every so often, only to be told by the older lads to keep out of sight. They sent a couple of spotters to see when the game had finished and they soon came running back to say the fans were coming out.

There were only two coppers on horses where the little mob hid, with the majority of police by the Billy Bremner statue with the rest of the lads who had been in the North East Corner. They could see them trying to get through the police lines to Millwall and fights breaking out. The hiding group broke cover and charged, spreading out across the road and smashing into Millwall. Leeds chased them back into the ground as the two mounted officers lashed out at them. Then Millwall came again and stood for perhaps thirty seconds before Leeds piled back into them and forced them into the ground again.

R clambered up a fence by one of the exits and some Millwall were lashing out with their keys and chucking coins. They had been caught out and looked a bit shocked. Those at the back were making more noise while those at front didn't look too keen to go out, and they were pushed back for a third time. 'I looked to my right and saw carnage,' said DS. 'Missiles were flying through the air and there was fighting all over the car park of the Peacock pub.' The rest of Millwall's supporters were hanging back in the ground as they knew what was going on outside. One copper got dragged off his horse in the melee and DS took a kung fu kick in the chest from a Millwall lad but cracked him back and went after him. The FA subsequently investigated events but issued a statement saying that no further action would be taken against either club, after discussions with Leeds and West Yorkshire Police.

When it came to the match at the New Den, R said he was arranging a luxury coach. So when he pulled up in a Transit van and told twenty IHS to get in the back, they weren't too pleased.

They met about 150 others in a pub in central London before heading off but the police caught up with some after following a taxi. Hull City were also in London and rang to say they were going to Kilburn, so the lads headed off there. They waited around for them, as no-one had tickets for the Millwall match, but they didn't show. Manchester United were also in London, as they were playing West Ham that weekend, and were apparently around Euston, so the lads then got the train over there instead.

When they got onto Euston Road, most went into a pub, but R, his brother and another lad from Donny decided to try the Euston Flyer. They got chatting to about twenty lads at the bar who said they were Blackburn Rovers fans. Another lad was looking over from another side of the bar and when they asked him if he was Blackburn, he ignored them and walked off. He came back with fifteen friends and they started putting black coats on. Straight away, the trio sussed that they were probably Man United's so-called Men in Black.

'You're fucking Munich, aren't you?' said R.

'Yeah, and you're getting it first, you cunt,' came the reply.

They gathered they were Reds from Barnsley. One tried to headbutt R's brother but hit him instead, as the others stood by, seemingly a bit apprehensive.

R threw a stool, shouting, 'Have one for George Best,' the United legend who had recently died. The stool clipped a bouncer before landing in the middle of the Man U group. The Leeds three then started backing out of the pub.

'One mouthy kid with ginger hair started giving us shit and saying we were pathetic, so I invited them up the road where there were more Leeds,' said R. 'They followed us out of the pub as we rang the others to come down and when they saw a couple of them walking down the road they started to back off a bit. Fighting kicked off by loads of chairs outside the front of the pub. It was toe-to-toe for a bit then we started to back them off into the pub.

'The ginger kid got a chair over his head, eventually, as me and my brother were fighting over a chair to hit him with. When thirty or forty Leeds arrived, we all steamed into the doors and United darted backwards onto a raised level inside. We chucked bottles at them and they threw chairs in return and ultimately the pub got trashed. As more and more of our lot appeared, more bottles were thrown and the fighting continued for a while before United went through a door to the toilets. There were a few laid out on the floor. We tried to get them out, as they were trapped. The pub was empty by now and the sound of sirens could be heard in the background. We hit the door with a chair just as the police came in and started nicking people.'

* * *

By 2006, most of the younger lot had stopped going to football for about a year. Trouble was now rare and was more likely to occur away from football. For example, three of the IHS were out in town one Saturday morning when they got word that a group of thirty-five Barnsley were in a pub singing, 'We hate Leeds.' A handful of their mates were in the pub and called them down, thinking things could turn nasty, so they felt obliged to go and help. They walked through a mass of lairy Barnsley to reach their mates.

'We thought Barnsley were away to Cardiff that day and presumed the group was their older, banned lot and big lumps out on the piss,' said DS. 'There were more lads down at the cricket ground watching a game and they got a call to come up to the pub, but after an hour the police came and moved Barnsley on anyway. We heard they were round at Arc bar and once the lads from the cricket arrived we went to find them. We saw the police were parked at the top of the road and we came out of an alleyway opposite the pub and went over, calling Barnsley out. They wouldn't come out, so we went to them and it went off in the doorway for a few minutes, with Barnsley lobbing a few bottles from the back. About five of us crammed into the doorway, jostling to get to Barnsley, and the doors were shut a couple of times but we managed get them open again and keep at them. The police came down and closed the pub and we scattered. Those that hadn't fought for a while got the buzz back, momentarily.'

The older lads were at a wedding that day and the younger lot rang them, winding them up all day for missing out on some rare action. They said they would come out at some point and later on a few of them did appear, still in wedding suits. They bumped into the same Barnsley crowd in Wetherspoons at the train station, and five went steaming into them. When one of the younger lads arrived he saw two older men coming towards him and assumed they must be chasing Barnsley but they were in fact backing away from them. They got a battering but kept going back for more until they and the younger lads ended up getting legged over to City Square.

Leeds United's latest descent into the lower divisions has coincided with battle fatigue, bans and CCTV taking effect on football hooliganism around the country. Mass fights have largely become a thing of the past. The IHS caught the tail end of a floundering scene, one that Leeds and only a handful of other firms have been involved in since the very beginning. Now, as the club goes through the most turbulent time in its history, the headlines are about the on-going saga of power struggles at Elland Road, the aftermath of administration and the fifteen-point penalty imposed on Leeds United and endorsed by the other seventy-one Football League clubs. The controversial, outspoken Ken Bates remains in control but after other clubs voted overwhelmingly to uphold the punishment put on Leeds, supporters feel aggrieved. Scenes at Elland Road at the end of the 2006/07 season confirmed that the fans wouldn't go quietly – a re-occurring theme over the years. The final home game of a disastrous campaign saw Leeds fans invade the pitch after a goal by Ipswich Town, forcing the players off the pitch for half an hour as bottles, coins and lighters were hurled. Several Ipswich fans were injured and police made eleven arrests for public order offences. A month later, demoted Leeds went into administration. They were subsequently deducted fifteen points from the start of the new season for failing to follow Football League rules.

Media loathing for the club and its supporters has never abated and there has been much rejoicing at its current situation. But, as one slogan on a fan's T-shirt said at Derby the week after the Ipswich game, it's a case of 'marching on together, forever, wherever'.

The *Yorkshire Post* summed up the dire season numerically in the summer of 2007, after a last game at Derby County:

> After nine tortuous months, one administration, 44 players, three managers – or four if you include Dave Geddis's stewardship of last October's Carling Cup defeat to Southend United – 17 loanees, eight captains and 26 League defeats, the worst season in Leeds United's history is finally over.
>
> A future in League One now awaits and the United fans who held up a banner reading 'We don't deserve all this' at Pride Park yesterday will hope the 2007/08 campaign signals the club's re-birth.

But while the club looks forward, the days when Saturday was all any lad lived for are most definitely in the past, the days when skinheads, suedeheads and casuals were just a few of the warring tribes out on the streets and it was obvious what people were about and into. It was an exciting and exhilarating time for the thousands involved across the country and a decisive part of social history. Nowadays, the lads say, everyone looks and acts the same.

Yet sometimes a drop down a division can rejuvenate interest and travelling support, both among ordinary, law-abiding fans and among the hooligan element. Leeds United have proven resilient over the years and their run of form in League One bodes well for the future. Fan numbers are still huge and it is inevitable that there is a welcoming committee ready when the 'mighty Leeds' arrive at lower division grounds, bolstering attendance figures to record proportions. Trouble is still never far away. Millwall at Elland Road saw police charge at Leeds fans baying at the three coaches containing the visitors, who were equally goading the lads. The two firms were kept apart by a heavy police presence, with Millwall also being kept back after the match. A week later, twenty-one people were arrested at Carlisle as Leeds took over the streets. Fights broke out in several pubs and missiles were hurled between fans inside the ground. But as one lad says, if and when the names of troublemakers appear in the newspapers nowadays, the hardcore often don't know who they are. It seems Leeds still has an extra, hidden element within its fanbase that can't be stopped.

For the ageing football hoolie, despite many no longer taking part, that initial feeling never goes. As one of the older lads said, 'Being a football lad encourages you to put a force field around yourself, toughens you up. You develop a swagger, like when you walk out of a train station. The opposition knows you're scared but you have to do it. When you're a skinny little kid, you do it, and nowadays you don't realise you are doing it – we're nearly fifty and we're still doing it. It's an addiction.'

It may be an addiction, but it is one that many of the lads have had to conquer, even if the urge always lingers. 'Although football lads around the country – decent lads that is – had a fantastic time, it is coming to an end,' says Eddie Kelly. 'We are taking a back seat and letting others do it. Lads who are lads have got the same respect for each other. It's a game of us and them with the police, so let's stay out of jail, boys. If it wasn't for the fact that I got a four-year ban, this book would never have happened, and I got banned for fuck all. There was some debate about whether a Leeds hooligan book should ever be written, some umm-ing and err-ing about it, which has been overcome. I know none of us like to think we have been done but we know it does happen. Everyone has had their chance to have their say, which I appreciate. Others who haven't, I understand, but if we all sit back and say nothing then we're all guilty of hiding the truth. And this is the truth.'